All About Meditation

Other Books by Ashok Tyagi

- **All About Hinduism**
  From Vedas to Devas and Past to Present
- **All About Spirituality**
  Practical Way for Self Realisation

ALL ABOUT
MEDITATION
Art and Science of Fulfillment and Euphoria

Ashok Tyagi

SHIPRA

Price: Rs. 1400; US$ 56

ISBN: 978-93-88691-85-7

First Published in India in 2021

All About Meditation:
Art and Science of Fulfillment and Euphoria

Published by:
SHIPRA PUBLICATIONS
LG 18-19, Pankaj Central Market,
I.P. Ext., Patparganj, Delhi-110092, India
Tel.: +91 11 2223 5152/6152, 9650028065
E-mail: info@shiprapublication.com
www.shiprapublication.com

Preface

We often do not do what we know we should do. Knowing, dreaming or even obsessing about things important does not make its way into reality. This very norm perfectly applies to practising Meditation. Most of us are well aware about meditation and varying degree of assured benefits expected out of practising meditation. Inspite of all this, only a few enthusiasts succeed in continuing their meditation practise over longer periods. Experience suggests that meditation is easy to begin and even easier to discontinue. Perceived benefits of meditation certainly pull people to explore it but conceptual, physical, mental and practical obstacles involved in its comprehension forces many enthusiasts to drift back to their earlier routines rather quickly. These roadblocks, in particular, inhibit maiden learner's motivation to continue beyond introductory stage.

However, benefits of transformational proportions reported by those continuing with it over long periods compel us to look at real issues behind practitioners becoming weary of meditation. Helping beginners to cross over initial perplexities on their meditational journey, on a road less travelled, therefore, clearly comes out as a righteous attempt worth all the efforts involved in doing so. Precise identification of right issues is expected to pave way for effective redressal of all those issues. This very desire is the fundamental purpose behind this book. Idea here is to take all those issues in desired details, and in a sequential manner, to help every enthusiast grow his/her meditation sapling into a well flourished tree.

Normal person regularly faces multiple aspects of mental agitations, anxieties, work stress, lack of creativity and issues like anger management. Limited supply of virtues like will power, concentration and commitment get exhausted in fighting those very challenges. As a result, the energy required for attending to things planned invariably runs dry on most occasions. He/she is fully justified to spend whatever little left out time and energy into activities offering assured success and higher returns. Working on practice like meditation, demanding sustained efforts over years, is certainly a tough call to make under such conditions. That is where complete understanding about meditation plays a critical role.

You are expected to do better when you know better. Let us consider the fact that Eskimos have fifty different words for snow. Snow plays a very critical part in their entire life and each of their word for snow describes its specific feature. While meditation impacts multiple dimensions in human life, all we got is a single word to explain this giant phenomenon. No wonder, meditation sounds simple to understand but extremely intricate to comprehend. It provides varied connotations to different people from 'sitting in a corner seeking peace of mind' on one extreme to 'being the most advanced spiritual practice to connect with the Universe' on another extreme, and everything falling in between. On philosophical level, one looks at it as a practice helping mental attention to focus inward. But it is amazing to realise that travelling this distance between 'mental attention' (mind) and 'inward focus' (heart) can take years if not decades. Beginners, in particular, lose steam and abandon their journey seeing this small distance only expanding over time. To that extent, meditation is similar to human knowledge about outer space; stronger the telescope, more you keep knowing about its limitless expansion. Here again, the devil is in details.

Meditation is like Education. Understanding education requires deeper comprehension of its multiple dimensions; formal or informal, learnt or taught, general or specific, scientific or commercial, basic or advanced, primary or secondary, bookish or realistic, theoretical or research-based. Imparting education starts in adolescence age and over years moves to primary, secondary, higher secondary, and college levels. Over its normal span of over a decade and half, education goes over many changeovers in terms of role of self, parents, books, teachers, methods, environment and peers. All through this process the word 'education' remains common but is barely used and understood without a precinct or succinct or both. It is simply because the vastness of education makes it impossible to comprehend it correctly without reference to its underlying level, stratum, branch, offshoot or phase. Meditation is even more vast, complex and unique than even education. But unlike education it is yet to be formalized, institutionalised or structured to convey its real context. All we got about meditation is out of individual experiences shared by other practitioners and that makes contextualizing meditation all the more complex.

Most of the reading material available or courses offered by teachers are based on their individual versions where being unique is celebrated. But such uniqueness fuels ever-expanding confusions for practitioners. Reading material on meditation also carries many stories exhorting how it enhances critical virtues like acceptance, concentration, mental focus, contentment, self-awareness and intuition etc. But most of these stories remain focussed on highlighting how quality of meditation gets improved to the level where all those benefits start accruing. It is like explaining what all is available in heaven without laying out clear roadmap to reach heaven in the first place. The layout of subjects dealt in this book, and its mix of theoretical and practical aspects, have been finalised with this particular aspect in mind. This indeed may be considered solitary approach of this book.

Nothing grows in isolation and meditation is no different. It is not like learning to ride a bicycle that you can decide one fine morning and expect to gain enough confidence to ride after a few falls here and there. Successful meditation practitioner has to master the art of preparing the fertile soil before seeding and expecting proper germination, growth, maturing and flowering of their meditational sapling converting into a flourishing tree. He also has to learn about right watering, pruning, and sustaining efforts to help that plant grow over period. Meditational tree also needs guarding against weeds, climatic events as well as frequent attacks from insects like any other tree. Required 'dos' and 'don'ts' must be learnt and mastered to perceive the bright light at the end of this long tunnel. It is the rarest of rare pearl that needs perfect physical, mental, emotional and spiritual conditions to initiate, sustain and grow to desired levels.

Why should One Pursue Meditation

Of all species on this earth, human beings are unarguably the most creative, intelligent and evolved. But every individual has personal choice to remain indulged in enjoying basic urges and primitive instincts or to ascend above all those temptations. The first choice allows status quo of evolution while the later leads to advancement of that very evolution process by expanding awareness of entire humanity. We also know well that enhancing awareness and pursuing spiritual advancements are always considered as pious efforts for their contributions to evolution of humanity all over its history. However, a big majority of humanity at all times has remained preoccupied in serving basic urges and gratifications alone and advancement of evolution process has always been fuelled only by selected few. Ever expanding intelligence on this earth bears testimony to those selected few alone. It is up to each one of us to decide which category of descendants we wish to belong.

Remaining subservient to primitive instincts, unfortunately, is our genetic inclination. Humanity, under normal situations, is known to generally prefer easier way of living. Pursuing superior human goals, on the contrary, calls to pursue difficult path due to intense purification and transformation requiring strict disciplining on multiple levels. Such transformation is achieved by developing right insights through real awakening. Awakening leads to advancement at deepest levels of self-awareness. Ultimately the advanced Self paves way for the Universal connectedness. Meditation is undoubtedly the most accepted practice used over millenniums to help achieve the objective of that very purification and transformation. Practising right meditation is summed up as the journey starting from 'Selfishness' to 'Selflessness' and finally to Universal oneness. In that process, the practitioner also stands to gain several incidental physical, personal, social, mental and psychological benefits.

Experiences from normal life in due course accumulate in subconscious space generating constant stream of excitations and stimulations. With this extra baggage, pursuing journey of spiritual advancement prove a Herculean task. That is why practising meditation on a regular basis comes out as tough as climbing a snow clad mountain peak. Meditation helps in shredding this baggage surely albeit ever so slowly. Meditation facilitates peeling off layers of such experiences by picking up each one of these, seeing each of these for what they are, and finally let them evaporate from our subconscious space. Meditation allows practitioners to lower the mental stimuli by simply withdrawing from those experiences and memories. Life without this baggage becomes much more candid and unpretentious. Of course, the process also involves dealing with many myths and complex concepts.

Awakening the mind to new realities or a paradigm shift is important for excelling in fields like arts, sports, crafts, or every other branch of knowledge. Progress in these fields also demands superior perseverance, enthusiasm and regimentation. An awakened person, on spiritual path also, applies these qualities to gain discerning wisdom and intuitive ability by gaining profound insights in his own heart and mind. Later, with practice, some more practice, and refinements, one can expect to get awakened to higher truths and transcendental reality beyond this visible world. But called by names like enlightenment, liberation, or self-realisation, awakening continues to be the highest goal of humanity. Reaching this genuine wisdom founded on profound self-experience is the ultimate truth of being human and it is here that meditation helps immensely.

Meditation may be called an art or science but what it does is to help in living a fulfilling human life by enabling access to many tools one develops and works with to live a conscious existence. This consciously awakened life is not for improving unknown afterlife alone but it directly impacts our actual ongoing human life, here and now, by brining required changes for enhancing virtues of love, empathy and energy or by enhancing the equanimity to accept what is beyond change together with intellect to identify the difference between such changes or acceptance.

Being a comprehensive practice that it is, meditation, in its widest possible explanation, include systems, techniques, methods and routines that liaison intimately with our internal attitudes and convictions. Meditation is supposed to be the most effective tool of regulating our internal awareness and to enhance the same to the highest level where we become the world, where the entire world gets perceived as our own extension. Comprehending such a deep subject undoubtedly requires practical realisation because intellectual comprehension alone, even with use of best possible and precise combination of words, in unlikely to offer much help. That is precisely why meditation is more often called a self-discovery than a skill set intended for specific advantage.

Once perfected and practised for a considerable time period, it helps us to be aware about our Self at our deepest level beyond our usual divisions and segregations. Meditation involves knowing about our Self not only on conscious level but on unconscious and subconscious levels as well; it brings clarity and neutrality about our motives and helps us realise our true nature which otherwise remains hidden under the overburden of colored views of being socially and morally correct viewpoints. This knowledge later helps to acknowledge that a desire to change the world around involves change at one's individual level. In the process of such a change, meditation is the tool used for reprogramming our brain and rebooting entire mental working. If our intellect is our CPU, meditation works as the software that cleans all the sensors, indicators and activators to ensure correct reading and feedback getting exchanged with the CPU. It helps us remove subjectivity and replaces the same with increased objectivity at all levels. At this stage, meditation helps us in making our reasoning more reasonable and our logic more logical.

This book can be used in multiple ways. You can rely on it to improve your conceptual clarity over subjects explained. You may use it as a reference book for techniques and tools available to practise meditation. It is also intended to be used as a guide to navigate your journey of meditation even when it has already begun. Finally, it can also be used to find your own place within an unfamiliar territory set in unknown topography to help you get back on track. The book is certainly not for quickly turning over pages or for getting tossed on a shelf. It is more of a step-by-step guide. Effort has been made to expose the reader to various theoretical concepts and subjects at appropriate level of advancement. The reader is expected to initiate into practising meditation right from the word go. The book is going to be helpful only for the dedicated enthusiast as hesitant starter can lose steam in no time. The subjects are placed similar to climbing a ladder where, to avoid a fall, achieving a firm grip and consolidating the whole body weight firmly on a lower step is essential before hiking to the next step.

Yes, meditation is simple enough but sustaining it over years demands strong measures of conviction and commitment. Meditation being a perfectly neutral practice, the target beneficiary of this long process can come from any age, gender, ethnicity, religion, educational background. Meditation offers benefits to every segment of humanity. It helps the students, parents, friends, professionals, achievers, sports persons, artists, scientists or other mature adults alike.

This effort being more like a guide, it is expected that there is time gap between taking up of various Stages and Chapters. Keeping that in mind, some critical concepts have been emphasised at more than one place. This unavoidable repetition is considered essential to illuminate the underlying notions and to facilitate required continuity. The mention of meditational practitioner as 'he' in this book is just for the sake of brevity and it always includes practitioners of all genders.

Please feel free to share your queries, views, suggestions or experiences at indotyagi@gmail.com at all times.

Ashok Tyagi
Surabaya
March, 2021

Contents

Introduction

In spite of increasing popularity of meditation, a beginner comes across many smoke screens and complex prism making his comprehension only tougher and murkier. There is so much knowledge and expertise available for meditation in books, websites, blogs, articles, and every other media source that indigestion is difficult to avoid. Multiplicity of methods and practices for conducting meditation only adds to confusions even further. To make the matter more complex, suggestions offered by experts are, at times, seen sitting in diametrically opposite corners. Side by side, there is no escaping from its deeper comprehension irrespective of all the complexities involved. You also have no choice but try out alternate techniques to find what proves most appropriate at particular stage of your emphasised at more than one place meditation journey.

Practically speaking, meditation is the sum total of all techniques and systems used for achieving transformation of our mind aimed at developing a state of consciousness where the mind is free from all scattered thoughts, patterns, conflicts and divisions; where the mind is able to develop focus, bring clarity of thoughts, establish emotional balance and gain ability to see things in their pure natural ways with spontaneity and freedom. In order to do all this, the mind also must be perfectly in order. Each morning when we get up, the mind is much fresh as compared to the time we went to sleep. Meditation helps to achieve similar freshness at conscious level. Person in normal state of mind is seen busy doing one thing, saying another and thinking yet another. How can one expect creativity and bliss from such a distorted mental state? The mind needs to be restored with its order where all above activities are unidirectional, the direction of pure truth and reality. Meditation at advanced level is the art of achieving that state of our conscious mind.

Meditation at advance level requires a perfectly still mind similar to stillness of water in a clean lake where even a leaf lying at the floor, meters below the surface, could be seen from above, where even a single ripple could be traced to its point of origin. That level of stillness requires highest standards of morality and ethics, mastering of techniques, complete clarity for self, crossing over past memories and experiences, complete understanding of the working of mind, success in regulating emotions and feelings. That is why years and years of practice are required to achieve fair degree of progress on meditative path.

Practising meditation also generates great deal of impurity and dirt accumulated in untrained minds. Settling down of all those impurities and dirt happens gradually through prolonged meditation practice working as natural cleansing process. In addition to meditation, this process requires working on many other off-the-mat activities like improving compassion, empathy, morality and ethics. Any forced effort to speed up that process is always found counterproductive. The best way to clarify the mental fluid is to allow it to settle all by itself avoiding all sorts of repressions. One has to mindfully watch the mud swirl, without any involvement in the process. At last, when it settles for good, it is expected to stay settled for long. Obviously, this process is full of its own challenges. Overcoming all those challenges also paves way for progress in meditation. So, only a part of meditation battle is fought while sitting on the mat. This reality suddenly widens the scope of meditation many times over.

The equipment and laboratory used in meditation is basically practitioner's own mind. Success in meditation requires work on two streams simultaneously. On one hand, one has to reprocess stored impressions, experiences and memories; while on the other hand, one need to install a strong security system for regulating entry of fresh thoughts in the mind. If there is no gate keeping, all good and bad thoughts gain free access to that mind. Poor security works like open invitation to known burglars named anger, sexual desire, envy and jealousy. They are very deceptive but attractive and human mind loves to entertain them on priority. Positive progress on meditative journey necessitates denying entry of these thoughts into practitioner's mental space. Beyond a point, both meditation and training of mind go hand in hand where each strengthens the other remaining in perfect harmony.

Making Mind Still as a Self-improvement Project

The constant desire to improve, to do better than before, to find simple ways of doing the same thing, has continued all through entire journey of Homo Sapiens' evolution. We are genetically programmed to work on improvements. But for this dynamic principle humans also would have remained predators like other primordial beings sharing this world all through our evolution process. Barring few radical breakthroughs, the entire process of inventions and innovations is also all about expanding boundaries of human desire to improve knowledge, experiences and capabilities. Initiative to learn and practice meditation also, as such, should be looked as a normal step towards that very relentless self-improvement and nothing beyond. In that respect, trying meditation is an obvious activity to try for every evolved individual.

But in current age and time immediate rewards are desired much before committing our efforts; every time one puts in some time and energy, there must be sufficient, visible and quantifiable outputs here and now. Further, there are multiple options to invest time/energy and there are only few long time investors willing to wait for years and decades. And it is not difficult to assume why. After all, longer the term, higher is the uncertainty. As a result, for meditation to qualify as a fair and just investment option of time and energy, it must yield direct, visible, countable returns. All the mighty gains and life changing benefits associated with meditation may, at best, be considered as blue sky options to be counted only as extra bonus.

Meditation also faces competition with other practices/options available for investing spare time and energy and it better offer something practical and substantial before being opted for by a common man. There is also heightened risk of failures like fate of year-end resolutions which are undertaken very consciously but get forgotten within days and weeks. Unfortunately experience of common man with efforts guided towards making better version of his own, are not very encouraging. But meditation is much more than usual resolutions and deserves a try for the sake of positive feedback available from so many sources. One always has the option of walking out if it fails to come up to expectations.

For the moment, let us keep aside difficult sounding and life impacting claims attributed to meditation and see if it helps us improve on some of our immediate and pressing issues. These issues can be relating to health, relationships, achievements, work performance, management of stress levels, disturbed sleep patterns, loss of energy and vitality etc. As a fair play, practising meditation must deliver on each of these issues before any long term commitment. The logic is to be practical and rely on meditation only if it helps us in living our normal life better than before. If, and only if, it brings direct impact on regular real life, it will be fair to expect commitment to invest more time and energy to seek emotional, philosophical, psychological and spiritual advancements.

At this stage, however, the novice practitioner is advised to keep aside his knowledge or perceptions about meditation. There is a big risk in beginning with existing burden. Preconceived knowledge may or may not be complete, consistent or confined in nature. Such knowledge is destined to become a roadblock in beginner's efforts. It limits him from looking at meditation in its simple and pure form. Let the beginner start with a simple understanding that meditation is more about mind than body; that a normal human mind works non-stop 24/7 even when the body is at rest. Also that our body is better at telling us when it is tired but mind does not know how to complain. The beginner may also be advised to remember that existing understanding about the mind, its issues, its challenges and its complications are far more complex and are best addressed with far deeper understanding of many other underlying layers scheduled for later stages.

Dip-stick Test for "Does Meditation Work for Me?"

With this little comprehension, you are invited to start your humble journey simply by sitting in some quite corner for 15-20 minutes at a time, for about two times a day, at a time and place of your convenience, in a posture that you feel comfortable. No, we are not attempting meditation but just a simple trial of relaxing exercise for our mind. There is no need to name this exercise at this stage. Let mental relaxation be the only purpose of this effort. It is like starting to go to a nursery class without burdening the young mind about all the complications involved in the tedious process called education. The total period can be three to four continuous weeks as anything shorter may direct you to wrong results. But even when it is just a precursor to real thing, it should be good enough for you to indicate towards things to come. Please take a simple self-check and check yourself. If you do not find a positive impact in terms of increased output, improved quality of output, better mental peace, improved quality of sleep heightened creativity, it is clear that meditation is unlikely to work for you. You should have no obligation to continue on meditative path and better return back to your earlier routine.

However, if this simple sitting for a few weeks unequivocally delivers direct and substantial positive result, you should feel encouraged to explore the real meditation. This may be right stage for you to formally deal with basic issues about how to sit and how to breathe. Suggestions enumerated below may be gradually introduced into your daily sittings with the aim that the practice must always remain enjoyable and not being felt as a burden. Your patience will get tested many times, so keep it strong. Also, let your pace be suitable to your natural rhythm. Forced efforts to achieve too much in too little time are destined to backfire. Golden rule is to keep it simple by curbing all temptations to expedite the process.

Always start your sittings in a position that is comfortable to you. Feel free to sit on a chair, on a cushion, crossed legs or any other way that goes well with your sitting habits. The only caution is to ensure that your back, neck and head remain erect in a straight line as much as your body permits within comfort levels. The logic for keeping the body erect is simply to avoid falling asleep. Erect sitting posture also facilitates smooth breathing. In the beginning, until such time that you are comfortable in sitting and breathing, keep your eyes open and focused on any random object in line with your vision. Open eyes also help you to keep looking at your watch to monitor the time progress. Trust me, beginners of this practice find ten minutes to be too long and hence the access to watch. Other than these simple steps, you need not prepare for anything in particular.

Regarding breathing, all you need to do is breathe-in and breathe-out in a regulated manner. Breathing is a very normal and automatic activity that we all carry out rather unconsciously. However, during this sitting time, you must try to breathe consciously. To begin with, try to match the time of inhale with exhale. Another simple tip for conscious breathing is to breathe a bit faster than normal/natural pace followed at other times. It is best done by making a bit of extra effort while inhaling as well as exhaling. You may also try other options aimed at bringing a bit of conscious effort in an otherwise unconscious activity. Why breathing is so much important and critical for attempting meditation even its infancy stage? Well the sole purpose is to keep the mind engaged on breathing activity so that it is not left free to wonder as it normally does at other times.

Focusing attention on breathing at the far end part of nose instead on the outer nostrils is another significant part of this exercise. Shifting focus by a few centimeters inside the nostrils results in enhanced feel of perceptions and stimulations which, in turn, enables in holding mind's attention on breathing. Without this trick in place, you are permitting random thoughts to enter the mind allowing its monkey nature to keep freely jumping from one thought to another. Little deliberate effort in breathing and holding mind's attention immediately results into a fascinating wonder. Generation of newer thoughts subside and engaged mind does not get a chance to entertain thoughts entering in its periphery of attention.

First Glimpse of Meditation

The exercise explained below is still not a meditation practice but just a quick peep inside the complex conundrum called meditation. It is intended to help the novice beginner to gain personal experience about things expected to come in due course, like a teaser showing story line of a mega movie on a highly intrigued subject.

The first sitting for this trial is best done in early morning before starting your day. Being a new initiative try waking up half an hour before your normal time. After quickly getting over your visit to the toilet, find a corner for sitting in a relaxed mood. With eyes closed, the simple objective of this sitting is to make your mind quiet. For a few weeks in the beginning, you shall just practise your conscious breathing as explained earlier. You may have to continue for several weeks before achieving a degree of comfort and rhythm in your posture and breathing.

Leave your mind to remain engaged on ongoing patterns of breaths, flow of air entering and leaving your body, other sensations all through your nasal tracks. Idea is to prevent it from uncontrolled flying out, an activity so much liked by every mind. But due to inherent nature of mind, it will drift out to other thoughts sooner than later. Each time it goes out, all you do is redirect it back on your breathing again. This gentle looking effort may frustrate you to your complete dislike but that is well expected. In our daily life ten minutes passes without ever getting noticed but while sitting and breathing consciously, you will realise that ten minutes takes pretty long. On lucky days when you get used to achieving around ten minutes of breathing with mental attention remaining within your sight you are certain to realise that your remaining day gets filled up with a new flow of energy, making you ready and willing to carry out your usual activities with positivity and eagerness. One should feel happy to get this realisation within first three months of starting this routine. It may be faster and more effective for those who can repeat the same sequence around evening time as well.

After sitting for ten minutes or so of conscious and concentrated breathing you can come out to your normal waking state and relax for a while. You may take mental notes about the shortcomings felt in your practise so that you may try avoiding them in your next sittings. After your introspection of few moments, please continue for another five minutes or so to mentally go over all the activities that you intend to attend on that day. Idea is to clearly review the activities needing your attention and prioritising the same in order of significance. Depending on what works for you, you may also like to list the activities down for reference and working as reminders. Some of us shy away from making a written record but experience suggests that a written down 'To Do' list helps achievers better than mental noting. As it is, our mind and memory has far more important points to focus than getting burdened with a long list of pending points, so better start writing down your notes.

Such a list may have to be referred a few times each day to tick out the points attended and getting reminded for the ones pending. Over few weeks, you can feel the improvement in your output levels as against earlier period. By going over the 'To Do' list soon after revitalising the mind by stilling over the sitting session, you are able to have better priority setting and increased energy for your work demands. Next day, the five minute session after the ten minutes of stilling the mind will help you review your progress of previous day and thereby fresh updating of the new priority list for the coming day starts emerging.

Second sitting of ten minutes is highly recommended just before going to sleep. This sitting also involves focus on breathing similar to sitting in the morning. The desired conditions for sitting and keeping back straight apply in the night time exactly as discussed for the morning. The focus at night is to disengage the mind with the thoughts and actions of the day gone by. At night time our mind is expectedly tired and stale. So your aim is to let it unwind and relax. But sit for this session only after you are through with all your activities for the day including last minute messaging and connecting on social media. For the sitting session to be effective, you must hit the bed straight after this session. This sitting brings tremendous improvement to your sleep quality making you feeling fresh in lesser time than before. Time saving so achieved by cutting down on sleeping hours makes meditation sittings time neutral. Improved quality of sleep more than compensates reduced time of sleep in all cases without exception.

Initial hiccups aside; you should be able to comfortably settle in this routine in a month or so. The second month may be considered as the effective practice time. Around the end of two months in practice, you are advised to conduct a simple self assessment of sort similar to a monthly test at school. The questions that you may like to pose for such an assessment may go like those listed below:

- Is there a perceptible difference in my energy level for activities attended, especially towards the end of the day?
- Do I see better control over critical activities of my daily life?
- Do I see a level of better discipline in my life in general?
- Do I feel more positivity and hope as compared to earlier period?
- Is there any improvement in my interactions with other people at home and work?
- Am I more conscious for better health and happiness than before?
- Is there a significant reduction in my nightmares or improvement in quality of dreams in general?
- Do I feel more rested when I get up every day in the morning?
- Do I sense lower stress levels in general?

If the answers to most of these questions are in positive, you are surely ready to explore more about this beautiful journey. It is time for you to increase the ten minutes sittings at a pace permitted by your body, mind and live issues in life. Needless to mention that the benefits you experienced so far are just a precursor of the fulfilling experiences waiting on way to your meditational evolution.

But if the answers fall in negative territory, you have reasons to be concerned. Most likely you have not been doing your practice in right manner. In such situation, please go over your entire approach and see if there are missing links and be ready to fix the same before trying again. Only in extreme cases, there may not be much progress even after a few more trials. If and only if, you still do not succeed, you may conclude that meditation is not for you and return back to your previous life.

Journey on spiritual path seldom take pre-defined progress. This is known to be a long and twisted route where there are no paved roads or clear footpaths. Each one of us, therefore, travels through different milestones. Meditation is a proven, effective and robust vehicle recommended to take us faster on this journey. But like all other big vehicles, its progress depends on proper signage, speed and direction of winds, traffic on the road, access control, smooth visibility and such other requirements to move fast and safe.

After getting positive stimulation from the initial experience of pre-meditation precursor, it is now time to get ready to be introduced with it in a formal and detailed manner.

General Understanding about Meditation

In its simplest understanding, meditation can be looked at a systematic training to withdraw thoughts from the external world and observe, analyse, regulate and finally reflect them after directing their focus towards inside. Over long periods, this process results in complete reflection over mind's accumulated contents and patterns and removes all layers of false perceptions. This purity and clarity allows inward focus of mental attention for finally inducing sense of active consciousness. However, to achieve this global objective, there are host of philosophies, tools, practices, methods, and techniques involving different times, different geographies, different cultures, different religions and faiths.

Internal reflection is very common experience and each one of us must have felt it at one or the other time. But in spite of such universal connect with meditation most people have apprehensions for it being a practice, method or technique. As a result, it has as many meanings as contexts. But meditation as a 'voluntary internal effort for analysing and regulating one's own mental processes' can be clearly established as a common thread among all the variations of definitions in use across the globe.

Tracing its Original Roots

While one can easily find its footprints across all major religious thoughts, the origin of meditation is associated with Eastern Spiritual Practices right from Rig-Veda times, if not earlier. *"Om bhur bhuva swaha...."* the most popular and highly revered Gayatri Mantra from Rig-Veda that we all are familiar with, starts with the very words "We meditate on...." This goes to prove that meditation practice in India is as old as Rig-Veda in the least. By 5th century B.C., meditation can be tracked to have spread in Taoist China as well. Somewhere around 300 B.C., Maharishi Patanjali is said to have composed the famous Eight Limb Yoga where meditation (Dhyana) has been explained in great details. Further spread of meditation followed the transmission via silk route when it reached oriental countries in Central China by 6th century CE, Korea by 7th century and finally reaching Japan by 8th century.

Judaism also contains a central meditation tradition. Torah talks about it in Genesis 24:63. Starting at the turn of millennium and in between Philo of Alexandria and Plotinus, even the Greek developed full version of their own meditative practices. Western Christians also came out with their own meditation practices by 6th Century CE. Later, by 1200 CE, Zazen got evolved in Japan as a specific type of sitting meditation. In short, while methods may vary from culture to culture and from time to time, mystical branches of all religions have practised meditation all through the documented history of humanity.

Major expansion of meditation in North America is traced to early 20th century where it was first introduced by Swami Vivekananda and later popularised by Paramhansa Yogananda. Its real explosion in the Western World, however, is credited to Maharishi Mahesh Yogi who helped spread it among the masses like never before through his own unique technique called 'Transcendental Meditation'. Soon many other neo-meditative systems started evolving in 1950s which led to sudden big boost to meditation as an effective practice. Riding on its fast popularity, by 1970 meditation in US started attracting a number of Professors and Researchers from academia. Popularity among such neo-scientific disciplines quickly facilitated modern day scientific studies and tests to measure and establish its peculiar and marvelous effects on human mind and body alike. It is to the credit of such studies and laboratory trials that meditation got established as a multi-dimensional practice providing respite to many modern day disorders that were not getting addressed from other available systems.

Meditation and its Significance in Modern Times

> "Meditation is intermittent fasting for the mind. Too much sugar leads to a heavy body, and too many distractions lead to a heavy mind. Time spent undistracted and alone, in self-examination, journaling, meditation, resolves the unresolved and takes us from mentally fat to fit".
>
> —Naval Ravikant,
> Indian-American entrepreneur and investor and
> himself a great Meditational practitioner

Having initially originated for the purpose of advancing spiritual growth, the meditation in modern times is increasingly practised for benefits related to individual well-being in general and stress-reduction, relaxation and most importantly as a tool for self-improvement in particular. In recent years, we have been witnessing globalised expansion of centres and teachers promising all kinds of meditations assuring benefits ranging from ecstasy to bliss. In a way, meditation expansion also can be traced with popularisation of Yoga as both these streams attracted a common pool of seekers falling out of particular aspects of materialism spread in the Western World. But everything that glitters is not gold. Different people holding their diametrically opposite versions make Meditation a very complex system. On top of that many of the versions available in the market stand far from the real thing.

This fast explosion brings its own challenges as well. Its being old and common practice make meditation vulnerable to misinterpretations and comprehensions forcing different people to understand it differently. Even when it comes to actual experiences of practitioners, one finds that not all practitioners are able to experience uniform advantages. Thus, available versions and personal stories of practitioners are enough to confuse a normal seeker. As such, a beginner is well advised to identify what is 'real and central' versus what is 'incidental and peripheral'. That is where knowing meditation in greater details becomes so critical. Since meditation calls for lifelong commitment and extreme dedication with regularity, it is but natural to begin new initiative like meditation with extreme preparations. Else it will be so much more difficult to avoid failures and disappointments.

Meditation and Modern Businesses

Meditation is increasingly getting used as a practice for enhancing effectiveness of executives at all levels. Corporations of all shades, shapes and sizes are seen spending sizable portions of their human developmental budgets for helping their executives learn meditation. As per an article published in July 2019 by John Elflein, a research expert covering health and health care, the market size of meditation in US alone crossed USD one billion in 2017 and is predicted to cross USD two billion by 2022. More than the dollars involved, important point to appreciate is that modern businesses do not put their money behind any practice unless its benefits significantly outweigh the costs involved. There is a consensus among thinkers and writers that meditation is becoming popular among CEOs and senior executives simply because it really helps them focus on core issues and find alternate options better than other available techniques they have tried in past.

Researchers now find meditation contributing directly towards building leadership skills and achieving business goals. It is said to help businesses in their major spheres, such as, talent management, talent retention, finding innovative solutions, team building and collaborative approach to face business challenges. Meditation is proven to enhance agility and flexibility at the same time, the key skills which have become more critical in modern days of influx from competing technologies, broken trade barriers, online information overflows etc. Researchers are also finding meditation sharpening key skills of memory, attention and emotional intelligence. Meditation is also established to build resilience besides being most effective in decreasing anxiety and thereby ensuring better performance even under stress conditions.

Recent studies also establish role of meditation especially its unique quality of encouraging divergent thinking among its practitioners. This helps executives in considering wider range solutions to problems in hand. Executives having achieved moderate to good progress in meditation also report improved creativity in finding better responses to challenges in their respective areas paving way for better business results. Meditation also offers many other indirect benefits like increased compassion, increasing ability to control distractions, ability to retain focus for longer periods and maintaining peace of mind, etc., qualities that are generally useful among people from all walks of life.

Comparing Meditation and Education

Let us also look at meditation in comparison to education system where a child progresses from kindergarten to primary to secondary to graduation and finally for post gradation or specialisation. Learning and practising meditation also is not too much different than the entire cycle of informal plus formal education. Here also a practitioner will have to start from lower level, with simpler subjects and concepts before being exposed to higher and higher levels of topics, subjects and concepts.

For example, mathematics is a common subject that is studied in almost all levels of the education systems but mathematics itself progresses through several stages where level of complexities keeps increasing with the development of the student. Such stages of mathematics may look like elementary arithmetic, algebra, geometry, calculus, trigonometry, statistics, probability, complex numbers, analytic geometry, exponential and logarithmic functions and applied mathematics. Each one of these subsets of mathematics have their own level of complexities and have to be taught in a given sequence; you cannot teach applied mathematics to a student of middle school, for example.

Similar to education system subjects, concepts and techniques involved in mastering meditation do have their own level of complexities. It is critical for right progress to stage all those complexities in ascending order since the very beginning of learning meditation. Meditation seekers must be open for very slow progress and should not get scared or lose motivation to continue their practice over the years.

Meditation, however, does not follow specific progress sequence as applicable for formal education system. This is where meditation loses comparison with education. Meditation is more subjective in nature and its progress differs from person to person. Issues dealt in meditation are not as candid as the example of mathematics. It is safe to follow the disclaimer that progress in meditation does not move on well paved roads, numerically numbered milestones or predefined sequences. Experiences of various practitioners suggest that progress always remains open for jumbled sequences, regular overlaps as well as varying time required to move from one stage to another.

Caution Against Over-Expectations from Meditation

While there are enumerable benefits confirmed by most practitioners, meditation should not be taken as any ultimate practice for which one should actually abandon everything in life. At times, we come across examples of people from families of rich merchants or elite class leaving behind all the luxuries at their disposal and giving up all their riches to pursue spiritual advancements. But such examples are to be taken as rare exceptions and nothing beyond. Meditation in particular has no direct role in bringing such drastic measures. Subject matter of this book is meditation for normal people of this time and age where we want spiritual growth without giving up materialistic riches. Sacrificing all we got is too tough a call and can simply be branded impractical in today's context. However, preferences and priorities are bound to get changed over long journey of meditation where ultimately significance of materialism will automatically get diluted in favour of other critical superior goals of human life.

Beginners are specially advised against taking meditation practice as solution to all of their ills. They should not leave other things in life and go after meditation as a hungry wolf going for its prey. Please avoid having all types of preconceived notions and expectations. It is best to start working on it just like a landscape architect looks at a green patch of land that is full of shrubs and weeds. He has no idea of the real surface to be worked as the surface remains beneath all those thickets. It is foolhardy for the architect to plan real landscape before the overgrowth is all cleared, trash is removed, actual contours of the land are known and soil testing is completed. In our normal life also we got much denser shrubs and weeds and many of which are proudly planted and watered with great satisfaction. Ignorant being continues to suffer from the ignorance of not knowing his inner consciousness and its overburden accumulated over years. So, recommended option is to start your meditation practice with 'zero' level of expectation. You should start with "let's do it" approach and wait for positive results to flow from different directions.

Some people start their meditation practice as a fashion statement. They are due for titanic disappointments as there are no thrills or adventures in meditation. Like every other important thing in life, it is just boring hard work to begin with. It is a constant battle which is much more demanding than losing sizable body weight or gaining biceps of superhuman size. Those going to gym for months and pumping hard, day after day and month after month, know how frustrating it is to bring the body in desired shape. If anything, meditation is many times more hard and dry. One has to be fully prepared for frustrating episodes, unwanted realities, non-desirable learning about self, and many more hitches and glitches standing in your way. On top of everything, you are also expected to enjoy the process without which sustaining it over years will be considerably more difficult. Meditation, unfortunately, is a journey without any settled destination.

For those familiar with the game of cricket, learning meditation is like net practice with bowling machine. There are no score cards, no statistics, no run chase, no spectators, no umpire and no selectors on the scene. You get your own time window and must make the best use of the opportunity to learn and improve your techniques. If you are able to improve your game, your performance on the field is expected to be better than before but there is no guarantee. Depending on skill of the opposition bowler and so many other factors, your batting on the actual game scenario may be same or even worse than before. But ultimately, over the long periods of time, those who sincerely sweat it out at the nets and work on their shortcomings prove to be the better batsmen. Yes, there is no applause or cheering but the foundation of the game gets built only through that net practice. Similar is the case for meditation.

Also, expecting meditation to work as a solution to all problems of normal life is absolutely wrong. No doubt sustained meditation practice brings about many transformational changes in life but continuation of all its benefits are inversely correlated with continuation of negative activities like stress, anger, envy, lust, bond with materialism and attachments. All these demerit factors are powerful leaks and quite capable of draining out accumulated grace of meditation practice of any proportion. Anyone desirous of filling the bucket has no option but to plug the leaks it got. So is the case with meditation. Let us remember that everything, small and big, happening in our normal life has impact on progress we make in our meditation. Let it be understood beyond doubt that transformative changes credited with meditation shall keep moving away so long as those known leaks remain unattended. Meditation goes in tandem with daily life activities and behaviour maintained.

Benefits to be Expected from Meditation Practice

> "Meditation will not carry you to another world, but it will reveal the most profound and awesome dimensions of the world in which you already live. Calmly contemplating these dimensions and bringing them into the service of compassion and kindness is the right way to make rapid gains in meditation as well as in life." – *Zen Master Hsing Yun*

There is no denying that meditation is good for us. Multiple sources do swear about this or that benefits from meditation practice. Some of these benefits are mere physical while others may indicate different types of positive impacts on attitude. Some benefits may be linked to normal happiness while others may touch upon its transformative impacts. On a broader perspective, this extreme categorisation may be due to fundamentally differing approaches emphasised in western and eastern cultures.

Western culture focuses on individual where primarily tangible outcomes of one's own actions are measured and valued. Western view defines well-being as optimal functioning with reference to normal daily interactions, activities and social roles. That is why its commentary on meditation is full of practical outcomes for physical health parameters, productivity at work, performance in sports or music, recovering out of specific medical conditions in particular and improving individual's well-being in general. These can be clubbed under physical, mental and psychological categories much more than social or spiritual benefits.

On the other hand, eastern traditions prescribe Moksha, the release from the continuing cycles of death and rebirth, as highest stage of human evolution. It defines human endeavour as a constant attempt for detachment from the world of objects and removal of false image of individual self-being different than universal self. To that effect, Indian traditions, in particular, prescribe constant use of meditation practice as a key instrument to cross over attachments to sensory objects and ultimately to attain identification with pure consciousness as supreme objective of human life. Eastern traditions do provide for achievement of individual goals and fulfillment of desires for enjoyment as well but they also raise flag that 'striving, enjoying, striving again' is a vicious and unending cycle. Due to this basic difference in philosophy to human life, Eastern culture primarily highlights spiritual benefits of meditation.

However, in between these two obvious extremes, there exists a long list of advantages reported by people pursuing meditation as a regular practice. These advantages can broadly be grouped under physical, individual, mental, social, emotional and spiritual domains. Beyond any segregation, a normal person is happy with as many benefits out of his practice, and as fast as possible. Luckily, benefits of meditation start appearing just after first few sessions. As the practice intensifies further, more and more benefits continue getting added to the list. However, the ultimate benefits of spiritual advancements start accruing only after several years of concentrated efforts.

The deliberate purpose of listing progressive advantages, at this very stage of this book, is just to arouse the curiosity among the readers/practitioners so that they do not get scared with the difficulties involved in dealing with arduous and complicated concepts getting laid out subsequently under various topics. It may never be overstated that meditation has never been for the weak hearts and exposure to potential allurements is dangled in the beginning itself to boost their commitment to continue pursuing it. Listed advantages, therefore, are to encourage and motivate readers to continue investing their time and energy for learning and practising meditation.

These benefits are not merely play of words or fantasies. There is no room for doubts or over-expectations about these benefits as these have been confirmed by actual practitioners over time and off late most of these are also backed by scientific studies conducted by multiple researchers. Let us list the benefits in the order that they are expected to normally accrue. The reader may also take note that while some benefits are linked to specific types of meditation practices (to be individually discussed at a later stage), most types of practices accrue general benefits to different practitioners in varying proportions.

1. Physical Benefits

- Improves digestive system by calming the mind and body and protecting against stress, anxiety and fears. Result is marked impact on improved gut, inflammation, acid reflux, ulcers and even food allergies. Meditation helps the body to perform its biological functions at a level higher than normal. In due course, it also induces the practitioner to opt for healthier food as a choice.
- Normalises blood pressures up to five points on an average. Hypertension poses big threat to adults from across cultures and lifestyles and is already identified as most widespread disease of modern times.
- Reduces stress levels under all conditions, yet another challenging health hazard of modern days. Stress has its origin among pleasures, excitements, worries and fears alike affecting a mighty majority at present.
- Improves immune system. Enables people to strongly fight common infections and communicable diseases. As experienced in Covid-19 times, the need for stronger immunity is never overemphasised.
- Helps you to sleep better by improving quality of sleep. One can get better recuperation in lesser time without any adverse impact on health. It is like getting one or two extra hours each day over and above 24 hours received by everyone.
- Helps in bearing physical pains by increasing ability to cope up with even chronic pains.
- Activates body's healing powers helping in faster recovery post operative or post trauma conditions.
- Reduces chances of heart ailments including chances of strokes.
- Takes care of several eating disorders.
- Improves longevity by increasing age and improving mortality.

2. Personal Benefits

- Improves productivity and efficiency at every occupation/ profession being pursued by its practitioner.
- Self-Awareness gets enhanced offering multiple choices in

taking actions with improved consciousness.

- Decision-making capability gets improved both quantitatively and qualitatively.
- Helps in shining personality and self-esteem. Develops feeling of worth and promotes benevolence.
- Helps controlling instant reactions to responses thrown back by people and circumstances.
- Improves higher self-esteem, satisfaction, ego-strength and trust in others.
- Enhances both alertness and awareness, at the same time, towards happenings taking place in the surroundings. This sharpens the skill of generating appropriate responses to emerging situations.

3. Emotional Benefits

- Helps in exercising control over anxieties, worries and impulses enabling proper appreciation of opportunities offered by life in general.
- Results in reducing bouts of depressions and fears.
- Empowers to fight the feeling of loneliness due to lack of connectedness with loved ones and friends in particular and society in general.
- Cultivates optimism and guard against adverse influences of fantasies.
- Helps in avoiding cynicism by making individuals more realistic. It reduces dependence on external conditions for one's own happiness.
- Works as a booster for enhancing self-esteem grounded in self-acceptance by pushing idealism out of the system.
- Balances mood swings by inducing emotions to operate within a lower range; avoids extreme impacts of emotions on either side.
- Improves Emotional Intelligence Quotient by first correct identification of emotions at play and then by harnessing those very emotions in finding solutions.

4. Mental Benefits

- Improves memory retention and recall power by simultaneously increasing focus and mental strength. This has exceptional positive impact on acceleration of knowledge acquisition process.

- Increases intelligence, both cognitive as well as intuitive. For examples, it directly improves performance in exams at school, college or at competitive levels.
- Facilitates higher speed in decision-making process without compromising on quality of decisions made.
- Enhances creativity and problem-solving capabilities by improving brain integration function. This augments mental alertness and also induces original thoughts.
- Brings about qualitative consolidation and reformation in imagination and inspiration.
- Elderly meditators can exploit the phenomenon of neuroplasticity to continue rewiring their own brain throughout their lifetime.
- Results in better activation of all mental faculties associated with artistic and creative qualities associated with right hemisphere bifurcation of mental capabilities.

5. *Social Benefits*

- Enhances noble virtues of compassion and sympathy helping better connect with one and all.
- Increases activity in the pre-frontal cortex area dealing with part of brain responsible for managing happy feelings.
- Brings about qualitative changes in all relationships by inhibiting attitudes stalemating social interactions. Enhances proficiency in solving interpersonal problems.
- Improves communication and hence collaboration with others.
- Broadens one's ability to comprehend views of others with open mind without being too critical or judgmental.

6. *Psychological Benefits*

- Helps in peeling away conditioned psychological aspects generated from subconscious systems.
- Helps in controlling generation of stress.
- Allows better access to higher levels of consciousness.

- Allows transcendental experience by suspension of sense of body, time and space.
- Enables practitioners to successfully fight addictions to alcohol, nicotine and use of substances of all kinds.
- Helps in faster recovery from traumatic experiences or stressful situations.
- Increases receptiveness to extra sensory perceptions; helps sensors to operate with increased keenness and sensitivity. Makes telepathy work.

7. *Spiritual Benefits*

- Brings subtle balance between concentration and detachment. Helps in keeping all unwanted distractions at bay.
- Helps is achieving self-actualisation leading to become best possible version of self.
- Helps in discovering real purpose of human life and in finding fulfillment in life.
- Provides access to inner silence and peace by allowing access with one's personal sanctuary of bliss.
- Develops the interconnectedness that all fellow beings are traveliers in the same journey called life with similar abilities, ambitions, failings and limitations.
- Aids in realising that there is a power well above whatever is visible in this physical world and inspires to see direct connect with 'That'.
- Makes a person capable of remaining in the state of heightened Awareness for self, others and the whole Universe.
- Helps being to connect with higher consciousness.
- Brings about a true personal transformation.

Over thousands of years millions of people have reported getting varying degree of these benefits from their sustained practice of meditation. Needless to mention that benefits accruing are always proportionate to the efforts invested in practice. The length of practice, comprehension of concepts, consistency in practice, mastery on implementing right techniques, strengthening of moral and social values are all very critical aspects to be worked upon before expecting advanced level of benefits out of one's meditation practice.

Interestingly, researchers are increasingly claiming that most meditational benefits can very well be replicated under laboratory conditions. This re-emphasises the original thoughts that meditation works for each and every human being without exception. Meditation certainly keeps you healthy, makes you happier, improves your performance across all activities including mental and physical, and greatly enhances your positive scoring on social and emotional quotients. Most importantly, meditation nourishes your psychological and spiritual well being like no other known practice.

No wonder the number of people opting for practising meditation is exponentially growing in the developed world. As per a study on the subject by National Center for Complementary and Integrative Health, USA, (NCCIH) carried out in 2012, over 18 million active meditators were found representing about 8 per cent of entire US adult population. Even more interesting finding from the study was a count of 927,000 children going for meditation, a healthy 1.6 per cent of all children. Many US schools now include meditation as part of their curriculum.

According to TheGoodBody.com, an organisation based in the USA and engaged in case studies, insights and analysis for health products, equipments and gadgets, the number of people practising meditation globally have tripled in between 2012 and 2019 and are estimated up to 500 million strong. According to their study updated in 2019, over 14 per cent of all adults in the US have practised meditation at least once with females being at 16 per cent and males at 12 per cent. The percentage distribution over different age groups also make interesting reading as 18-44 years being at 13 per cent, 45-64 years at 16 per cent and 65+ years at 13 per cent. The listing of major benefits as reported by their respondents in their survey conducted in 2016 also provides an interesting insight about over-all expectation of people going for meditation in the US. General Wellness tops this list with 76 per cent followed by improvement in Energy and Drive reported at 60 per cent. The top two benefits were closely followed by Aid in Memory and Focus at 50 per cent. Anxiety Relief at 29 per cent, Stress Relief at 22 per cent and Depression Relief at 18 per cent were other major benefits reported by people. Similar trends are also visible in all developed societies and certainly indicate significant growth potential of practitioners in developing societies as well in due course of time.

Stage One

Curious Explorer

Meditation is often described as a life-long journey. All long haul journeys pass through rough terrains and unknown topography. Sharp turns, undesired twists, blind spots and ditches are also to be invariably expected on the way. Imagine a journey where even roads are not properly laid out barring some foot paths crisscrossing in unfamiliar topography. Meditation is absolutely like making a way through dense forests without the luxury of proper signs, leads or familiar milestones.

Practising meditation is more like 'a lone wolf's approach' where one does not have much help from others. All one may have is some theoretical knowledge and experiences of others. Other person's experiences, however, are unique and rarely guide others in perfect ways. Still, a new explorer stands to benefit from familiar markers from whatever source. Even rough signs help locate one's own position and may point in right direction. This should indeed help in avoiding detours, glitches and pitfalls to ensure faster pace. As such, advance preparation becomes all the more critical for pursuing meditation.

Similar to a particular student outshining his other classmates in the school, practitioner's own diligence, discipline, dedication, and perseverance play significant role in making right progress in meditation. It happens as the dimensions impacting meditation are infinitely boundless as against a fairly defined and limited syllabus used in a school class. Also, there are far more transitional steps in meditative journey creating endless obstacles on the way. But qualities just mentioned always come handy in acquiring specific skills and mastering techniques to help practitioner taking his practice to whole new levels. One might read about claims that certain professions, life styles, cultural backgrounds or individual make-ups provide better headstart in meditational progress but that may just be some insignificant fraction. Yes, each individual has unique strengths and traits and progress made is never identical there are always many subjects to discuss falling within the general arc. So please do not make or think about comparisons or competitions with others.

Readers, who have undertaken reasonable number of sessions spreading over months, may well have realised that most concepts to be learned are sequentially connected with each other. In the beginning of your practice, you have to comprehend the concepts before actualising them into your practice. Later, your level of mastery over concepts and actual practice start helping each other in an intertwined manner. But you should take up one problem at a time and master it to desired levels before starting on the next issue. If sitting continues to bother you, deal with it before you start working on breathing. Starting on one issue and leaving it in between is not going to help in the long run. Make peace with the fact that no one can work on improving all skills at the same time.

Another reality to be faced in meditation practice is about shortcuts not working at all. Neither have you got option to pick and choose as nothing is optional. Some levels in formal education allow you wider variety to choose your questions to attempt. There you can always skip some chapters and still aim for higher final score. Meditation progress does not offer you that luxury. As such, patience has to be default setting over the entire journey. Attempts made by many overenthusiastic practitioners, unfortunately, run the risk of corrupting the practice altogether. Such an expedited approach ends up in pushing real benefits of meditation further away. So, do not aim too much or too fast. Master patience and be ready to travel light with focus on mastering a single issue at any given point of time.

Most practitioners face bigger challenges to their meditation in the initial period. My personal experience is a testimony to this fact. And it is not difficult to assume why. The impacts of negative forces at work in normal life have stronger pulls and pressures in the beginning. In this stage you have to learn and practise concepts and also confront old habits and attitudes. That is why many people cave in even before giving meditation a serious chance. Please generate additional motivation to somehow cross this stage, have patience, show your commitment, remain dedicated and do not give up. Once you are over the first stage, all you do is scale up your practice qualitatively as negative powers are destined to get significantly weakened over time.

Launch of space rockets offer a perfect case study to understand real impact of negative forces explained above. Weight of the rocket is always maximal in the first stage where a large amount of propellants and strap-on engines are used to lift-off the rocket from the launch pad. This stage consumes much larger fuel to obtain desired thrust, covers much less distance before obtaining desired ascent. The weight of the rocket by second stage is significantly reduced and only a sustainer engine is able to generate enough speed to achieve escape velocity. Finally, in the last stage only a maneuvering booster is required to guide the payload to its desired orbital position. Both the engines and propellants used in different stages are also not similar. This is exactly how progress in achieved on our meditational journey also.

In this background a curious explorer needs to comprehend a broad picture of the entire journey. It is like unfolding a large map to find out one's position and getting idea for future progress. A bird's eye view of the entire terrain of meditational horizon, even if general in nature, is likely to help a new seeker starting his journey in right earnest. The seeker can look out for rough milestones to get a fair idea about direction of progress, journey completed, and pace of journey undertaken and also get a general idea of things to come. This knowledge will certainly help him enhance his clarity about the whole process and make preparations required with responsibility and commitment.

1

Crossing Over Preparatory Issues

Popular proverb of 'Well begun is half done' applies for meditation completely. To begin with, all we have is an enthusiast who is curious to try out meditation and is willing to test waters. Notions at this stage are in fluid state with no deep understanding or conviction. There is no real comprehension of issues, challenges or obstacles. Identification with this stage is very simple as most people live this life all day long. Usual Concerns, perceptions, judgements, thoughts and their continuous rerun keeps them busy with no room for peace or letting go. Most thoughts are founded in dead moments of time bygone or fears, or 'what if' scenarios about things to happen. Concepts like silence, stillness, insights, and fulfillment are just empty words with no real forms or substance. Body is not ready to offer the stillness required for contemplating on any subject; mind refuses to obey no fly rules; thoughts keep originating endlessly. Even if one forces body to sit and contemplate, it uses the forced sitting to induce sleep. No wonder many people are seen enjoying deep sleep in their introductory meditation sessions.

This stage is like primary school in formal education system. Objective is to obtain primary knowledge of the subjects. Simply attending the school physically suffices to move on to next class. There is no pressure of performance. You can count on your guides to get reminders of your responsibilities which are simple and easy to follow. Most things are grasped in a single effort. Assignments, if any, are short and simple. The outcomes expected are generally in black and white and obviously clear in scope and approach. There are lots of holidays and you are not expected to bother any learning while outside the school.

Novice meditation starters in this stage struggle with very basic and physical issues like finding sufficient time, sitting in the sessions with ease, besides usual struggle with regularity and sincerity. As and when one sits for meditation, the mind starts showing its efficiency by pointing towards urgencies seeking immediate attention. Forget about subtle matters, the very physical issues are found beyond solutions. Basic issues like when to sit, how to sit, how long to sit, what to think and how to start practice acquire immediate priority. Importantly, these issues are of high significance for a novice as well as a seasoned practitioner alike. So, we better deal with all important preparatory issues in sufficient details before moving further.

Theoretically it is not important that one prepares to meditate with any specific routine but we all are busy people and desire to get the most out of what we do. Recommendations mentioned below are optimum level suggestions to deal with all physical and environmental issues so that no time gets wasted in doing things in wrong manner. How and where to sit, how long to sit and how to deal with temperatures, noise levels, intervention from people are some such issues that need to be faced from the very first meditation session.

One must have seen an infant in the family learning to stand and walk with lots of trouble taken by people around. The child needs encouragement to put one foot in front and maintain a balance and all those steps must have been repeated many times over until she could do it all by herself. That support as well as instructions from family is nothing but a formal practice in the art of walking. Before you know, the same child turns out a sprinter and starts helping others to run faster than before. Basic preparations for getting ready for meditation are similar to learning the art of walking. Once you learn to walk with baby steps, you keep refining your art all by yourself. Later you not only improve your own practice but can also extend your hand to others in the vicinity.

Mastery over these issues may not contribute to the success of real meditation but good practice of these points remove the nagging worries that play spoil sports especially in the beginning of the practice. Accepted that we are all real people from actual world and face very pressing demands from family, work, self and society and, as such, we must look at these preparations from practical perspective rather than just looking at ideal scenarios that do not fit in our life. So deviations forced out of our individual situations are well acceptable provided we remain committed to the objective behind each suggestion listed below.

A. Setting a Suitable Schedule

Establishing a formal practice schedule, a specific time when you resolve to do meditation and nothing else, is very important to begin with. It may prove a bit difficult for some because it requires back working and rescheduling of other activities and appointments to make sure that the schedule remains available on all days. It may also necessitate making some lifestyle changes which normally have their own challenges. For example, fixing a morning time calls for sleeping on time, which means saying no to late night parties, movie shows or missing live match telecast of your favourable sports or favourite TV programme. Some people are very adjusting and for them changing any schedule earlier or later is no big deal. Well, that may be called flexibility, a worthwhile trait to feel proud of. But that does not work with meditation. Flexibility in changing time for practising meditation qualifies as a negative character. Actually, flexibility in schedule makes mental focus all the more difficult simply because the mind gets the signal that it is ok to not follow strict schedule. And mind loves freedom as much as it hates discipline. You better fix a particular time and stick to it no matter what.

Learning meditation is like acquiring most difficult skill set. People familiar with the training schedule of accomplished sports persons will vouch that they rearrange all their activities and restructure their environment so as to ensure that there are no distractions or interruptions to their training schedule. Learning meditation is no less. Yes, you start this skill learning quite late in life by which time you are already conditioned by your habits that are difficult to kick out. But you hardly have a choice. Experiences of people who start meditation and try to keep their earlier habits in business are not encouraging at all. Habits have to be dealt with, discipline in life has to be introduced, and scheduled time must be spared for this pious initiative.

It helps to accept that our life thus far has been similar to muddy water flowing in a river. Meditation is intended to clean that stream, remove all the sludge, promote the aquatic life and regenerate the water sources. Needless to say, all streams discharging into the river shall have to be purified to attain this objective. Similarly, all our daily activities, all our habits, all our routines and thinking processes will have to be refined and readjusted to support learning of this great skill from the very start. To some people all this schedule fixing may initially sound a big effort. But people who are good at learning new skills will look at this favourably. Actually, your resolve to be open for making changes in your habits and life style is a nice pointer showing your determination to use your sessions on scheduled time.

B. Creating a Cozy Corner

Second important physical preparation is to find a place where you can sit for your sessions. There are not much to expect except that the place selected should not be noisy or frequented by other family members. The place must offer you the privacy to prepare yourself battle ready. Depending on your individual situation, it can be a separate room in the quite corner of the house or a small makeshift corner or anything in between. No, it does not have to be some ideal spot on the bank of a river, near a lake or amidst a forest. Basic requirement is to get a place where you can sit comfortably without being distracted or being conscious of happenings in the vicinity. You cannot meditate if you start feeling as if you are on display. Again, you are advised to practise your sessions at the same place every day. Our mind body entity respects continuity. So if you frequently change your place, you will have difficulty in stilling your mind to be ready for meditation. Later you will get introduced to the enormous difficulties faced in concentrating the monkey mind. Even the remote possibility of some people crossing your sight while you sit with closed eyes is enough to let this monkey continue its jumping.

Sounds of all types also need to be dealt with. For that your place has to be away from sources of sound. All types of sounds are distracting. Pious bhajans or solemn classical music is no exception to this rule. Unfortunately, out of all sense organs our ears are most disobedient. Ears cannot be closed at will the way we can close our eyes. On the other hand, meditation demands highly concentrated attention. It certainly does not mean you have to go for a sound proof room but lesser the sound better it is to dissuade the mind from deflecting concentration.

Some people go to the extent of especially decorating their seat area to invite better vibrations. They burn a candle or a lamp and also burn incense stick to create a mood. If you are devotional type, may be such routines help you during your initial sessions but ultimately you will have to move over such practices when you start realising them as obstructions. For example, whispering smells from incense stick will ultimately qualify as a distraction as it is capable of inviting mental thoughts about the smell itself. My personal experience suggests that once you have conducted your session in your fixed place over few months, you start feeling the unique tranquility that helps your concentration. So, even if you prefer to start your place with your paraphernalia, be ready to get rid of the same as soon as feasible.

In addition, there are a few sacrosanct principles for your selected space which need to be maintained at all times. Let your space be reserved only and only for spiritual activities. Activities that are even remotely associated with entertainment, sensual/erotic/carnal or violent in nature must never be allowed near your selected space. Let this place develop its own aura and splendour so that your mind is motivated to regain its purity the moment you take your place for conducting your regular session. These subtle issues ultimately play significant role in success or failures of your meditation efforts and you better take care of them from very beginning of your journey. With all above precautions duly taken care of, your mind gets ready for the required surrender no sooner you take position for conducting your session, and you will soon realise that it is a big positive factor.

Some people prefer to meditate in their home temple area. It may be obvious choice as they consider meditation as an extension of worship itself. While it is ok to use such a place but the real difference between the worship and meditation should never lose sight. Speaking loudly, worship involves a somewhat *quid pro quo* transaction where a person offers his bhakti to his chosen divinity and in return expects a certain blessing, be it peace or positive culmination of desire or prosperity in general. So there is a person desiring and an authority being approached to seek favours. But there is nothing like that in meditation. Here one makes his own efforts to touch base with his own inner self in an effort to understand its true nature and, as an extension of one's existence, establish a unique connection with the entire universe. So use your worship area for meditation so long as the differences involved are clearly understood and appreciated. If it helps, and only if it helps, you may use the temple bell before starting your session or you may light a lamp to help you jump start your sessions. Later you can always get rid of these rituals similar to scaffolding being discarded after construction of a building gets completed.

You should feel free to try out all possible aids and use them as long as they help you in your practice. For example, one person prefers to sit in a dark room to avoid disturbance from indirect daylight while some other may be fearful of dark and may need a bright lamp even in night time. Feel free to try whatever works for you. Your objective is to attain a nice mood to sit for some extended period in pure contemplative posture. A special spot reserved for meditation and nothing else works for most people. Please ensure that your place feels conducive for your practice and do not forget that it always requires a bit of experimentation. Please try out all possible options at your disposal and get a feel of how the place responds to your desire to sit with lesser distractions and avoiding all sorts of self conscious feelings.

C. Pledge for Perpendicular Posture

Right posture is indeed critical for obtaining maximum possible gains out of meditation. But in the beginning one can sit in any posture, either on ground or on cushion or even on a chair. There is practically no bar for any posture in particular. Your posture must facilitate sitting for entire duration of the session without giving rise to pain or uneasiness. Once that happens, the body keeps sending sensations to mind forcing it to lose its focus on anything else.

However, let us not lose sight of the experience of million others who have invested their years and years in learning the fine tricks and eventually using the Lotus Asana. Common visualisation of a person in meditation is always someone sitting straight with crossed legged and eyes closed. This has been so for all time periods, cultures, religions as well as geographies. So even when we, due to some or the other reasons, start with any other posture, ultimately we have to follow suit and get used to Lotus posture because it is only there one experiences mind feeling complete freedom from the physical body.

The practical requirement from the sitting pose is to ensure back, neck and head remaining erect, without having any tension, in a straight line similar to a pile of coins resting one over the other, perfectly balanced. Let psychic currents pass without any obstruction from base to top. Erect spine makes inhaling and exhaling possible without disturbing other parts of the body. Similarly, open chest posture with rib cage lifted slightly allows obstruction free abdominal breathing. Without this feel of uplifting, the breathing tends to attract mental attention. Erect posture frees mind from paying attention to the body. That in turn facilitates attention remaining fixed on nasal track for breathing alone. Erect neck and head also makes falling asleep that much more difficult. Ultimate perfection in this posture brings breathing into auto mode so much so that one loses difference between inhaling or exhaling at a given point of time. The idea is to treat your body as a vehicle parked in a secure lot with only engine running at a slow speed without any vibrations or sounds.

Full Lotus, Half Lotus or Quarter Lotus positions meet all above requirements. That is why these are most popular positions among all practitioners. Some people find Vajra Asana more comfortable. One can try out and settle for what works best. For either posture, sitting on a firm cushion provide additional balance and comfort. If you do not have a firm cushion, a simple cushion used on your couch or just the pillow from your bed can be used to get the same benefit. Resting of hands, similarly, can be on the lap or stretched out for resting on the knees. Idea is again comfort and convenience. In order to ensure relaxation for muscles of neck and back, shoulders also need be relaxed by slightly opening the front body and pushing shoulders back.

Dealing with the gaze is yet another important point to discuss. During initial sessions, it is recommended to try meditation with eyes open. Fixing the gaze loosely in the front in an unfocused manner is found helpful because the wondering of mind increases exponentially with eyes closed. Beginners may like to keep eyes open without actually noticing any patterns or pictures or objects in the front. Keeping eyes open also helps to avoid falling asleep.

Avoiding thoughts and day dreaming are bigger distractions for the beginners and keeping eyes open certainly helps for the same. Later, most meditators can be seen practising with closed eyes.

> "Mere physical sitting is not enough. You have to sit carefully and attentively. Let your body and breathing sit. Let your mind and emotions sit. Let your blood circulation sit. Let everything sit. Then your sitting becomes indestructible, immovable".
>
> — *Maezumi Roshi*

D. Managing Duration of Sessions

Every person has different experience for learning new skills. Some learn during the dawn, some in the afternoon and others in the evening time. Meditation is considered as one of the most crucial skill a person can ever learn. As such, one should combine own orientation with traditional wisdom out of experience of others to decide the best time to conduct sessions to begin with. Third aspect for deciding the right time is of nature since it plays a role in stilling the mind and thoughts.

Conventional wisdom suggests the twilight time zones, when the day turns into night or when night turns into day as best times for sitting for meditation. This is a time when physical activity level is generally low. As per Sanatan traditions, this time of Godhoolivela encourages activity only among Asuras. Devas on the other hand are advised to remain inactive during this time. The fact that most human beings are seen experiencing inertia around twilights is also established through scientific studies. Whole surrounding is quieter particularly at the dawn. Daily life of people around has yet to start, the body is well rested and mind is at peace. There are no calls, mails or messages expected to be attended to. You feel more agile and energetic. These natural factors makes this time most suitable for meditation.

Keeping practicalities in mind as well the best time suggested is early morning before breakfast. Mind and body are at their best to fight dozing off into sleep. Sessions in morning result in better clarity. Morning meditation also helps in setting exquisite tone for starting a great day. Morning time comes out winner from hygiene point of view as well which enables better blood circulation allowing pain free longer durations in desired postures. That also facilitates practising Asanas and Pranayam exercises before sitting for meditation. Statistically also, most people conduct their meditation sessions in the morning itself.

After work hours may also be a workable idea especially for those who use their muscles at work. For such people, a good session after work helps relieve all tensions harboured by the body making their remaining hours more effective. After work meditation also facilitates a smooth switching from work to personal life. There are some who normally start their work in early hours and they normally finish by early afternoon. Early evening time may work best for them as well, unless they can pre-pone their wake up time and squeeze in meditation before starting their work.

Considering the importance of meditation for rest of your life, it deserves to be first most important activity of each new day. Those who do so, enjoy many overflowing benefits in normal life as well. Let news and mails wait for later. World is unlikely to go anywhere if you do not update yourself before your daily session. The habit of getting updated with news headiness is the worst of attachment to begin your day. News Channels and Newspapers seek your attention as their esteemed customers. You better avoid their trap and behave like a responsible customer and connect with them at a time of your choice. Kicking out this lousy addiction, by itself, is a great by-product of your practice.

Taking a good bath before each session is highly desirable. Bathing in Indian culture is taken as a cleansing ritual which helps you feel fresh and clean inside out. In addition, a good bath help soak away both muscular and mental tension. No wonder, Indians take bath before every important activity, meditation being no exception.

Some people prefer to meditate just before hitting the bed at night time. They report lesser mental activities at that time. Well, this can never be a good idea at all. By night time your physical and mental energy is drained, your stress and fatigue levels are at peak. Constant mental processes of the entire day convert you into a bundle of contradictions. Due to these factors, you are unlikely to perform at your best for any activity you undertake at this time. Fatigue leading to dullness should never be taken as concentration of mind. Aiming for progress in meditation in such overwhelming condition is a disaster in waiting. In any case, meditation is the life changing and most difficult skill to be acquired that just cannot be left to be the last activity of the day. However, practising meditation before sleep has some obvious physical advantage in so far as it helps you unwind mental processes active during the day. This directly contributes to better quality of sleep and you can expect fewer dreams and even fewer nightmares. So, it is good to make it a worthwhile habit, albeit please do not count this sitting as meditation.

Psychologically also, morning time proves better over other options for practising meditation. After few months into your practice, you will be dealing with raw stuff involving feelings, emotions, moods and attitudes. The time you select must also be sensitive to these factors. Morning time is best suited from this angle as well because later in the day your attitude is likely to get conditioned by happenings of the real world. During morning time you are fresh and look forward to your sessions with hope and positivity rather than exasperation or desperation.

Much later, when other peripheral issues get resolved, you gain freedom to sit at any time of the day. By that time you stop getting impacted by the happening of day to day, and every hour of the day is the same for you. At that stage, hour of the day is no more your concern. But that is couple of years down the line, not now.

Irrespective of your choice of time, please make sure that the temperature of your surroundings is moderate, air is fresh, body is well oxygenated and fresh oxygen supply is not inhibited. Your muscles must be well stretched. Your clothing must be as per prevailing climatic conditions and not too tight or too loose. Please ensure that you are neither deprived of minimums nor you are tilting towards luxury because in either situation your body will find it that much more difficult to keep you free from its twinges and frenzies. And if the body is not well attended to, it would not allow your mind the freedom to focus inward. It is indeed so simple.

E. Settling Sufficiency of Sessions Duration

This is yet another critical point to deal. Generally, the golden rule for practice for every other trait is more the better. But meditation is different. In true spirit of words what matters here is quality and not the amount of time spent. The theory of middle path shown by Buddha is found most effective for determining time for meditation practice. In simple words, it just means 'Don't overdo it' as much as 'Don't underdo it'. This means you sit for that much length of time where your body supports you without aches and irritations plus your mind feels fresh and willing to listen. Uncomfortable body and unwilling mind are equally bad omen for positive progress in meditation.

The key for settling optimum time for your practice is patience. Please be ready to wait for years before finding your sweet spot. Make a cautious beginning. Keep your expectations low. Do not get disheartened as you realise in the beginning itself that even ten pure minutes of real meditation are good to make a difference. Just remember that every practitioner faces frustrations in the initial periods. Remain open to add precious minutes to your time but only bit by bit. Remember that you are not here for endurance test. The use of alarm works as a double edged sword. On one side it reminds you that you are still not there but on the other hand it provides a very nice tool to your fickle mind to keep expecting the alarm to go off any moment.

As a general suggestion, a period of 25-35 minutes is considered a safe target. During initial periods, you have many challenges like posture, uneven breathing, fighting sleepiness and such other irritants. As such if you are able to meet even the minimum target time of clean ten minutes, you should feel satisfied with your progress. There is no point in torturing yourself if your body is not supporting you happily and your mind starts turning rebellion. Be generous and let your duration increase rather slowly. As a definite yardstick, if you are able to comfortably sit for 30 minutes after about a year of your effective start, you are absolutely on track.

> "You should sit in meditation for twenty minutes a day, unless you are too busy—then you should sit for an hour".
> Zen proverb

In the beginning of your practice be ready to face testing situations rather regularly. Your practice will experience highs and lows without any specific reasons. One day you will feel like pro while the very next day, with most other things remaining same, you find it impossible to make your mind quite even for few moments. It is all natural and the best way to deal this situation is by getting used to it. This phenomenon is experienced even after years into your practice. But frequency will drastically come down as you continue your practice over years. Another practical experience worth sharing is to mentally fix your time for that session keeping in view your schedule of the day and state of mind on that day. Telling your internal system in advance helps it to respond accordingly. This way you are taking away this decision from your subconscious system and telling it to stick to the time already finalised beforehand. Incidentally, subconscious system is a good servant but bad master.

Over months and years, length of your session will be less and less your challenge as both body/mind and your externals demands get adjusted to your routine. By this time your internal alarm system itself gets activated to achieve set targets without any intervention on a daily basis. Seasoned practitioners are known to sit even up to 3 to 4 hours at a stretch but most people in their earlier years suggest a time of 45-60 minutes to be most effective.

F. Beholding the Breath

Breathing is a subconscious activity shared by all living beings. It might sound funny to have a lesson about this basic and most common activity. We learn it automatically and it continues subconsciously all by itself without any interruption or intervention. But breathing for meditation is a different ballgame altogether and it comes out as one of the most critical barrier for success. Meditation involves transforming breathing from subconscious to a conscious and deliberate activity. Breathing acts as the most effective exercise for keeping mental distractions and diversions at bay. Holding focus on inhaling and exhaling not only brings calmness of body and mind, it also eliminates distractions and turn out as most important activity for beginners in particular. They must detest changing the duration of their breaths and continue with natural rhythm. Not worrying for anything being right or wrong and just paying attention to respiration is enough to bring desired relaxation.

Beginners are advised to bring their attention to breathing in a willing manner without exerting any kind of pressure. Let the natural activity of breathing remain as natural as it ought to be. Some people find keeping count of breaths useful. It helps them to keep the mind engaged on breath as otherwise the thoughts start wandering into no fly zones. One may try keeping a target of 10 or 15 breaths per cycle and start another cycle all over again. Please remember that this number counting is not for keeping score but to keep the monkey mind entangled on breathing and not go out. Whenever it does go out, please bring it back and start counting once again.

Sensations provided by breathing meet all critical features advised for an apt subject matter for conducting the meditation. Breathing involves multiple movements, variations in pressures at different stages, changes in temperature for inhale and exhale, sensations at different locations of the entire respiratory track coming in contact with breath. Normal understanding about breath is about nose or, at best, nostrils. But breath passes through nose, throat, voice box, wind pipe and finally in the lungs. Feeling a breath at all these locations, and with all its variations, offers a very vast opportunity to become the subject matter for advance meditation progress. All this make it ideal subject for engaging mental attention.

Later, when you have reached to certain level of progress, this breathing alone is your most effective instrument for deepening your practice. At that stage you will have to further learn conscious and rhythmic breathing which is entirely different than the auto, involuntary and unconscious breathing used in the beginning. But considering superlative complexities involved in that process, discussions for explaining issues for that stage are best kept for much later.

G. Minding the Mental Matters

Having settled all physical and environmental issues it is now time to focus on issues related with the mind. Before sitting in daily session, it is advisable to remind yourself that you have made the choice of sitting as your own conscious decision, that there is a motivation and commitment behind this endeavour. This fires up the clarity of purpose and helps achieve good outcome. Equally advisable is to fix some basic targets for every session just after taking your posture. One may recall problems faced in last session and make a mental note how to avoid those in this session. Yes, it is a serious business and deserves to be approached with all seriousness.

Initial sessions offer you several easy goals to achieve. Not falling sleep may be the first such goal. Continue to maintain the desired posture for some length of time may be another. Abstaining from day dreaming about some pressing issues is yet another reoccurring issue. Ignoring that pain in some part of body will need persistent efforts. Reducing the number of times attention gets lost from your breathing demands multiple attempts. There are many more specific issues that you have to remain conscious of over a long period of time. These issues may not appear so significant but experience suggests that these very harmless looking petty but nagging issues remain strong enough to dilute desired balance between body and mind.

Let us also look at other soft issues playing critical role for fruitful meditative sessions. First of all, please hit the cushion only and only with a calm mind. Heading to your seat straight from agitated mind with work related or relationship issues is never a good idea. Even if you are indeed a multitasking expert, you need a break before starting meditation. Meditation is effective only after a smooth change over from gross mental state to subtle state has happened which is impossible to achieve at the drop of a hat. You may not realise but even normal activities build up pressure in the muscles and other organs which needs to subside at a natural pace. Let first few minutes of your sitting always be dedicated to letting the body and mind achieve this transition.

Please ensure that your body is well oxygenated, limbs are relaxed, muscles are stretched, blood flow is stimulated and mind is serene. Also, always approach your meditation session with a loving attitude. Maintain a friendly and accepting view on your feelings and thoughts. An agitated mind is the biggest enemy of meditation. Please remember this statement all through your journey. Overlooking soft issues mentioned above carry big risk of pulling down quality of your practice irrespective of presence of best of physical environment.

Having dealt with all preparatory issues, it is time to dig in with conceptual subjects to be learned, understood, contemplated and realised one by one. Please allow sufficient time to help sink comprehension of these difficult and at times philosophical subjects but only at your leisure pace. The placement of issues involved is following the order of criticality for growing your practice and degree of challenges involved. Ultimately, all the issues explained represent one individual step of the ladder. To climb over to your desired place, you will need to cross over each step irrespective of its placement being at the bottom or near the top.

> "If you just sit and observe, you will see how restless your mind is. If you try to calm it, it only makes it worse, but over time it does calm, and when it does, there's room to hear more subtle things – that's when your intuition starts to blossom and you start to see things more clearly and be in the present more. Your mind just slows down, and you see a tremendous expanse in the moment. You see so much more than you could see before". — *Steve Jobs*

H. General Dos and Don'ts for Getting Prepared

Starting meditation without bringing some basic changes in our day to day life may not be very effective. While you sit on the mat for few minutes, good progress in meditation is dependent on what you do and how you do to your off mat activities. Let us briefly look at some useful 'Dos' and 'Don'ts' which prove effective in pursuing meditation practice in right earnest. Investing time in these practical tips also permeate in other walks of life including work, family, relationships or pursuing passions and hobbies. Therefore, one may practice them irrespective of commitment for meditation. Practised well, these suggestions contribute in augmenting psycho powers which also play critical role in pursuing meditation:

1. **Unplug electronic gadgets** — While it is right that 24/7 access to internet and smart gadgets bring us instant access to current affairs, news and people but these very gadgets and Apps are indirectly damaging our brain by curbing its attention span. Constant access to smart gadgets also plays havoc with human memory muscle. Let us not forget that humanity has survived so long without internet and all these gadgets. World is not going to end if we use these gadgets

only at appointed times. So apply your own rationale, decide how much time and frequency is logical and access your gadgets accordingly.

2. **Move away from disturbing environment**—Loud sounds, unpleasing scenes, foul smell, irritating music, hot or humid places are all realities of our normal city life today. No, you never get insulated to their adverse impact on your overall performance. Realities like physical fatigue due to lack of sufficient rest and attachments with shining objects make us believe that we do not get impacted by these or that we got used to these. This also is never possible. Such factors continue to disturb your mental peace subconsciously irrespective of how long you have been exposed to them. Try isolating yourself from these disturbances and distractions for as long as feasible. With their presence in your system, you can certainly forget about meditation.
3. **Maintain a disciplined routine**—Good health demands all subconscious systems to work optimally. Human body is relatively rigid when it comes to adaptability. Maintain a tight routine as much as possible as human physical systems do not like adjusting to frequent variations in routine. The key processes of food digestion and sleep cycles in particular work best following a strict regimen. Right eating, regular exercises, following natural rhythms are all too important to keep body and thinking healthy, positive and productive in whatever we do. Like any sport played at highest level, meditation also necessitates well oiled machinery in terms of our body.
4. **Avoid company of distracters and parasites**—If we are not conscious and careful, unwanted people in the surrounding end up consuming a good portion of our quality time by forced involvement in their useless issues. Distracters have a common habit of dragging others in their follies under the pretext of seeking small guidance or help. While offering help to those in need is advocated, it is best done after taking care of own needs. Parasites are pure burden on you and better leave them at their own peril. Move away from their company. It is good to be humane and allow conscience to

get some kick by helping others but parasites and distracters impinge on your valuable energy and time leaving your mind agitated just for nothing.

5. **Always focus on the big picture**—Focusing vision on the big picture placed at some distance helps avoid too much attention on the nagging issues in immediate vicinity. Our thinking process generally thrives on entertaining immediate emergencies even at the cost of the substantial but distant. If you continue nibbling on the starters, you will have no appetite for the main course. It is strongly advised to find a minimum 30 minutes slot once every week for thinking and generating ideas for longer horizon issues in your life. Later this very slot can be merged with meditation session. Also, important is to pick specific goals for medium to long term and prioritise your efforts. Remember that it is your life and nobody else is as interested in you as you yourself.
6. **Be here and now**—Make an impressive mental placard with signs of "Be Here and Now" and flash it to self as and when your thoughts gravitate to either past or future. Untrained mind loves to dig in old memories or create scare out of fear of future. Such wandering is useless in totality. Be conscious to bring it back to present to focus on ideas and actions. It improves both output and quality of whatever we pursue at that point of time. This harmless sounding habit has qualitatively significant impact on our outcomes. As we will see in due course, this is also a primary mantra for success in meditation.
7. **Reserve some time in evening for worries**—The *sandhya* (meeting of two time zones) time generally makes our mind little dull and inactive. It is a time when our heart is really not into the job at hand. Our productivity takes a hit bringing down performance irrespective of what we do. It is equally true for students, sports persons, professionals, executives or those engaged in blue-collar jobs. This time is best used for worrying. Worrying cannot be avoided completely but we should not allow it to creep in any time without our permission. Please work on your skill to allow worries to meet you only on appointed time or by invitation alone. By

having a fixed exclusive schedule for worries, you prevent it eating your productive time.

7. **Take regular breaks at work**—Scientific research recommend taking smaller breaks from work frequently to keep performance above par. Most people avoid taking breaks to achieve more in less time but it is not effective at all. Human mind is not equipped to work in robotic manner. Our mind is genetically engineered to concentrate only in smaller intervals. Get up and move away from your work station every 40-45 minutes for small breaks of 5-10 minutes. You can count on any day that you perform better with breaks. You may have tried studying for long hours during college time and seen its resultant impact on quality of retention. Mind's working in adult life is no different.
8. **Mix-up your environment**—Best of a single place can only satiate you so much. Mind enjoys flying. It helps to regularly visit natural settings be it lakes, hills, gardens, valleys, forests or beaches. Equally important is to visit social settings having festivities, marriages, rituals. For the same reasons, visits to places of worship, spiritual lectures, congregations or visits to artistic settings like art galleries or places of performing arts, all contribute to change in environment. Mind regains freshness from such environments and fresh mind is a natural ally who is willing to stand with us in our time of need. Find some such opportunity at least once every week. You may not imagine how satisfying such visits can be for broadening your horizon and boosting your compassion and empathy quotients.
9. **Picking one job at a time**—We must cultivate the virtue of picking one activity at a time and take it to its logical conclusion before picking up another activity. Multitasking appears very fashionable but is terrible for final output. Through deliberately involving in more than one activity at the same time, we are unknowingly feeding to dirty habit of mind of wandering, habit that continues playing spoilsport on our long journey of meditation.

2

Body or Mind not being Who We Are

"Who Am I"? It is a basic question troubling spiritual seekers from times immemorial. But we intend to deal with it with reference to practical understanding of a common man of today living an incredibly busy life juggling pressures of career, family, society, finances and many more. Without entangling in the web of philosophies and difficult sounding concepts, it is true that identity of each one of us is truly unique. This sense of unique individual identity, generally called as 'self', comprises of the physical body, mind, intellect and some other force which makes these elements work together in harmony. Interestingly, this very individuality is always a work in progress; it is not something static, rather it continues evolving with every moment passing by. Its ever evolving nature brings its own complexities that we will understand in greater details in due course.

This single entity comprises of very unique subsets of feelings, emotions, thoughts, memories, imaginations, opinions, and experiences etc. Generally we look at it from a first person's perspective but at times we also look at it from third person's perspective. Actually, both perspectives are established as valid and imperative to define this entity. Interestingly, for a common man, discussions about 'himself' are rarely black or white because one's own commentary of 'self' is always circumstantial and multidimensional which is largely influenced by time and mental state. Still, let us attempt to understand it by dissecting the whole into smaller forms. Looking at individual parts helps in understanding the whole with greater clarity. Let us take one part at a time, define it, understand it, evaluate it and later put all parts together and see where we reach.

Are We Body Alone?

Our physical existence is certainly identifiable with our body more than anything else. It gives us a name, a specific image, a sensory system, limbs to act and a physical address where we live and can be reached by others. It is real as we can touch it and feel it in many miraculous ways. It is visible, functional, and movable and in general sustains our entire life. No wonder we remain attached with it and invest a lot of our attention and efforts on keeping it shining. Indeed, it works just like a brilliant machine that consists of highly complex systems and functions. But is it enough to define ourselves?

On the molecular level, our body consists of innumerable cells that are continuously replaced such that every cell gets replaced in maximum of 12 years. But our sense of identity remains unchanged all through our human life. Yes, body is operated by some very complex systems which function in auto mode for most part of our life. Imagine how our breathing continues, pulse runs, blood circulates, food digests and retinal images are conveyed to mind all through our lives. But all these activities ultimately come to an end and in a fairly predictable manner. At times, it comes to abrupt end even when all its functions are at peak of performance. On elemental level, 99 per cent of the mass of human body consists of oxygen, carbon, hydrogen, calcium and phosphorus. How can such a composition be associated with the uniqueness of its identity?

On atomic level, everything related to our body, its organs and processes are ultimately composed of atoms, which are made up of interacting subatomic particles, and can be called as 'matter' for general discussions. The 'matter' generally includes atoms and anything made up of particles (or combination of particles) and can exist in various states (also known as phases). All elements of 'matter' are always temporary and are known to change its combinations in due course. There is nothing new out here as all these points are well established in 'particulate theory of matter' put forth by Greek philosophers in 5th century B.C., just over 2600 years ago.

Closer study of anatomical aspects of the body and its working reveals multiple sensations like pain, hunger, thirst, injury, tiredness, fear, and pleasures, etc. All these sensations are nothing but regular reminders from the body's functional systems like Digestive and Excretory, Cardiovascular and Respiratory, Nervous and Immune, Skeletal and Muscular or system relating to Reproduction, etc. But all these functional systems are like equipments/processes and nothing beyond. These are all there to support body in its working just like a vehicle has engine, transmission, cabin, air pressures in tires, air conditioning, lighting, etc. together with their indicators and metres on display at the dashboard and nothing beyond. These equipments and systems work as per their nature and are mostly repetitive and identical for most beings. The moment we start thinking their direct correlation with our being what we individually are, the reply is in firm negative. These systems operate for most individuals with more or less similar intensities; they do not separate us from others for sure.

Yes, our body is a machine that allows us experiencing this world in physical form. It is similar to a vehicle assigned to us for a particular journey. We must take good care of it to get smooth ride but let us not forget that irrespective of body's qualities, at the end of a predictable time cycle, the end of the journey, it will have to be just left parked. Too much shining of it or too much flashing of its external decorations do not help it to go any faster or further; what takes it long and far is well serviced internal systems, cleaner fuel, periodical servicing, avoiding over-speeding, stoppage at recommended stations, lane and sane driver, careful steering and protection against collisions with other vehicles on the road.

So human body is an amazingly complex entity but simply not what we are.

Are We Mind and Not Body?

Some people say that we are a mind having a body at our service. Body and mind share an intimate but awkward relationship. Modern day neuroscience teaches us that organs working inside our minds are purely physical entity, conceptually and casually embedded in the natural world. Our mind receives millions of signals every moment from inside as well as through sense organs and remains busy in processing them together with experiences, memories and impressions stored from past realities as well as projections for future.

Others say that we are what we think and that we are nothing but a unique collection of memories, experiences, feelings, opinions or beliefs. But a close look at these claims will reveal the reality and very quickly. Thoughts and emotions are work of hormones like testosterone. Our mind creates all thoughts not by working alone but through its inextricable links with the body and the environment around. Our thoughts and feelings are also momentary in nature and are influenced by many other things like attitudes evolved over years, beliefs held and people we interact with or think about. Memories, beliefs and opinions are also not set in concrete. These change almost continuously and are just work-in-progress. Our recall of same event of past is different each time and our opinion about a particular thing changes all the time depending on the hat we wear at that point in time. Opinions are merely ways in which we attempt to link ourselves to a given situation, issue, time and circumstance. Thoughts generated by mind result from interplay of emotions, intellect, memory and ego which all are momentary and fail to define us as a unique identity.

Opinions and beliefs can refer to some specific elements about ourselves but not the entirety of our identity. Unfortunately, working of mind is not as much a matter of common knowledge as other organs but modern neuroscience has successfully tracked most of wiry neurons, electrical impulses and inter-connectivity of neuroelectrical signals operating in a human mind, leaving almost nothing unexplained. Mind's working, therefore, is quite comparable to the working of an efficient machine like a computer server that operates in line with its software(s) installed (and updated from time to time) and data base created over its useful life. One can even brand human mind as more complex than other machines. But all machines, at the end of the day, are machines. One cannot identify any machine with a unique identity.

Interestingly, our mind is not so much ours as we wish it to be. If it was ours, it should listen to our command and should surrender itself without resistance. But in reality, mind is a rebellion and hates to operate under rules and controls. Whenever we ask it to focus its attention as per our choice, it starts behaving in disorderly manner. All attempts to control it bring us to its reality of being like a monkey jumping from one branch to another at all times. Mostly, it does not listen to us and remains busy with its own agenda. How many times our mind is filled with thoughts and feelings that we do not wish or like? Even when we try to get rid of those thoughts, it embarrasses us by not letting go. Hence saying that mind has a mind of its own appears to be true.

Close observation of mind reveals it to be turbulent ocean with lots of creatures lurking below surface; an ocean that is always drifting, that gets blown by typhoons, that has undercurrents; a sea where 'I' is just like a boat which keeps surfing above, somehow. So, the mind can be anything but that very helpless 'I'.

Mind is a process and not a state; mind is a verb and not a noun; mind is a journey and not a destination; mind can be trained and enlightened, albeit, with concentration, patience and tons of efforts. If rest of the body is gross physical body (including brain), mind is just a subtle material body which also comes with 'use before' warning; it does become weak slowly but eventually.

Interestingly, at times we tend to look at things going on in our mind from purely a third party perspective. It is just like a person watching a movie on the screen.. On such occasions we also listen to a feeble voice suggesting us to do the right thing, the voice of our conscience. So if we can see ourselves from a distance or if we can have a pure independent voice well within our own self, and we are able to process such observation and pure counsel within our own mind, surely, we cannot be that very mind. The 'observer' and the one 'observed' ought to be different entities.

Surely, the 'self' we are looking is different from our mind and cannot be the constant and abiding entity that we know we are.

Are We Someone Defined by Others Around?

Others interacting with us look at us as a postal address having a distinct name, job title, relationship status or member of a particular group including religion. Agreed, these identities contribute in bits and pieces to define who we are but do not represent the whole of us. These are mostly not fixed but keep changing almost continuously. An attempt to link our 'self' with some or all of these identities is surely incomplete and undesirable.

Besides body, mind and changing identities discussed above, there is certainly another aspect that feels, judges, reflects and anticipates; one that is not visible but without which both body and mind entity is reduced to being just a big mix of material substances. It may also be understood as 'the voice in our head'.

The bond that keeps body and mind together and functional is called by names such as soul, consciousness, conscience, life breath, or 'atman'. Modern writers call it by the name of 'conscious awareness'. So they define 'self' simply as a form that is aware. Everything else is explained as simply projections of life situations. This force is the real principle of life, got distinct entity, never changes, and remains with you all through your life including when you sleep, dream or even when you are actually unaware. This 'awareness' is completely different than all mental processes involved in thoughts, actions, memories or feelings. This very element is immortal and is beyond time or space. This also is the spiritual part of human. That is how we are called spiritual being having human experience.

The experience of being human is supposed to be normal. But most of us take it very seriously and get entangled in its endless drama involving constant stream of thinking and chaos of emotions. Enjoying this projected experience consumes too much of our energy and attention leaving no quality time for serious thinking. The life vortex proves too tempting and seductive that the voice of frequent reminders coming from within, the sound of conscience, does not reach to our ears. On the other hand, conscious awareness is inherently still and silent. Without perfect silence, you cannot even experience it or feel it in any way. Many people live full physical life without ever listening to this unique silence.

Meditation is most effective reminder that enhances our ability to receive signals that life is timeless and the normal life drama is destined to come to an end, sooner than later. Meditation is that very reminder that makes us realise that we are part of eternal consciousness and occupy this body/mind entity only temporarily. Meditation is that serious thinking that lets us understand that the mirage being chased by us without differentiating needs (defined and minimal) of this body/mind from what it wants (countless and insatiable).

Should we not try to replace our acceptance of self from current perception to correct comprehension? Should we not behave responsibly and see through the web of desires and attractions? For sure, there is no use putting blame on genes, brain's biochemistry, constellation at birth, upbringing, immediate environment or even external pressures. No, none of these issues limits our potential except 'we' alone. Thinking, feelings, actions occupying us at all times are just a matter of habit flowing through our existence similar to free flowing powerful rivers. But the choice of flowing with the current, and allowing streams to take us where it wants, or swimming upstream, against the current, is entirely our own. Surely, swimming against the currents demands preparedness for tough breathing, bruises, scars and tons of caution but those are the real test of winners. This choice separates adults from teenagers or special from ordinary and makes us qualify to become first among equals.

After continuous practice of meditation for good period of time, you learn to being a unique personality and disengage yourself from your feeling of a physical body/mind. Continuous meditation practice alone activates your process of recognising your true nature. But you have to work hard and wait for a long time before you start visualising yourself as a bundle of conscious energy with no worries for body or mind. Until such time, all you need to do is develop understanding, refine the same by practice and undertake more practice.

Meditation Exercise for Regaining Vitality

> "No apps, no noise, no guidance. Sit in a comfortable position first thing in the morning, back upright, but ok to use cushions etc.. One hour at a time, no less. Just surrender to and accept whatever happens. No energy for and no energy against. Resist and reject nothing." — *Naval Ravikant*

At this early stage of your practice, expecting you to sit in proper meditation session will be too much of asking. But this book is not about increasing intellectual understating devoid of practical experience. Having covered basics about sittings for meditation, let us try some simple exercise hoping some direct and immediate benefits and get a feel as how it works. Since lack of physical energy is very common condition and impacts most of us in varying degree, even at this stage, you can try out your sessions for recharging your physical energy, if nothing else. Extra flow of energy will sure bring a welcome relief from exhaustion and feeling of fatigue that we are so used to.

Fatigue is a common symptom and is not always due to obvious reasons like hard work, prolonged work or poor sleep. To the contrary indirect factors such as worry, boredom and lack of exercises are more likely bigger source of strained feeling of weariness. Other factors leading to fatigue are pressure of dislikes, failure in finding solutions, conflicts with colleagues/seniors, sense of under-achievement, lack of opportunities, unreasonable demands from relationships, lack of job satisfaction, etc. Fatigue puts breaks on our ability to think with clarity and positivity and invariably pulls down our performance on all fronts. Besides physical energy, mental energy is as vital. Let us not forget that mind consumes about a fifth of our total energy and it does that at faster speed. Let us find how our experimental sitting can be used to restore positive energy and enthusiasm.

- Find a nice corner, a cushion and make yourself comfortable in your preferred position with backbone and neck in an erect line.
- Start deep breathing at your normal pace and feel the relaxation.
- Few minutes into your deep breathing, you will feel normal noise of your breathing settling down as a sign of relaxation and count of thoughts running through your mind getting progressively reduced.
- Bring your attention to your heart area. Remember that all our creative insights, ideas and breakthroughs originate from our heart only.
- Feel enthusiasm and inspiration entering your system with breathe in.
- Let lethargy and negative tendencies get thrown out with breathe out.
- Continue deep breathing with these feelings for a couple of more minutes.
- Let your thoughts go to people you idealise.
- Recollect instances of your ideals inspiring you with their words, actions or thoughts.
- Seek their blessings and compassion. And feel motivated by their examples.
- Feel responsible for people who trust, it may be parents, spouse, children, friends or trainers or some such other person(s).
- Uplift your imagination's thinking about past occasions when you felt fully charged.
- Imagine yourself as smiling or dancing or some such activity where you got completely absorbed.
- Try this sequence over and over for several minutes.
- Slowly come out of your session and get busy to face the world with renewed vigour in full roar.

3

Advancing Indisputable Acceptance

> "Reality is neutral. Our reactions reflect back and create our world. Judge, and feel separate and lonely. Anger, and lose peace of mind. Cling, and live in anxiety. Fantasize, and miss the present. Desire, and suffer until you have it. Heaven and hell are right here, right now." — *Naval Ravikant*

Finding faults in words spoken by others, expecting others to work as we deem fit, believing accuracy of own view point, unfulfilled expectations from dear ones, taking gestures of others in poor light, pronouncing judgements on others, finding faults with religious/social/political systems/players/groups, are incidents filling normal person's life from dawn until night without an end in sight. We go through these incidents on daily basis with full sincerity and responsibility under the disguise of making some difference. We take great pride while discussing these matters privately with friends.

We also expect others to appreciate our views/opinions and inculcate those in their lives as well. In reality, however, these are all obvious and clear instances of non-acceptance. Yes, normal person's life is indeed filled with countless mistakes in form of inability to accept things as they exist. Non-acceptance makes our mind agitated, it robs us of our mental peace, it generates negativity in our entire system, it pulls down our self-esteem, and it makes us feel small. Little we realise that it does more harm to us than to those blamed (people and situations) behind our non-acceptance.

Having strong views about a subject or desire to improve a thing appears harmless and obvious thing to do. But deep down, the very desire to improve a thing comes out of hidden non-acceptance for the same. After all, you will rather not think of improving a thing that is acceptable in its present form. In reality, this desire to change originates from premeditated resentments which in turn are embedded in non-acceptance. Being very subtle, seeing through this difference necessitates far deeper understanding. Unfortunately, most people of modern day continue harbouring negative feelings like resentment and disappointments even without being properly aware about them. Later, getting rid of these habits pose even bigger problems. Just like a stubborn tenant refusing to leave the leased house, such thoughts continue occupying our mental space no matter how hard we try to wish them away. Advancing your acceptance for things as they are, without any colour or judgement, remain the only remedy to pass by these resentments.

Most importantly, non-acceptance sows seeds of frustrations and anxieties. Each time there is non-acceptance, it works like developing a hole in our reservoir of happiness. All efforts to fill that reservoir go waste so long as holes are not plugged. You must follow a golden rule if you wish for peace in life that 'it comes only when it is made with everyone and everything around'. Agreed that world offers things that are imperfect but realistically it is also not possible to change most of the things on offer. Accepting them is the only lasting solution. This understanding alone helps in getting rid of brooding from daily life. Meditation is a proven and most effective antidote of such non-acceptance.

Besides acceptance, all you can do is to change all irritating things standing in your way. Well, one may try to change the world as hard as feasible but ultimately reality of one's inability to do so is bound to expose. You may also try arguing with others and refute their arguments at the top of your voice using strongest logic possible. But how many times you can recall people changing mind based on logic? After all their views are formed by their judgement which only tend to be stronger after discussions with people holding alternate positions. Their ears are as deaf for your arguments as yours are for theirs. Fighting something that you cannot alter is detrimental to your physical and psychological health and nothing else. This is a battle no one has ever won.

Understanding True Acceptance

Genuine Acceptance involves person's admission to the reality of a situation irrespective of associated negativity or inconveniences. It means open willingness to experience ourselves as it exist, remaining at peace with issues in front without feeling the need of altering or modifying them. It is about voluntarily moving away from 'what we want' to the reality of 'what we got'. Acceptance brings an additional solution to a given problem which did not exist earlier. Acceptance means 'letting go', a state of mind that brings a greater sense of freedom. That freedom alone leads you to the source of happiness. Accepting life and its events at their own terms without offering resistance and choosing not to desire changes is a unique option of saying yes to life at it unfolds itself.

On a more profound level, true acceptance leads to harmony with self which, in turn, makes way for harmony with the whole world. Thinking that mental peace requires secure, still and calm environment is wrong, as it be momentary attempt. Perennial mental peace is Acceptance alone. Developing acceptance is not moving away from perfections neither it means settling things below par. Acceptance puts higher value on malleability against rigidity. Perfections and ideals are imaginary perceptions based on a falsely perceived vision of the real world. Developing this understanding, however, ask for stronger strength and commitment and that is precisely why many people remain lost in their delusions by persisting with non-acceptance. Let it be realised that Acceptance is the only ladder that helps you grow from your 'ego self' to 'true self'.

Non-acceptance does not operate only for external issues. It plays havoc at our own individual self and with far greater consequences. In reality, most of us are not very generous with ourselves. Our own perceptions about our own mistakes, failures, rejections and criticism are our greater enemies. Non-acceptance of self accentuates normal worries to become nightmares. Soon, even small failures get enlarged into bigger self-doubts and fears. Non-acceptance of self leads to constant self-judging. This converts into poor emotional and psychological well-being. Self-acceptance, on the other hand is similar to the process of self-certification that everything is within norms. This certificate helps a great deal in performing at optimum level.

Unfortunately, self-acceptance is not our default state. So long as the going is good, most of us accept ourselves as we are but not so when we are down and under. Much more than external world, peace needs to be established with our own frailties. One must learn and practice to separate actions without being judgemental about one's own personality. Mistakes happen or flaws create problems but it is never a good idea to define yourself with your faults. That is a pronounced homicide of self-esteem. Unfortunately, roots of non-acceptance of self-get formed during the parenting experienced in childhood where children are constantly told to act within strict behaviour norms. However, as proven by scientific research studies, strict parenting actually creates behavioural problems in children in terms of lower self-esteem. Such children get punished more than others. But let us not punish ourselves anymore.

Acceptance is a fundamental virtue that has transformative impacts on our lives. Cultivating acceptance makes us humane. At a philosophical level, it makes us realise that world is what it is; that we are just very insignificant tiny part of this universe, that we need not take situations too seriously, that those opinions and views are mostly irrelevant, that desiring outcomes of things in a particular way is unwanted burden. Acceptance of self and surroundings as they are, actually releases large pool of energy that can be used to do wonders in life. Let things move without our desire or approval, let people think as they please, let others comments in ways they do, let situations evolve as and when they emerge. Desiring outcomes in your particular way, even for the tiniest issue, creates stress for you and you alone.

Accepting is not being Passive

Critics of acceptance blame it to be an excuse for inaction. They believe acceptance makes them less competitive and less successful. While being competitive does not carry an ugly connotation, acceptance has nothing to do with being complacent. Striving to do better than before, in true spirit, is completely natural feeling and is part of being human. Acceptance is in fact a training ground for actions. When you accept current circumstances and stop focusing on negative feelings you open your mind for intuitive feelings which always lead to positive actions and superior results. Acceptance, as a choice, enables you to stop putting things in narrow brackets such as right, wrong, good, bad, fair or unfair. Acceptance replaces such qualitative judgements with just a neutral feeling of 'this is what it is'. Acceptance does not stop you from being a fighter. Instead, it offers better ammunition and helps to identify the exact spot where strike is needed.

Acceptance demands courage rather than inaction. In normal circumstances, finding faults with self is taken as a way forward for self-improvement. Taking stock of your fault lines is considered first step towards corrections. But acceptance helps you perfectly in the "Acceptance Paradox", the situation where instead of defending against self-criticism you accept the fact that you are deficient and imperfect. It does not mean you give up, rather it acknowledges that you are far more worth and can pursue changes for things that matter much more in life. Acceptance is found most effective in all inter-personal issues. Combined with self-compassion, acceptance erases old burden piled up and paves way for bringing transformative changes in our social behaviour and attitude.

Acceptance restricts the swing of emotions in a narrow range such that impact of all emotions is fairly limited. It takes out force of negative resistance and makes us receptive for exploration with curiosity rather than anticipation. Acceptance develops padded cells in our mind to absorb vibrations from thoughts thereby minimising bouncing back effect. Acceptance is like peeling off false and limiting beliefs about self, others and life in general. It removes the very need of negative self-talks, self-control, self-regulation and thereby brings end to useless worries, fears, and anxieties. Non-acceptance, on the other hand, is just like rubber ball, you throw it to the wall with force and it comes back at you with almost similar force.

Acceptance and Tolerance

Acceptance moves many steps ahead of tolerance. Tolerance, for example, gives birth to a feeling of "I can live with such and such...." while acceptance will say "such and such is actually OK and living with it is just a natural course". Tolerance is possible without acceptance but not the other way round. Just imagine your teen child informing you about some unwelcome career choice or some such life style issue or your adult child informing you about choice for spouse or sexual identity, you have option to use either tolerance or acceptance. But taking it with tolerance will bring negative feelings to surface every time you face the child or think about her. Acceptance, on the other hand, will help you maintain peace both inside and with outer environment. Acceptance alone, in this case, will allow family living together with harmony and mutual affection remaining intact.

> "Instead of 'Let it go', we should probably say 'Let it be'; this recognizes that the mind won't let go and the problem may not go away, and it allows you to form a healthier relationship with what's bothering you." — *Jon Kabat-Zinn*

Acceptance and Meditation

An innocent beginner may be baffled as to why such a lengthy discussion on acceptance is provided while he is looking to initiate his meditation. Well, non-acceptance is that first roadblock which can force you to get exhausted and give up meditation even before a proper beginning is made. So long as events of the world (self included) weigh on you, you cannot recognise feelings of being in the present moment and view your own experiences with compassion. In due course you will develop much deeper understanding that success in meditation depends on concentrating your focus on 'here and now' and finally going inward to see the pristine truth and serene wisdom lying dormant inside. Meditation basically means investigating into one's own inner self by withdrawing mind and senses from the nagging distractions and to contemplate on issues of substance. Such investigation requires a stable mind that is free from all types of preconceived notions and diversions.

A mind suffering from brooding or sulking due to unacceptable happenings in the surroundings is never stable and free to focus inside. The stability of mind necessitates practitioner's acceptance of self as well as everything around which become possible only with letting go of instinct to protest or make changes. Non-acceptance works as mosquitoes disturbing a student trying to study on a summer night in an open space. Even when a mosquito is not biting or buzzing, the fear that it can do so at any time is enough to puncture the student's attention. Acceptance, on the other hand works like most effective repellent allowing that student the freedom to focus completely on his studies.

Hours and hours of sittings in meditation, month after month, with an un-accepting attitude are destined to bring only failures. Acceptance brings in humility and a sense of surrender. It goes beyond admission of defeat or powerlessness. Its virtues progressively help the mind to retain its peace and tranquility resulting in faster progress in meditation. Beyond a certain stage of your practice, acceptance and meditation will become intertwined where one helps the other grow but practical experience suggests that in the beginning acceptance is most essential quality to develop before even starting meditation.

Practical Actions to Cultivate Acceptance

So the first step is being aware of the realities and second step is developing acceptance for that very reality. 'Accept then Act' is considered a proven strategy to succeed. But actions do not always mean moving forward. At times, moving back or opting for no action is considered a better action. Let us explore all such steps, forward or backward, required to cultivate our acceptance beyond philosophies and religious teachings. These steps are worth making efforts not only for meditation but to enhance quality of life we live:

1. **Develop liking for self**—We generally judge our self harsher than others. Our normal system is geared to focus on negative qualities of self and positive qualities of others. Our perceptions for own faults/pains/expenses and others qualities/comforts/income are always exaggerated. Be kind to yourself. You may not be as bad as you think. Being in love with your internal self motivates you to be positive and do more. Be kind to yourself. Remember that your self-view determines your physical and psychological health. Negative self-talk is destructive, move away from it. Be aware of your positives and connect to family and friends. It always works. Forget past: tough childhood, bullied or abused, troubled relationship are normal events that happen with many. Winners shake them and built over past while weak continue clinging with them. Move over your uncontrolled habits. If you look around, there will be plenty of examples where people come out winners. Why should not you?
2. **Everything need not be personal**—Contrary to what many people believe, others got no time to always conspire against you. It is useless to think that others are teaming to let you down. Most people do not enjoy hurting others. Few may end up doing it out of ignorance or without any ill will. Many things get lost in translation. Have faith in others. Guarding against others eats up too much of your precious energy. Direct that energy to productive use.
3. **Forget and forgive**—Be selfish. Not forgiving hurts you most. Forgiveness is power. It benefits you and others around. Else, you carry all the resentment, anger, sufferings and pain on your shoulders like dead weight. That costs you lot of time and energy and only promotes negativity. Forgiving sets you free instantly. This is best tool for feeling light and charged. Have no place for grudges, hatred, envy or malice towards others.

4. **Experience challenges but make peace with failures**—Mistakes are made by people who experiment. Safest way of not making a mistake is to do nothing. More you challenge yourself, more likely chances of failure. Failures provide you wisdom so long as you learn from them. Failure can be bad, indifferent or good depending on the learning made. No one wins playing blame games. Accept that being defensive all the times is too dull and boring.
5. **Grow faith in others**—A person with right empathy may easily develop capacity to see and appreciate other's point of view. It should be simple to realise that everybody does, think and speak as best they know. Also, there indeed is more than one right way or more than one truth. See the ways of others with open eyes and listen their truth carefully. The difference in explanations of a single object comes from the difference in angle used by people. Everybody wants to have a happy, successful, and live a fulfilled life. So if our end objectives are similar, our ways to reach those goals cannot be much different.
6. **Remember the all powerful Supreme**—Having a firm belief in the presence of some supernatural power, called with whatever name, also helps in gaining acceptance for happenings around. Firm belief in Him and his ways provide strength to accept every outcome in life as His wish. This belief is especially helpful to face adversities presented by life from time to time.
7. **Maintain arms length distance from emotions**—Emotions hold key to our feelings, thinking, and actions on a moment to moment basis. And it is so easy to get wrapped around them. Emotions are to be blamed for our perception of an event and our response that follows such perception. Knowing, understanding, identifying emotions require deeper understanding of working of rational mind versus emotional mind, which requires lot of work and practice.
8. **See through impermanence of the visible**—Looks, money, position, influence or possessions are all very subjective and matter differently to different people. Even if there is someone who seems to have more than you, how is that relevant? What do we get even if others see us or rate us in a particular manner? Can their approval ever feed us one time

meal? Yes, our ego loves constant comparison with others or our own scenarios with past or future but we must go past that ego. If you break things into smaller parts, you will get many good things to cheer about. The ugliest of person may have some personality traits that are worth appreciating after all personality combines looks, dressing sense, walking sense, command over language, general knowledge, manners, skin quality, hair style, features, etiquettes, courtesy, sense of brands, fashion sense, gadgets used etc. If at all you need to compare, do that between your potential and your current status. God has made all human different under a scheme, so stop comparing please.

9. **Stay Positive at all times**—We must remain positive under all circumstances. Every negative situation also has an optimistic viewpoint to follow. Spend time on activities and people who influence your positivity. Say no to sit with someone known to drag you down. Stop entertaining day dreaming about vague fears that hold you back. Best antidote for gaining positivity is to extend help to people in need. It is bound to cheer you up. Also, take regular physical exercise and watch out your food and sleep cycle.

Meditation for Calming Down from any Stressed Situation

Stress is part of every modern day life. During their hunting days, stress was a positive capability for our ancestors. But those kind of existential physical dangers pose no threat in modern times. Today also stress may be called a good thing for meeting a deadline or in emergency situations. But used frequently, stress unfortunately becomes a hazard. Interestingly, stress cannot be eliminated but certainly reduced. As a normal part of modern life, stress can be experienced from body, thoughts or environment. When stressed, the body thinks it is under attack and switches to 'fight or flight' mode, releasing a complex mix of hormones and chemicals such as adrenaline to prepare the body for physical action. This causes a number of reactions, from blood being diverted to muscles to shutting down unnecessary bodily functions such as digestion. It also minimises functioning of our brain leading to inability in thinking straight.

To make matter worse, remaining under stress for longer periods or too frequently turns out very detrimental for our mental health as well. "Stress" is already the biggest weapon of mass destruction at work in most urban societies today. More and more people, from all age groups, professions, income brackets, nations and ethnicities are experiencing stress today like never before. The idea of motivating the reader to use initial meditation sessions for inducing protection against this menace is to seek immediate and quick benefits for fighting against it as much as possible. Virtue of acceptance, incidentally, dilutes the guilt arising from issues giving rise to stress. Following exercise should be found helpful to reduce the stress on daily basis:

- Spray your meditation place with your favourite scent or light your incense sticks as the case may be to use aromatherapy. It works best for stress management.
- Settle down on your cushion in crossed leg posture with back and neck erect. After taking comfortable position, start deep breathing at your usual pace and continue for five to seven minutes.
- Zero down on the most obvious issues of your stress, one at a time.
- Assume a dark stage in front. Place the issue in some imaginary form in the center of that stage.
- Now assume a roof fitted focus light illuminating the identified issue in totality, beginning from the middle and expanding towards its outer edges.
- Slow your breathing and retain your attention on the illumination until all parts of the issue get brightly illuminated.
- Continue the illumination for a minute or so. Soon you will see a possible effective solution/understanding emerging out slowly. Soon it becomes more and more clear.
- At times, you may expect more than one solution hovering around the problem, including some immediate and some long term in nature.
- Park that solution in your mind for action at a later stage.
- Now think about a relaxing subject and focus on that to the exclusion of everything else. This diversion is to work as a break in between two issues.
- After some relaxation, pick up the next issue and go through same sequence.
- Repeat this sequence of illumination and diversion for couple of times until you start feeling unburdened from your stress.

4

Practising Santosha

Contentment with Gratitude

A normal untrained human mind loves indulging in wanting more of everything it likes. Most people do not get tired chasing higher fame, prominence, better title, better car, bigger house, better financial status, etc. Pursuing all these is recommended worthy pursuit of adult life (Grihastha Ashram) even by ancient wisdom and scriptures. But continuing with this very chase to the exclusion of other prescribed objectives of this stage is entirely a different situation. This otherwise noble and justified pursuit runs the risk of becoming a formidable nightmare when we refrain from prioritising other compelling pursuits like raising family, educating children and helping needy, poor and orphans as well as extending hospitality to guests, saints and sages besides serving social causes for the just sustenance of society at large.

Scriptures provide that person in Grihastha Ashram must attend to Kama and Artha while remaining founded within Dharma. Let us also not lose sight of the fact that same scriptures have allocated second half of life span for Vanprashtha and Sannyasa Ashram where all you should do is attend to Moksha alone. Going by pure Arithmetic, twenty five years of life is invested for two and half objectives while remaining of expected fifty years is advised to be dedicated for a single objective says it all about comparative importance of Moksha. Chasing Artha, collecting more of the same, and keeping most important of all objectives suppressed in deep freezer is asking for severe consequences. In such a scenario, desire to collect more is destined to turn into disappointment, unhappiness and dissatisfaction. Alas, this mistake is being repeated by a large majority of modern day's population. This perennial chase for what we already got not only keeps us away from enjoying what we got but also and robs us of opportunity to pursue what is recommended but we do not have.

Anytime one opens this discussion with a common man, pet comes the reply that their pursuit of rat race is just to secure minimum requirements for a financially secured life. This is a compelling argument and it is difficult to find faults with it under normal circumstances. Real problem is to understand what necessity is and how much is enough. Interestingly this is a deeper question troubling mankind for ages. Socrates, the classical Greek philosopher and one of the founders of Western philosophy called contentment as natural wealth and luxury as artificial poverty. He is also credited with another very strong quotation on contentment which goes as under:

> "He who is not contented with what he has, would not be contented with what he would like to have."

The views of most other cultural and religious streams on this issue are no different. Even Buddha said, "Health is most precious gain and contentment is the greatest wealth." Actually, there is no need of any teachings on this. That desires know no limits is individually well known to us already. Who does not know that chasing desires is an unending journey without destination? Contentment is the only recommended virtue to deal with desires.

Understanding Santosha

Sanskrit word of 'Santosha" consists of two parts of Sam and Tosha. Sam means completely or in entirety while Tosha means contentment. Inversely, it is a state where craving for everything not available is willingly lost. Spiritual state of contentment is considered essential for optimism where no effort to change the future is considered necessary. Philosophy of Yoga, credited to Maharishi Patanjali, beautifully defines contentment as the inner state where, "exists a joyful and satisfied mind regardless of one's environment, whether one meets with pleasure or pain, profit or loss, fame or contempt, success or failure, sympathy or hatred." The English word 'contentment', therefore, is but only a partial translation of 'Santosha' which must also include the sense of gratitude for whatever one is bestowed with. In the current day context, it may be simplified as a state of happiness enjoyed by putting a lid over desire of accumulations or gratifications.

Let us also briefly look at why discontentment is the norm of the day. Surprisingly, the most fundamental psychological reason for the feeling of discontent among adults is their self-doubt and sense of insufficiency. As explained under chapter on Acceptance, a person's desire to change themselves invariably results in self-dislike or feeling of self-insufficiency. Real life situations like stagnant careers, failed relations, unending complaints against others and finally absence of happiness, offer many reasons for such feelings. Usual but ignorant escape from such feelings is seen into acquisitions, possessions, drinking, excessive socialising, adultery/ infidelity, gaming or accumulation of wealth. Unfortunately, these are temporary escapes. The sense of self-insufficiency is destined to surface soon after indulging in these pursuits. The real solution is developing right knowledge about self and making peace with what you already got. That is where contentment works as a sure shot catalyst for brining fundamental changes as against patchworks of gratifications, acquisitions or accumulations. To grow this virtue in desired proportions, you are going to need sustained practice and nothing else.

Necessary to have the Riches Before Growing Contentment

There is, however, an important caveat before one starts working on growing this virtue. Right contentment can be developed only when the person has actually fulfilled some minimum criteria. The practitioner for contentment must have achieved a certain level of success on all parameters applicable to an adult in householder stage explained earlier. For example, someone who does not have access to materialistic abundance or who has not been exposed to luxuries of life is not expected to feel real contentment. Giving up something is possible only when you have got that thing in the first place. This is clear from the Ancient Indian systems where graduation to Vanprashtha requires successful completion of Grihastha Ashram. Only a man who has already fulfilled his desires, who has been there and done that, is capable of giving up, else the giving up is a false delusion. A poor man struggling to meet two ends meet can never appreciate the urge of giving up materialism.

This point has been proved with several scientific studies also. Abraham Maslow, known for his extraordinary work called 'Maslow's Hierarchy of Needs' establishes a pyramid shaped hierarchy of needs where physiological needs sit in the bottom of the pyramid, followed by Safety, Love/Belonging, followed by Esteem while the top slot of the pyramid is occupied by Self Actualisation needs. As per Maslow's conclusions, contentment belongs to top of the pyramid and can be attained only after progressively fulfilling the defined needs starting from the bottom. For example, so long as you have not fulfilled your needs including safety and esteem, the desire to cultivate contentment must remain postponed. It is quite amazing that even modern scientists working in the field of Positive Psychology are only reemphasising the teachings of Ancient Eastern wisdom signifying importance of contentment and calling it a critical ingredient for a happy and fruitful life.

How to Grow Santosha

Santosha needs to be learned, understood, appreciated, and eventually perfected. It is a matter of practice but comparatively a difficult practice to master. As seen earlier, human mind is engineered to seek, acquire and enjoy more of what it likes. Striving continuously is another default setting that cannot be thrown out of the window easily. But striving about a thing is less about achievement and more about the underlying feeling that drives us to perform at our best. So it is more about the process than a certain target. The real answer is enjoying present moment with a sense of curiosity filled acceptance for what you already got.

Practising contentment involves crossing over obvious default setting mentioned above which is possible only after rewiring of the mind. From desiring more, the mind has to be trained to celebrate whatever it already has. You must keep away from worrying about future or sulking about past and bring your entire focus on basking the offering of 'nowness'. Surely, it is a mammoth task as rewiring of mental processes is easier said than done. Because of the difficulties involved in this process, many spiritually advanced individuals can also be seen violating the concept of Santosha. After all, we do come across frequent examples where even Babas and Yogis, known for their decades of commitment to spiritual awakening, are seen indulging in increasing their followers, sale of their merchandise, number of their centers, or their place on high tables. All such desires, after all, are in complete violation of the spirit of Santosha.

Let us now look at helpful practical initiatives for cultivating this important virtue. The objective of discussing these initiates is actually two-fold. To begin with, we must introspect and spot these symptoms within our self and later work to get rid of them one by one. Success with this process helps in positive advancement of meditation as well as in other spheres of normal life.

- **Do not fancy too much on possessions of others**—Worrying for what others have is a wasted effort because there are so many things that just cannot be seen. What we see, may not be true or important. Nobody gets here everything and there is none who got nothing. In between these extremes, there are over seven billion people on this earth today. How can comparisons or competitions with others be meaningful? To begin with, we generally have limited knowledge what others have. May be they lack too much on many other equally important blessings of life. Reality is much different and far bigger than the anecdotes floating around. Stories about riches of others are always based on fictions. Looking at others, assuming untrue things and behaving like a cynic is just too demeaning for your own self.
- **Comforts are fine but do not get habitual of the same**—Life is never constant and it better not be so. Like a river, human life passes through innumerable turns and twists before it merges with the ocean. One who goes with the flow normally avoids getting drowned. Getting habitual for the smallest of a thing or routine is painful in the end. Let there be nothing that you should not survive without. Then alone you enjoy the freedom from being habitual. After all, each environment has something to offer and will soon change, so best is to feel comfortable with it. Look at life as a glass half full. Break your life's monotony as often as possible. Keep yourself physically and mentally ready to face ups and down life has on offer. If you live in a city be prepared to

enjoy life in a village or town. To be open and happy for every situation provides a unique sense of excitement and liberation.

- **Minimal is modest and manageable**—Become minimalist and enjoy the simplicity of life. Managing possessions is a serious obligation by itself. Travelling light brings lesser stresses in times of disturbances in plans. A friend has many properties rented out, smart equity portfolio and multiple currency holdings in banks. Each tenant, share or currency at times behaves in erratic manner. Now, he is technically retired for years but does he really feel mentally free? The answer is a big no. It is always difficult for a man with baggage to focus on things crucial for superior living. Contentment is the life blood of minimalism. Refuse to acquire things just because you can financially afford. Apply filters of necessity every time you go for shopping things, big or small.
- **Build trust with self**—If we count our self-conscience as a separate identity, it is like we living life with a very close friend. Work on establishing trust within. Setting tall goals and failing while trying brings your self-trust lower than before. Chances of success with multiple baby steps are brighter than leapfrog. Set smaller targets and work to achieve the same before picking another. Finally, you will be able to achieve more with self-trust intact. Trust in self reduces lots of fears and unwanted worries and prepare you to willingly feel happy without expecting more than what you already got.
- **Give away what you do not need**—Giving away of whatever you do not need is one of the simplest ways to secure karma credits. Identify things that you do not need anymore and find a person who needs the same. Giving develops a sense of satisfaction and positive esteem. It also frees some valuable space that can be used for accommodating something more meaningful.
- **Get rid of your ideals**—Many a times we hold certain tough ideals which we are unable to live by. Simplest of unfounded ideals harm a lot as you remain burdened with subconscious comparison with those ideals. Please let go your ideals and embrace reality. Comparisons force you to make changes to

improve things. Efforts to change rarely succeed but keep you disturbed. Sticking to ideals stands in way of your positive world view and colour your memories in the least.

- Religions, ethics, historical facts, politics and even science are all matter of perceptions which forces people to hold opposite beliefs. How can there be a single ideal position in such scenarios? It is wrong to pursue ideals as they replace principles as well as reality and can turn very violent at times. Let there be no place for fixed ideals in your system if you are sincerely keen to find your place in this universe.
- **Gratification is not the solution**—No one has ever been able to fulfill their desires by indulging in gratification and you stand no chance of being exception to that rule. Gratification is always harmful on more counts than one. Let us take the current example of harmless and free information flow through internet and social media. While these new options have certainly made connecting with others and accessing desired information easier than before, these very channels have turned people to become impatient, distracted as well as socially disconnected. Self-control has always scored over gratification across ages, cultures, civilisations, and religions without exception, period. Gratifications of all types weaken your resolutions and drain your freedom. In the end, you are left with despairs and frustrations only. Contentment, on the other hand, is always fulfilling and gratifying.
- **Do not forget that final voyage is always empty handed**—This simple fact is significant enough and deserve due consideration. We come to this world with empty hands and cannot carry a dime while leaving it for good. But there are karma credits that accrue for use in next life. The wisest of all must prepare for the afterlife in the best manners possible. This divine reality needs regular reminders. Let us not be a moron chasing money and other materialistic things which are destined to remain behind unused.
- **Refrain from too much of social interactions**—Lately, social interaction is too much overrated. Having as many contacts and acquaintances is considered trophy. In the past, social interactions were more common at congregations

or participating in festivities where people with common interest came together to collectively interact with each other without compromising simplicity. But today social interactions are events used as open platforms for showing off material possessions of the host and those participating.

People are seen displaying their designer outfits, expensive cars, precious jewelry, individual styles and even unique looks. How can such vulgar and preposterous display promote anything other than envy and jealousy? Every word of spoken at such interactions is to score over others. Food served is unhealthy and drinks served are aimed at intoxication. Conversations are indirect taunts or aimed to let someone down. Every person is seen boasting 'if you're a quarter then I am a quarter and a half'. Surely, being part of such gatherings is bound to make you stressful and mentally disturbed. It compels you go one step further or be ready for ridicule. Unfortunately this cycle keeps going in never ending circles without an end in sight.

If you wish to cultivate contentment better abstain from all such events. Being labeled as 'anti-social' is much lesser a price to pay. Living in silence and spending maximum time in solitude, on the other hand, is largely relaxing and allows you to contemplate on substantial issues far away from the glitter of materialism and showoffs.

- **Be spiritually minded**—In all your efforts of reading, watching, listening and discussions with others, please work on finding space for spiritually influenced topics. The moment you are spiritually awakened, your desires to acquire more or hold on to unwanted objects, opinions and thoughts will start losing its tight hold. One needs to work on intuitive awareness that one is in essence divine or an integral part of divinity. This space is far above the worship methods of all types and shades. Evolving belief in life being in a constant cycle of life after death, where good deeds and pains endured add to your karmic credits and bad deeds and enjoying pleasures deplete the karmic credits, prepare you for possible salvation. For every spiritual person Santosha works as the foundation for erecting all subsequent structures.

Contentment and Meditation

Second step of the famous eight fold Yoga, the Niyams or spiritual observances, talks of Santosha as the second of five Niyams. As discussed, contentment enables us to enjoy peace of mind reducing stress on both heart and mind. It comes very handy for regulating thought process in later stages of our meditative journey. The attitude of contentment and gratitude allows the mind to feel relaxed resulting in urgencies and emergencies remaining at bay. This harmless looking attitude holds significant influence over letting the mind willfully surrender for focusing inside on subtle matters of contemplation. Discontentment results in constant chattering and endless dialogues within one's mental space. This makes quieting the mind almost impossible.

Contentment results in considerable shortening of 'To Do' list and thereby brings mental peace. Sitting in meditation with a long list of activities fighting for attention is a gigantic roadblock in letting the mind surrender willfully. Contentment clears clutters and gratitude suppresses your dissatisfactions. That is why contended people make faster progress in their meditative journey, especially in the initial periods when the practitioner is seen fighting multi front battle for influencing the mind to surrender for contemplation. Later, however, when a practitioner starts enjoying initial success in his meditation practice, meditation starts paying back by supporting the growth of contentment. Meditation also produces a surge of endorphins, the beneficial brain chemicals, which result in an instant experience of the power of contentment in normal life.

5

Living in the Present Moment

> "Nothing is more precious than being in the present moment. Fully alive, fully aware".
>
> — *Thick Nhat Hanh, Zen Buddhist Master*

Present is a time falling in between past and future. Past is mostly about memories of experiences laced with negativity and struggles. Remaining in past is all about recycling and all you get is guilt, remorse, self-doubts or regrets. Similarly, living in imaginations of things to come in future assures you only anxieties and fears. But remaining in present is all about enjoying what is actually happening here and now; it is lived with direct perception, it is fresh, it is real and it has never happened before. Present can be enjoyed on physical and emotional dimensions. It also lets you experience feelings and emotions rising or falling in the real time and space. Living in present is actually awakening to events unfolding in front of us right now.

But if present is so good, why do not we normally live in present? Well, simply because living in past or future is our default setting. This shocking conclusion is well supported by findings from well established studies in the field of human psychology. During entire evolutionary process, human beings have remained blessed with abilities to 'learn' and 'plan' and we owe our survival and thriving to this very approach. Learning involved dwelling in past and planning involved thinking about future. These capabilities have put us ahead of other living beings which survive only on limited instincts or restricted reflexes.

The problem starts when we indulge in glorifying past rather than survive. Soon, glories of the days gone by become yardstick for measuring achievements in present. Apparently it appears a tiny trivial issue but little do we realise that it directly results in neglect of present. Similarly, we must think about future to avoid mistakes, failures or setbacks about things to come. Problem arises when we start worrying for things unlikely to happen. At that stage thinking about future turns out a complete waste of energy. What gets ignored is that every moment spent on past or present is at the cost of present.

Mother Nature is by far the most powerful and continuing reality of this universe. Nature is known to perpetually evolve within the cycle of interdependent impermanence. Come to think of it, there is no past or future that impacts Mother Nature in any way. How can past or future become more important for human beings? It is simply because we are victims of time; because we have tendency to accentuate our memory of past and inhibitions about future much more than logically justified.

By dwelling in past/future, which is scientifically more of an illusion, we invariably sacrifice the all important present. No, this is not only an academic discussion. We can see examples of past and future destroying our ability to live in present all around us. An executive at office working to meet the deadline to deliver a project on time without actually enjoying the activity is burning example of present being destroyed. Stressing hard to impress the boss and not working at full potential, worrying about Monday morning, and not focusing on help to children to learn a new skill on Sunday, preventing an opportunity from flowering in the present by remaining caught up in the past are all daily life examples. There is a dire need to change this and focus only on things that arise now, in present.

Observing Present, the First Step

Right observation requires full mental attention and agile sense organs. It demands conscious awareness for everything happening around us; be it dawn turning into life enriching warm light as Sun rises; or being aware of the air that we breathe in and out so regularly; appreciate blue water displaying different shades in lakes, rivers and oceans; be alive to the landscapes, flora and fauna, and mountains around; look at grass, plants and big trees for their softness, flowers and colour of leaves. Listen to sounds of all types of noises life offers. Savour happenings of every moment without evaluations or comparisons.

Surely, we do not observe present as much as thought we do. Living in present charges our emotional response with positivity pushing stresses away. Focus on present makes things complete and unburden us from past mistakes or missed opportunities. It also keeps us completely unaware of fallible failures of future. Focus on present does not stop thinking but it prevents stopping on thoughts. Thoughts are very deceptive. One can have thoughts about vacation while on work and vice versa. Under both situations, even such apparently harmless thoughts end up destroying your being in present. Focus on present also makes us more creative because creativity ignites only in present.

> "Touch your inner space, which is nothingness, as silent and empty as the sky; it is your inner sky. Once you settle down in your inner sky, you have come home, and a great maturity arises in your actions, in your behaviour. Then whatever you do has grace in it. Then whatever you do is a poetry in itself. You live poetry; your walking becomes dancing, your silence becomes music."
>
> —*Osho*

Practical Techniques for Being in Present

In addition to past and future, there are other factors hampering being in the moment. Normal day life revolves around work, family, social media, urgencies, news, digital distractions, daily chores and leaving alone the hobbies or other essential activities like daily exercises. Being in present is not to be in conflict with such activities. On the other hand, it can qualitatively help you attend to all such activities better than before. All it asks is your total attention on the one activity you wish to attend at a given moment. For example, if you are attending to needs of your child, let everything else wait. Deal with it as if it is very first and only demand being made on you. When you watch a player playing your favourite sport just watch him as if you have nothing else to do, as if you have not seen that player or the teams playing anytime before. Thus, you can attend to your activities and be in present at the same time without being in conflict.

Living in present is even more important for meditation. There are several key topics necessary to master the art of being in present for progressing on path of meditation beyond the initial level. But all that has to wait for our advancement to reach a certain level. Let us take those subjects at a later stage. In the meantime, suitable for our existing stage of progress, we can look at some practical steps for a beginner to remain in present at the conscious level.

- **Get rid of old memories, burdens and belongings**—Memories are dead moments and are best burned or buried. Both physical and mental space is always limited. Carrying old useless stuff/thoughts always has implicit complications. Dead weight of memories/things is unwanted burden on shoulders for every step taken. Attachments, relationships, achievements of past are not important today. Lay them to rest in peace at the earliest. Life is often compared to journey and extra luggage always adds to troubles. Travel light and keep it simple.
- **Trick your evolutionary disposition**—Learning and planning is our core default setting but it is possible to trick this process and increase our attention span on present. Look at your 'self' of today and not of yesterday. Since we are always selfish at heart, we shall automatically love to stay focused on latest self which alone is open for transformation. Practice and some more practice, they say, bring changes even on evolutionary processes. (This point is adopted from an article by Prof. Eyal Winter, Ph.D, Hebrew University of Jerusalem titled 'Why Is It Hard to Live for the Moment' dated Sep. 19, 2016 published on Psychology Today).
- **Make every day a new day**—Every day when we get up from our bed, our attitude is, for sure, relatively under our control. Why not resolve to start every new day with a positivity of making it better than yesterday? Let us be conscious and try to make every day a new day, a day that is not coloured with happenings of yesterday. Starting the new day with a smile helps in forgetting the hurts and failures of days gone by. Be in present and avoid pulling by negativity. Let today be the only day of life. Let us make efforts to work on everything we do today with our full involvement, commitment and using our total potential. Do not bother even if results are not positive.

- **Flare up potency of your sense organs**—Our senses are a God's gift but we often let them work at suboptimum levels by letting their subtle sensations invariably go unnoticed. Notice sensory inputs of your sense organs with greater attention because senses always work in present moment. Recall of their sensations is always a second hand activity. Look around for things you consider beautiful, pay attention to pleasing sounds that your ears listen in far and near, do not miss the beautiful smells that exist in your vicinity, appreciate the loving feel of various textures and surfaces of things you touch.

  If you pay attention to even a simple activity like brushing teeth, you will be amazed to see how many sounds, smells and sensations exist there. These newer sensations attract and hold your attention in present and letting you know about yourself in an entirely new manner. If we call these senses to be special gift to humanity, why not respect their potencies and enjoy their blessing on a continuous basis. Let your emotions rise and fall. Notice them filling you with flows of pleasures and displeasures. Do not let these go stale. These feelings and emotions can never be exactly recollected ever in their purest form except in present.
- **Do not let your routine be dull and boring**—Mind is known to wonder because that is its nature. But can we consciously try following it and keep track of its likes and dislikes? Do not try stopping it to go out but you can consciously divert its attention back to present. One simple way is to keep changing your routine on a regular basis. Do not drive on the same road every day, do not eat at the same place too often, do not take morning walk at the same route every day, do not watch the same TV channel, do not go to the same mall all the time, even do not use the same Prayer every day. We do not notice but every time we are changing the routine, our mind gets willingly ready to pay more attention to happenings around. The moment it finds the same activity getting repeated, due to its own smartness, it quietly finds an excuse to wander out of present.
- **Wipe out both wins and losses of past**—Past is gone and never going to repeat itself. Both hits and misses of past

are worth nothing. Dwelling on past accomplishments is as harmful as clinging on to past hurts. Our recollection of past is always coloured by our desires and wishes at the time of recollection. That is why a recollected version of past event is always different and linked to mental condition at the time of recall. Projecting past as valuable for avoidance of mistakes in future is a very weak argument in the fast changing world of today. People not alive to the realities of present alone advocate usefulness of past.

Keeping old hurts alive is very detrimental for present. More often such bruises hurt you more than those being blamed. Waiting for an apology from others is a bad bargain because that keeps postponing your happiness. Take responsibility of past, own it and jump start either by pardoning other person, circumstances, happenings or by getting over them through other course corrections. Be a protagonist and end the story of being a victim forever. Please remember that blaming others in and every situation makes you powerless or certainly less powerful. So, come back to present and build on new innings afresh.

- **Scan your body parts**—Scanning different parts of your own body regularly is, to the least, a good way to connect with your own body. It may sound funny but generally our mind remains busy with its own stuff leaving the body to act on its own. Consciously taking your attention to your body parts, one at a time, not only keeps your focus on present, it also helps release of accumulated tensions in those parts. Scanning body parts, thus, is also a good way to bring both mind and body at a single point.
- **Indulge in activities you love**—Morning walks, jogging, cycling, gardening, sports, swimming, fishing, singing, photography, writing, cooking, worshiping, cleaning or even dish washing are some of many activities which may have power to absorb your attention completely. All you need is to find which all of such activities works for you in particular. Do indulge in your activities of choice and get absorbed as often as possible. Every moment you devote to such an activity indirectly wean you off from past as well as future.

- **Think beyond old tricks**—Rules applied for living life, in modern times, are changing with lightening speed. Changes are too rapid in pace and disorienting in character. But everyone has to learn these for surviving and thriving. What may have been valid a decade ago may not be as relevant today. Many solutions of yesteryears are obsolete. Adapt to current scenarios, the new norms. Look at human relations. Just two decades ago, elders were getting respect just because of their age. But now technology has created a unique level playing field where a person with guts can outshine like never before. World does not give a damn who you were in the past and does not care who you may be later. What matters to others is what you are at the moment. Step up your adaptations and be ready to face the present moment as a warrior.
- **Accept the world around as it exists**—Perhaps the biggest stumbling block to living in present is unceasing attempt to refashion the universe as we wish it to be. We love commenting on everything and hold strong opinions about everything under the sun. It is very rigid and stringent hobby to live with. We know well that we cannot change this world and all we can is to exercise some influence over self. Still, we keep harboring the desires to see the world exactly as we wish it to be. Let it take its own course. You have no choice but to go with the flow. If you try obstructing it you are destined to get crushed and washed out. Work on being adoptive and identify yourself with your rightful tiny place in this big world.
- **Stop being a control freak**—Many normal people are seen attached to a false illusion that they can control people and events around them, to achieve whatever they seek at a given time. Although this illusion gets shattered almost every day, they keep clinging to it nonetheless. Speaking psychologically, only those who do not have control over their own life have stronger wish to control life of others. Force your mind to give up shouting on others as a shortest path to attain lost control and force it to face your own major problems and work through the same. It is better to restrict

yourself to your responses to the events offered by the entire world. Controlling the events of this world is beyond your control and all you lose in the process is your focus on present. Let things happen under whatever design they happen and respond to them as best as you can.

Steps suggested above are helpful to every person in general and may not directly relate to meditation, the subject under discussion. But construction of any edifice calls for clearing all types of vegetation along with roots. You also have to remove all types of boulders stopping you from progressing on howsoever heavy they may be. Adopting measures listed above exactly equate to preparing the ground for construction of desired superstructure. Being "in the moment" is one of the most significant requirements of meditation. Actually, both meditation and remaining in present moment are like twin sisters who help each other grow well in the initial years. Years later, of course, meditation starts encompassing many more other traits in addition to being in present. "To be in the moment" helps meditation deepen, and it also happens to be a fruit of the practice.

Being in Present and Practising Meditation

One comes across tons of published material explaining how meditation helps in living in present moment but you are likely to draw a blank if you start looking how living in present helps your meditation. Now, do we keep our goal 'to become good at meditation' or 'to become good at living'? Surely, meditation is a means to an end by itself. And even if better meditation helps us improving our focus on present, how can we get better meditation in the first place? Is it not like saying a clean environment will help improving green covers? Yes, clean environment will certainly help trees to grow better but which comes first? Can we have clean environment without first growing of lots of trees? Being in present is like planting trees, which eventually helps the environment becoming clean. The actions taken at present shall ensure improved progress on meditation.

Mindfulness, a very important technique for advanced meditation, subsequently explained in greater details, is basically advanced version of this very concept.

6

Cultivating Art of Detachment

The usual trick applied by monkey catchers uses a transparent heavy jar partially filled with nuts. The jar mouth has a small opening on the top such that monkey can just put its bare hand inside freely. Monkey picks up fistful of nuts but is unable to bring the fist out of the jar. Greedy as it is, monkey tries hard to bring out the fist without letting go of the nuts but in vain. Soon it gets overpowered by the catcher. Only if it knew how to let go those nuts, the monkey could have remained free.

We human beings behave no differently except that our nuts are of varied types. We remain busy in chasing money, power, ideas, anger, influence, relations, people, and what not. These are all our nuts that we refuse to let go. Why blame only poor monkey, how often we see human beings letting go their own nuts in order to regain freedom and happiness? We remain strongly glued (attached) to all types of allurements; major portion of our life goes in collecting them and we refuse to let them go out of our hands at any cost.

Speaking generally, the word attachment is considered as affection, sympathy or fondness for someone or something (as if limited to people or objects). Yes, that is most obvious form of attachment and do not need examples to bring the point home. But even bigger menace, and equally compelling, is attachment with one's own ideas, views, opinions and beliefs. More people get killed in the world by people holding diametrically opposite views and beliefs as against people killed guarding their materialistic assets. Even more dangerous is attachment with own sense of right and wrongs, the sense of judgement. This attachment ignites us to pass so many sermons and you may also call it as 'fatwas' (a ruling on a point of Islamic law given by a recognised authority) for things big and small where everything in nonconformity is immediately called out as wrong or inappropriate. Attachment to titles/positions is yet another bond forcing many people to behave in a typical manner.

All types of bonds and actions induced under attachments keep our mind agitated and we know that. Attachments stimulate us to behave in selfish manner. Selfish motive immediately narrows our horizon where other important aspects get ignored or bypassed. Being attached to our own interests, we neglect rightful causes of others turning us less compassionate. Extreme end of this phenomenon extends right up to harming others and igniting suspicion even without genuine reasons. Yes, they always please our ego but attachments result in downgrading mental standard to a level that is clearly unfit for meditation. Meditation, as we know by now, requires a pure, willing and voluntary mind ready to turn inside in search of pure truth.

Even when we know otherwise, the charms and temptations of attachments are just too strong to let go. The glue that keeps us bound with attachments is nothing but our desire to own, possess, prove, collect, hold, navigate all things, people and events, outcomes towards our preferred desires; our child should get highest grades, I must have the corner office ahead of all others, we should have house in that locality, my daughter should get such and such type of match, so and so should accept my romantic proposal, this particular political party alone deserves to come in power, my taste in fine arts is just unique, my style and knowledge of cooking is better than that friend of mine, my style of dressing and makeup is best among all, etc. are all examples of our attachments. We know how much of our mental space is occupied by these thoughts.

At this stage let us understand the difference between detachment and non-attachment. At times, we use these terms as mutually exclusive but in reality there is a big difference between the two. Detachment, for example, signifies making one's distance from the world driven by lack of interest or efforts. A detached person likes to live life of an aloof by separating himself from the world at large. It may not be out of place to essentially define it as escapism. To that extent, detachment is anti-social and anti-progress and it runs risks of its own pains and sufferings. Non-attachment, on the other hand is essentially a situation where sense of 'self' is abstained from a given situation. It means to be in the world, but not of the world. A non-attached association with any person, situation, thing or idea is open, healthy, strong, loving and filled with effortless natural traits of kindness and compassion. (Allowing common parlance also to mean the real meaning, use of word 'detachment' anywhere in the entire book must also be understood as non-attachment only as explained here above.)

Non-attachment is basically the art of withdrawing attention from desires and refocusing the energy on purity of thoughts and actions. Non-attachment is a state in which a person overcomes his bond with desires for things, people or concepts of the world and thus attains a heightened perspective. It is considered a wise virtue and is promoted in all religious streams evolving from Indian soil. Practising non-attachment attains greater significance today when attachment to worldly possession is often too common and increasing like never before.

The forces of attachments are as strong with the common man today as was the plight of Arjuna. In particular the verse 47 of Ch. 2 of Bhagwad Gita *"Karmanye vadhikaraste Ma Phaleshu Kadachana, Ma Karmaphalaheturbhurma Te Sangostvakarmani"* (translated as 'You have a right to perform your prescribed duty, but you are not entitled to the fruits of action) is a living example of non-attachment without giving up action. Never consider yourself to be the cause or beneficiary of the results of your activities but never get detached from doing your duty, is possibly the greatest lesson for practising non-attachment.

Non-Attachment not Being Passive

Confusion between detachment and non-attachment, misleads people to look at non-attachment as an escape for running away from responsibilities. They advocate attachment as essential glue to effectively discharge just demands of their responsibilities at home and at work. But nothing is far from truth. To see non-attachment as running away or withdrawing from affections or withholding from emotional bonds only reflects lack of understanding. It does not mean inaction. Think about it, every person is always busy in something or the other. One may be lazing around or thinking, but engaged he is. There can be no life without action. Quality of actions may always be different, e.g., our actions may be influenced by goodness (Sattva), activity (Rajas) or lethargy and ignorance (Tamas) or a combination of these three natural qualities, the three Gunas. But avoiding action for improving non-attachment is not even an option worth considering.

Non-attachment also does not mean underperformance. Virtue of non-attachment empowers you to lose emotional bond of desiring outcomes of your efforts. Under non-attachment, doing everything is like discharging a pious duty. Actions undertaken with truly non-attached attitude qualify as a noble obligation where you perform at your best capacity, irrespective of results being success or failure or anything in between. And it will be wrong to believe that such a concept is impractical for householders. Non-attachment is not for the ascetics or people living in caves or forests. It is actually more practical and useful for people like us living modern day life amidst all its chaos and complexities.

A non-attached person gets blessed with positive behaviour which enables the individual to act with authenticity, elegance and compassion. Therefore, virtue of non-attachment cannot be used as an excuse not to earn livelihood or support family. Non-attachment makes you smarter professional, loved parent, dear friend, dedicated executive or devoted social worker, all at the same time. Non-attached people are known to have superlative performance levels in every field they belong. Non-attachment has nothing to do with being careless or indifferent, not at all. Non-attachment practised as a skill does wonders by infusing life with sense of purpose and grace. It awakens beings into superior goal of transforming this human life in a meaningful way.

In modern context, one can also look at non-attachment as a very effective and cheap emotional health insurance policy. It protects you against many possible illness attributed to emotional attachments. A person looking for longer life, richer experiences, and loving people around, stand to gain significantly as long as he practices non-attachment in its purer form. You can look around in your family or social circles and cannot miss non-attachment as the common quality among all people blessed with exceptionally longer life. Attachment leads to compulsive emotional complications while non-attachment provide solid defense against such entanglements.

Non-attachment is also highly recommended for improving your work life balance. Only a non-attached person switches off his mind from personal matters while at work and vice versa. Such a person isolates self from the results, so no stress gets generated in his life. It is a reality that stress has less to do with burden of the duty and more to do with our habit of expecting results as per doer's desire.

Non-attachment tells us how to put that burden down for taking rest and pick it back only later when you wish to deal with it. Practising non-attachment, however, is just too much to pursue for the control freaks. They normally are intimately attached to their strong thinking and giving up that for them is like ending the life. It must, however, be agreed that one need strong guts to let go attachments. Unfortunately, the entire process is exercised through regulating mind resulting in neutral thinking. And thinking itself is one of the strongest attachments we have. Thinking generates inner commentary. This commentary itself is an enemy of our mental peace.

Non-Attachment and Meditation

There is no denying the fact that attachment, with all its attractions, pulls and pressures, forms and situations, is biggest roadblock in the way of making progress in meditation. So long as a person remains bound to attachments of any kind, his mind does not acquire the right state for turning its gaze inside—the fundamental first step for effective meditation. There is no middle path here. Attachment and meditation perfectly falls in either or situations. As such, people sincere enough to aim for progress in meditation have no choice but to loosen the grip of their desires and preferences. They have to focus on their actions and thoughts without the shades or reflections of their selfish motives influencing them. Over weeks and months, when selfless efforts become their second natures, they will find their mind getting ready for sitting in meditation. Then alone the practitioner makes real progress on that path.

Eknath Easwaran, the famous India-born spiritual teacher and author, makes a great point in explaining the importance of non-attachment in his article titled "The Art of Detachment", as posted at www.spiritualityhealth.com dated 24th April 2015. He compares attachment as gravity pull of planet earth which sucks in everything within its sphere. He further compares detachment (non-attachment) with the multi stage rocket where each stage fires for increasing speed and thrust of the rocket as it lifts to cross the gravity of earth. Each stage does its job and gets separated from the rocket to make the rocket lighter but faster as it moves out into space. Similar to a space rocket, each progressive stage of detachment requires different practices which later make way for progress to be achieved using other practices.

Those familiar with aviation and aeronautics will vouch that a single stage rocket may never get to the speed required to reach Escape Velocity (approx. 25,000 kms/h) because rocket's own weight will not allow it to generate required thrust. Bonds with attachments are as powerful as gravity pull. Nothing less than a multistage non-attached vehicle is required to get out of attachments.

Meditation Exercise for Looking through Emotions

Mood swings, anger over something or someone, frustration over failures, situations leading to strong likes or dislikes, etc. are all too familiar to all of us. Their ride on the emotional roller coaster keeps us occupied in endless loops. At times, we are not even sure if we wish to come out of these. Let us see if the practice suggested below helps us in reducing the gripping force of such situations:

- Sit in meditation and start deep breathing for a couple of minutes.
- Become aware of your emotional state at that very moment.
- Assume yourself to be a trained Doctor sitting in a clinic. And your emotional state being the patient visiting you for treatment.
- Look around your entire body and feel for any physical sensation like, goose bumps, butterflies, stomach ache, sick feeling, high blood circulation, tired legs, tired eyes, dryness in the throat, etc. arising out of the prevailing feeling.
- Spot out the main sensation and try linking it with your mental state.
- Think logically and identify which attachment is prompting the emotion at work.
- Contemplate on the bond until you are able to conclude that the attachment is uncalled for and need to be dispensed with.
- Slowly, with few sittings at most, you will start feeling detached with such feelings.
- You will get a sense of perspective out of the self diagnosis.
- The span and degree of your reactions or outburst will start narrowing down from earlier extremes.
- After tasting success for one dominant emotion, select the next in your sessions to follow.
- Continue your cycles until all emotional reactions get dully covered.

7

Crossing over Myths Surrounding Meditation

Meditation has been practised across cultures, religions and civilisations over millenniums. Something so vast, so historical and so subtle is bound to get riddled in countless different interpretations about its real meaning and scope. Even in its purest forms, 'old school' meditation consisting of Buddhist and Vedic traditions is quite different from its 'new age' versions centered on mindfulness. You may pick up as many books and videos at random and you invariably come across different versions floating below the surface. To make matters worse, as part of their marketing strategies of base product with USP, various part time Teachers and Practitioners have been selfishly spreading half cooked product variants in attractive packaging. Many times their variant approach starts denting the real understanding about meditation, which always was, is and will remain nothing but a pious practice.

Although, in this book, we are focusing on use of meditation more as a tool for overall improvements, it is essential to remove all misconceptions and myths surrounding the very concept of meditation and its real spectrum. Unraveling myths generally requires deeper understanding of esoteric and philosophical aspects of every complex subject in hand, including meditation. Considering such complexities, clarity about myths should preferably find place towards later part of the book. But that runs the risk of the reader advancing to the later part of the book with shadows of unfounded beliefs looming large risking their snowballing effects.

Placing this chapter at this stage of our journey is, therefore, a well considered decision. End of stage one, with practitioner having covered some ground and having suitably dealt with initial roadblocks, it is most appropriate time to deal with the myths surrounding meditation. In worst case scenario, at this stage, you may glance through this chapter with cursory look on the issues involved and later revisit the specific sections as many times as required to develop deeper grasp.

People of wisdom have used the time tested method of narrowing focus of light on a core subject by breaking myths surrounding that subject one by one such that, at the end, only real substantive core remains illuminated with full clarity. Let us take each of the prevailing myths about meditation and evaluate them briefly to either bring them closer to the core or push them out of the periphery. Since our purpose is to reach to the very foundation of our understanding, sometimes, very harsh and strong words may have to be used to bring the point home with conviction. Use of such words is a matter of accentuation to forcibly filter out traces of grey shades out of understanding of the readers at large, and must be considered accordingly. (This important disclaimer should be remembered by each reader lest their sentiments get hurt in any way. Strong words are used only where there is a need for segregating all particles of grey into black or white for infusing added clarity and nothing else.)

Let us pick some of the popular myths in a random order.

1. Meditation is about controlling mind—Many teachers and authors are seen advocating meditation practice to control the mind to perform on desired lines and get focused on desired objects/subjects only. But this is all farce. Decades of practice does not help people to control their mind. In reality, all efforts of controlling human mind are destined to fail. The DNA of human mind does not recognise 'No fly Zone' signs. One can put as many notice boards as possible but mind is meant for wandering free without any rhyme or reasons.

So, please guard against your desire to use meditation enabling you to control either generation or repetition of thoughts. Thoughts are the result of working of human mind. Similar to other organs like kidney, liver or heart, we have to let our mind work for what it is designed, i.e. thinking. All you can do, however, is understand its working. It has a predictable mechanism similar to other complex machines. Machines are not managed correctly; all you can do is operate machines correctly. Human mind hates vacuum even for a second. Mind and its processes are constantly working for indulging in desires or avoiding aversions. This indulgence and avoidance are like two monkeys living in our heart; while they continue to shake and agitate the tree, it is futile to expect total peace or total control. However, what is left unsaid is that better results require training those monkeys in desired manner. Once they get suitably trained, they will jump but in right direction.

Another misconception is about meditation helping the mind go blank. Certainly, meditation practice requires curtailing online thinking going around endlessly but that is not possible by going blank. Most of us are plagued with thoughts that arise seemingly without cause. It is rare to experience more than a few moments without some thought arising and replacing earlier thought. Meditation allows us some rest from relentless onslaught of thoughts. Not arising of thoughts is said to happen at the most advanced level of meditation which can only be envisioned and is beyond the reach of any normal being. The ultimate objective of meditation practice is not so much of blanking the mind but to redirect its focus on inner contemplation. What best can be done to regulate the mind, however, will be taken up in much greater details in due course.

2. Reciting mantra being very helpful in Meditation—Some preachers advocate use of mantra as a tool for suppressing thoughts and distractions. In their opinion mantras work like big tools capable for motivating mind to positively agree for meditation. Repeating a mantra is also advised during times of stress for bringing relaxation and while facing a crisis. Depending on one's belief system, the mantras may also be advised to let you get in touch with your God spiritually.

Some people indeed find chanting specific mantra as an effective help. People go all the way to secure mantra from particular Gurus hoping quick success in their practice. And it might indeed help the beginners. But reciting the best of best combination of words or sounds, ultimately, is merely a repetitive mechanical exercise. Even when it may appear working with select practitioners, mechanical repetition at best is a good vocal exercise and nothing more. Human mind cannot remain glued to endless repetitions of the best of best mantras for long. And you cannot expect creativity from a mind riddled in repetitions. Further, following anything mechanically may be called by any name but certainly not as meditation.

The moment a person starts repetition, DNA of his mind is designed to stop working. Human mind is very intelligent organ and it hates being kept busy where it has nothing new to experience. Mind loves being active and creative at the same time. It opts for flights of fantasies rather than repetitive engagements. Passages or mantras are able to engage the mind only until the time these are learnt and become part of our sub-conscious. Once that stage is reached, the repetitions become robotic actions leading the mind to go back to its previous self. As such, serious meditation seekers are strongly advised to detest their chase for sacred mantra of any type.

3. Systems from experts being the best way of learning Meditation—This is total misconception that meditation learning is dependent on others. This view is largely due to complex nature of the subjects required to be dealt. Learning meditation is certainly tough; it demands lots of discipline and dedication but it is more of an art than science and hence, need to be learned by developing conceptual understanding and self practice alone. Others have but only a limited role out here and that too in initial phase. Each one of us is blessed with different orientations and no outsider can ever know or track what goes in our mind 24/7. Meditation is like learning underwater swimming in a tunnel on a dark night. You just do not have a person to lean on when it actually matters. Hand holding for long is just not an option in this long journey.

Others may have succeeded in overcoming their own challenges and may provide general idea to others but nothing beyond. Their system may have worked for them but need not or may not work for you. Time keeps changing everyday and systems propagated by others generally get fossilised very quickly. Each person has to dig his own well to quench his thirst. No one has ever found heaven with the dying of others. If heaven is what you need, please be ready to go through your death yourself.

Meditation is not knowledge which can be acquired or taught. By following others, you are reducing yourself as a clone or a substandard human being who is not willing to use his own intellect and wisdom. Our own truth has to be accessed by us singularly with our own efforts. Experiences of others are good to get general directions. But in tough topography called meditation, you need to make your own way to. Subtle understanding of this fact goes a long way in making right progress. The path is accidented, with serpentine trails, through the bushes filled with lots of uncertainties. Still you alone have the power of making your way through it. You have to be ready to fall down or get lost. Prepare yourself to retract, rearrange, re-motivate and keep going. Holding somebody's hand may save you from some such problems but will rob your chances to pursue your own individual unique destination.

4. Meditation is all about concentrating the mind on an object, subject, organ or thought—Some people look at meditation simply as a practice aimed at improving concentration. This view is especially promoted among students as concentration helps them secure higher grades with same efforts. But it is too narrow an approach. Concentration of mind is a faculty which focuses one-pointedness on a subject without interruption. It can be taken as a tool and nothing beyond. But like all tools, it can be used for good or for evil. Unless its quality is free from greed, hatred and delusion, even one-pointedness is of no use for meditation. Concentration demands strong determination. Experience suggests that strong walls need to be erected in the mind to let it engage in selected thoughts for a longer duration. Those of us who has tried concentration can vouch how little success is possible in erecting such barricades. Concentration has its own challenges to be crossed making it difficult by itself. But even when developed, concentration by very definition is coercive in nature and any coercive attempts are known to fall flat as far as meditation is concerned.

Concentration involves duality of forces at conflict with each other at all times. In achieving concentration we have an entity active in forcing us to not pay attention to distractions and another entity paying attention to the object of concentration. Interestingly both these entities are not different but just two different aspects of the same mind. Existence of two separate entities is, in reality, a great impediment in the path of effective meditation. Mind is the linesman as well as Centre Forward at the same time. Mind alone is also busy in generating thoughts. Mind is the watcher and the subject being watched is also controlled by the same mind. One aspect of mind seeks freedom while the other wishes to control. How can a mind involved in ongoing turf war with its own twin sibling, enjoying equal rights by birth, can ever achieve concentration on something under duress?

However, concentration is an important step in the journey of perfecting meditation practice and, hence, it will be dealt with in required details under a separate chapter where all its aspects including why and how will get explained. Merging two separate entities, discussed above, in one single stream is a small distance journey but can take years to complete as one-pointedness is to be converted into mindfulness where the mind is perfected to stop generating distractions in the first place. It calls for a long training in becoming aware of your feelings and emotions, letting them arise on their own, taking notice of them without any sense of attachment and judgement and finally letting them go. These simple looking steps, by themselves, however, are a subject matter of one separate book. In short, meditation is much beyond art of concentration where concentration itself is taken as a sub-process rather than a goal.

5. Meditation is just like worship or prayer—When we pray, invariably there is a Supreme God who is approached for His blessings. But deep down there is always an indirect desire to obtain a thing or two. It need not be material abundance alone but can be as simple as a clean heart or peace of mind. Tangible benefits of worship, falling in between above-mentioned extremes include desiring wisdom, protection against dangers, strength to face failures, opportunities to grow, possibilities to make quick bucks, power to rule, ability to stay peaceful, good health (without exercises and diet control), ability to hold on to morals, etc. In short, there is always a quid pro quo involved in worship, as we understand it in practical terms. In that sense, it is more transactional in nature.

> "Prayer is when you talk to God; Meditation is when you listen to God." — *Diana Robinson*

Worship in today's time is more about being visible, a kind of show. Many people end up undertaking it to please others, parents or well-wishers included. Some undertake to address their political constituencies. Many worshippers are seen worshipping with a long shopping list of items available for free or on deep discounts. Many others do it just mechanically. The idea behind using such harsh words against worship is limited for the purpose of drawing its stark difference with meditation where benefits are, at best, mere abstract in nature.

Unfortunately, worship is also associated with one or the other established religious traditions, which involves unique pride of being superior over other religions. But there is no such competition or comparison in meditation. Meditation is only about you and you alone. It has no connection with any religion, tradition or such other divisive practices. So whatever works for worship does not work for meditation. Worship and prayers, especially those conducted in groups, generally involve singing or prayers and all such activities take you away from silence. As against this, meditation necessitates a complete silence, a silence of inside where there are no thoughts rising, where emotions are at deep sleep.

Some people look at worship philosophically and say that worship helps them in surrendering the false sense of self. But if their heart continues to remain focused on where their treasures are (and sometimes where their sleepers are), where is the possibility of surrender? Surrender demands choosing between money, desires, attractions on one side and God on the other. Prayers to God, and all forms of Gods included, is more of seeking or bartering. If one is to look at Hindus system of offering 'Chadhava' (offerings of valuable gifts provided some prefixed desire gets fulfilled), the activity will even qualify as prearranged incentive scheme run by companies for their dealers or, even worse, a contracted bribing. Paying back a promised cut on successful happening of a pre-decided activity finalised privately, is branded bribing under even liberal legal systems of the world.

On the other hand, outcomes for meditation are more about losing; loss of ignorance, loss of pride, loss of false perceptions, loss of identity, loss of ego, loss of attachments, loss of memories, etc. Seeking meditation requires forgetting the world around, something where rituals have no space. Meditation impacts our body, mind and spirit; it goes to make our mind quiet and helps in reducing fears and anxieties; meditation enhances creativity and intuition resulting in expansion of our consciousness and thereby helps us to experience the infinite. So, meditation and worship do not have many things in common except the physical posture at best.

6. Meditation allows you to escape from something or someone—Meditation is not about running away from real understanding of your own core in its true form. It is also not to avoid harsh realities as an escape into emptiness. The emptiness felt in meditation comes after years of good practice and is felt only when all questions are answered and removal of all doubts pave way for pure wisdom. Meditation also does not make you immune to psychological pains. Mood swings do not get eliminated forever. Feelings and inadequacies are going to remain even after you have been meditating for long. You continue to remain open for life's ups and downs. See, you are going to meditate only once or twice every day. Assuming the session of one hour each, you still got to live normal life in remaining 22 hours of every day. Life in those hours continues like for others except that a practitioner gets equipped with better tools to deal with normal tenacious realities of actual human life.

Continued meditation over longer periods encourages acceptance for those realities head on rather than pushing them under the carpet. Meditation, for example, will prompt you not to find escape route in other distractions like getting active on social media. As we will realise in due course, progress in meditation heightens our observation skills as well as our awareness. These skills help in seeing the distractions as waste of time.

So people who get attracted to meditation as a "get away" exercise are destined to get disappointed with it sooner than later. No, this is no pleasure trip or an exercise to experience for few moments. On the contrary, meditation results in bringing all our fears and scars to surface and helps us getting over these with objectivity and practical approach. Meditation makes all our dark shadows stand in front of us forcing us to see through all negatives or grey shades of our personality. So there is no escaping from any issue or person. Therefore, people desperate to run from issues or persons need not start meditation at all.

7. Meditation results in some profound or transcendental experience—Experiencing is defined as an art of accumulating greed for repeating particular feeling over and over again. Further, all experiences are always grounded in past. Meditation, on the other hand, focuses on present with no connection with past or future. Focus on present does not involve any accumulations. So, notions linking meditation to experiences are absolutely far from truth. Let us take stock of reality that our normal mind is invariably busy in materialistic and sensuous engagements and such a distorted mind is not even capable for experiencing something great.

Meditation involves reaching to deeper levels of sub consciousness and that is neither an experience nor a matter of qualitative ecstasy. The state of mind for right meditation has to be pure, complete, natural and spontaneous. So if there is someone promising you profound experience, please call such bluff on the spot and move on. In real life there is no room for transcendental experiences.

Actually, when we succeed, even temporarily, in taming the mental process to relative silence, the agitation in the mind slows down forcing a sharp drop in overall energy levels. Such drop induces dullness increasing from subtle to gross and finally leading to strong drowsiness. Such state of drowsiness is similar to deep sleep where even dreams appear real. As soon as the meditators come back to full consciousness, at times, there is a recall feeling of that blissful silence leaving an impression of a profound experience. Unfortunately, some naïve beginners take such experience too seriously.

In reality, transcendental experience presupposes a non-dual state of awareness where one gets perception of a subtle pure being. Such being is without any phenomenon, distraction, intention, desire or even thinking. It is a state where default mode of the being switches from ego to consciousness, where there is no world of senses, objects or thoughts. In this state there is no doer, no process, no action and no thinker. Well, such a state is technically possible but only for someone who has reached the pinnacle of progress in his practice. But people struggling to make initial progress in meditation, therefore, may only consider having 'experiences' as flight of fantasies and nothing beyond.

8. Meditation involves unraveling of mysteries – A common thread among all different definitions of mystery is 'something not understood or beyond understanding'. While meditation deals with consciousness, something deeper than thoughts but there is nothing mysterious about it. Meditation can be a mystery only for those who could not experience its impact. It is a vast subject and a beginner may get confused with esoteric language used by many sources to explain meditation. Like many other subjects, more often than not, proper understanding about meditation also suffers from the fear of unknown.

Meditation involves intricate use of mind to know about itself and overcome the deficiencies noticed by the same mind. It is like a single person acting as investigator and judge for a cold blooded murder trial. The only way to demystify this enigma is through constant practice and experience. Meditation alone is capable of changing all types of perspectives, attitudes and mental processes. Stable practice of meditation begins to unravel all mysteries buried down in an ignorant mind, one at a time.

Yes, meditation results in fine tuning of your sensory system allowing you to listen to your own soul with clarity but that is about all. Being natural and spontaneous, meditation can be logically understood and practised by a dedicated practitioner exactly as most others skills are acquired, practised and mastered. What get revealed is not something exceptional but the real truth that was always there in the depth of our being, the one that remains invisible, suppressed or overburdened under ignorance or false understanding.

Meditation reconnects us to our own core of humanity burdened by many self made layers of ego dominated attitudes and habits. Once you reach there with your own efforts, bit by bit, one baby step at a time, you realise beautiful eternal reality of being human. Of course, that is going to take whole lot of time and practice and, hence, there is no need of worrying on that count in the beginning of your meditative practice.

9. Meditation relaxes you and calms you down from stressful situations—No, even the most clumsy and ignorant person should not recommend meditation just to seek physical benefits. Meditation is neither a way of getting a sense of serenity or rejuvenation in any way. But it is not to say that meditators do not feel relaxed or calmed in general. Deep breathing practised during meditation results in slowing heart rate, lowering blood pressures, relaxation of muscles and increasing the blood flow to mind. Yes, deep breathing by itself is a well established relaxation technique but the comparison stops here.

Relaxation results due to release of tensions from the body and mind from breathing exercises carried out for or without any link with meditation. Such physical benefits are purely incremental and incidental in nature. But expecting physical advantages alone from meditation, for example, amounts to firing real rockets for celebrating Diwali. Real meditation involves one-pointedness, internal reflections, introspections and ultimately achieving deeper states of consciousness. The breathing exercise in meditation is aimed to facilitate those. In that process, the body also gets revitalised.

However, many so called meditation sellers/dealers attract ignorant people to guided meditations using audio, music, video or a combination of such appealing tools. As physical relaxation is instant and visible, ignorant beginner may translate such relaxation as a great advantage. But you should know that relaxation in disguise of meditation is really a bad bargain. Deep into your practice you realise that all those sounds or videos which were being served as guided meditation techniques were in fact distraction in your practice and prevented you from connecting with your inner self. Real meditation requires complete silence and disconnect with all your sense organs. Relaxation, at best, is similar to getting served with starters much before a tasty and satisfying main course. So, please do not relish too much of starters as it ends up reducing your appetite by the time main course is served. Because starters are only for appetising while main course is for real nourishment of body, so why settle for less.

10. Meditation is all about sitting in the lotus posture and working on regulated breathing with the aim of some sort of unique enlightenment—These conditions aptly qualify as 'day-dreaming' or 'self-hypnotising' rather than meditation. People having tried meditation by sitting in such postures can directly relate to their own experiences and appreciate the link. Posture is all about calming the body so that it does not come in the way of guiding focus on the inner subtle thoughts which get broken with slightest physical distraction. Posture has hygienic importance and nothing beyond; it supports meditation but does not contribute much towards its success. One can have the best of posture and ability to hold it from sunrise to sunset but if his mind is unable to attain desired qualities such as concentration, mindfulness, inward focus, acceptance, etc., his end result in meditation will continue to be next to nothing.

Yes, keeping the spine absolutely straight, from hips to neck and head is an essential element of meditative posture but it is just to ensure detachment with the body while focusing on the inner world. Many people practice meditation sitting on a chair or sitting cross-legged on a cushion with good success. So meditation is not so much dependent on your posture but on getting freedom from the body to focus inside. So, people with some physical condition, that do not allow them to sit crossed-legged or in lotus position, need not have any concern about their posture. So long as they are able to find out a suitable posture that allows them freedom from the body and its senses over the entire duration of meditation sessions, they are in for reaping benefits of meditation in equal proportions.

11. Meditation is simply a self-improvement project—Big improvements demand changes in attitudes and behaviours. Sitting alone and going over 'what is' and 'what should it be' or 'how it can be' may be, at very best, a self-talk but it has no power to bring changes that are key to slightest variation in human behaviour. Actually, the very thought of self-improvements emanates from an unending sense of unworthiness. This tricky feeling gets formed with ongoing self-blame and poor sense of judgement about self by the critic sitting within. Without going in nitty-gritty of these issues, and as already discussed, the very desire of self-improvement and virtue of acceptance of things as they exist are in straight contradiction with each other.

With particular reference to matured adults, the very inclination towards self-improvement works as a trap. Longing for improvement arises from wanting more. That calls for striving more which disturbs the balance among competing objectives existing up until that time. Striving more calls for ongoing evaluation and judgement on progress being achieved. And forming judgement continuously becomes a way of life. This cycle got no end to it. In the least, it keeps our mind engaged on issues away from 'here and now'. A mind that is eternally busy in attempting for a better circumstance is certainly busy even after achieving set targets and, in the process, bound to generate dissatisfaction and sufferings. Just imagine the additional impacts of failures and frustrations due to under achieving of targets?

In contrast to all this, meditation is all about living in the present moment, the only true moment of life. Meditation focuses on love, peace and happiness. A person involved in self-criticism is inflicting severe kind of violence pushing love and peace that much farther away. Meditation strives for self-compassion and acceptance which leads to contentment. A person already blessed with treasures of contentment need not look for self-improvements. He will rather work for self-actualisation and self-realisation.

12. Meditation brings guaranteed results—No one is assured of results from meditation simply by following all the instructions. Even when sessions get spread over days and months, there is no guarantee of any kind. In other skills, efforts always lead to some progress but not so with reference to real meditation. There are examples of people putting in years and making zero progress apart from some physical benefits. It is not like perspiration after a session at the gym. There is no direct input to output ratio working for meditators. It is a long race with innumerable unknown obstacles at every step of the move. And not all people succeed in marching past known obstacles of meditation. That is why a practitioner must understand the underlying concepts, be aware of all potential obstacles, and prepare life filled with moral and ethical behaviour besides being regular in his practice. Tangible results in meditation, therefore, are far more demanding than many other skills honed in earlier avatar.

13. Meditation is only for Saints—Generally, meditation has been associated with people living in caves or mountains, the saints and sages from across cultures or hermits/ascetics belonging to ancient Indian traditions. All these people are highly revered in their respective faith systems. These people are known to survive under climatically challenged circumstances. While it may be right that all these people generally follow one or other meditational practice or something similar. A common man believing such stories cannot be blamed to associate meditation with people who have gone through hard penance.

But reality is entirely different. There is nothing that limits meditation only with selected few. It can be undertaken by every living person who is able to sit, feel and think or, using technical interpretations, who is able to reflect, ponder and contemplate. Age, gender, education, occupation, social or psychological background, or religious orientation make no difference for moving on with meditation whatsoever. However, people having positive orientation towards devotion, religion and philosophy are seen better placed for making faster progress on this path. Beneficiaries of meditation actually belong to very wide spectrum as it is equally helpful for scientists, eccentrics or tricksters. Meditation has been helpful to people from ancient times but its relevance in today's fast paced, stress generating, competitive and materialistic life has increased significantly; it is an old tool suitable for new ailments. It is very much for Karma Yogis of the real world like us. The only condition is that it requires strong willpower for getting transformed into a newer purer soul.

14. Meditation is a spiritual/religious practice—It is a very old practice which may have evolved within a particular religious context with the purpose of achieving spiritual goals but, in its present context, it does not belong to any religion or culture in particular. One can practise meditation without even basic belief in anything divine. An Atheist or an Agnostic may practise and seek benefit from meditation as much as a Christian or Muslim or Hindu or Buddhist, Meditation practice, in general, does not come in any conflict with any faith at all.

All religions work on faith while meditation works purely on mental abilities. Meditation is much beyond any kind of man-made divisions or segregations. However, one may come across some teachers propagating meditation by adding religious elements or adding rituals connected with specific religions. Such linking should only be seen as a variant of basic product aimed for niche segment or target group as a marketing promotion scheme and nothing beyond. Some people also recommend religious rituals to help beginners get used to kick start their meditational journey. They find a good connect with rituals and prefer techniques involving symbols from their own faith to help seek all important motivation to start meditation.

The role of such symbols and rituals in learning meditation is just like different types of scaffolding used to erect a tall building. No sooner the building gets ready; all the scaffolding is removed and thrown in some unseen corner. The occupants of the building do not even bother which kind of scaffolding was used for erecting the structure they use. In due course, after some basic progress in meditation is in place, all such symbols, rituals, elements are found of no use and every practitioner will have to voluntarily discard faith related elements without exception.

Any further linkage with any religious strand shall be seen as a roadblock. Continued relation of the meditator with his religion works as a unwanted distraction keeping his mind away from willful surrendering, a precondition to see reality in its pure and non-judgemental form. Unfortunately, all religions without exception are based on man-made divisions. Such divisions are best left out from very beginning of your meditational practice. Meditation by itself is a complete skill and can stand on its own feet without needing support from religions, scriptures or rituals of all sorts.

15. Meditation is not for people having no access to exclusive place—Not true, a good place for sitting is essential but there are no set specifications for that. A clean and airy place anywhere in your vicinity is fine to help you comfortably sit, breathe and focus inside. All you need is an interruption free environment. Meditation involves internal interruptions much more than external. Residential setups do have usual noise from the activities of its residents including neighbours and it can certainly work as a distraction but with practice it is possible to acquire state of mind where usual sounds no longer work as distractions. In any case, you are well advised to accept your external environment as given and it is easily done when, in due course, you develop Acceptance to desired levels.

One must realise that more than noise, it is your resistance or annoyance which distracts the mind much more. Acceptance of the environment helps you realise that there is hardly anything you can do about it except, may be, tightly closing your doors and windows.

But so long as your internal annoyance exists, you keep waiting for the noise to disturb you rather than focus inward. People with success in their practice actually suggest that uncontrollable noise in the background even helps them to get focused on present and enjoy the inner silence even better. Much later, there comes a time when the expert meditators are able to conduct a good sessions in the midst of full crowd.

In short, you can actually conduct your meditation sessions within whatever kind of space is available to you. Let it not work as a diversion tactic deployed by our intelligent mind to discourage us from looking inward. There is no empirical study to suggest that a hilltop, lakeside or lush garden helps your practise faster as compared to a crammed cozy corner in your home.

16. It takes years to get any benefit—The answer is a big no because benefits from meditation start immediately and keep growing with the growth of practice. The practice itself is the benefit. Even a beginner gets some advantages of each meditation session provided the preparations required are well in place. It is like learning to play a sport. On the very first day on it, you stand to gain the physical advantages to the least. The low hanging fruits of meditation include calming of mind, lowering of mental tensions, prioritising your time and energy as well as identifying important things to attend to. Meditation brings great physical and mental health benefits after even as little as eight weeks of practice and it has been proven scientifically.

Superior level benefits, however, may take varying periods and efforts depending on so many other factors to be discussed at length in subsequent chapters. All other things remaining same, length of practice and cumulative benefits can be considered growing in similar directions. Of course, just for example, a Buddhist monk with thirty thousand hours of meditation will have reaped more benefits than a person who started doing ten minutes of daily practice just last year.

Meditation has many levels of benefits. If you want to attain enlightenment, or be in a fearless state beyond all suffering, then yes, it will take a long while. But if all you want is better mental health, a bit more peace and balance in your life, you can start having that in few weeks. You will usually feel better after every single session. You feel more focused and more ready to go. It is in this context that meditation is getting prescribed for common man engaged in regular professions, with family to support and individual aspirations to do better in life.

17. Meditation will motivate me to abandon life and become a monk—If your interest in playing cricket carry the risk of making you Virat Kohli or your love for playing sitar carry the risk of making you Pandit Ravi Shankar or your visits to gym carry the risk of making you Mr. India than alone your meditation practice may motivate you to give up life for becoming a monk. Let us not forget that in the real world of today there are many more people who meditate and lead a "normal life" than people who meditate and live in monasteries or ashrams. It is too distant a fear to worry as there are far more important immediate hurdles to cross.

18. Meditation is anti-religion—Well, most part of meditation is carried out sitting in comfortable posture with regulating the mind and breath. Now breathe or mind regulation cannot be branded as being Christian, Hindu, Muslim or Buddhist. How can focus on attention on your breath, or repeating a sound in your mind, be anti-someone. There are thousands, if not millions, of Christians who meditate and gain from it without any conflict with their faith. If meditation is known to make you a better individual, and you are a Christian, it will only make you a better Christian.

Ultimate aim of meditation is to transform the mind to connect with our real core. Unfortunately, several traditional Christian old school followers fear that transformed minds lead a practitioner to think and act like a Hindu or Buddhist (free) away from their own teachings (regulated). Yes, apparently, some practised religions refrain from diktats provided by their books or traditions without room for any questioning or search of logic. Some followers may find compulsions to move away from such teachings and practice like meditation may certainly fuel such ideas on selective matters but that happens all the time even without meditation. So meditation cannot be singled out for such deviations at all. Apostasy in letter and spirit is a reality and was always so. It is futile to blame it on a religion neutral practice like meditation. People have said so for Yoga as well but look at how many Muslim and Christian practice Yoga regularly and confirm getting positive benefits.

19. One needs a master teacher by side to meditate—Again we can take example of learning a new sport. We do not require an expert coach to learn playing cricket from the day one as there is so much to learn from watching the game or practising ourselves. If your goal with meditation is simply health improvement and some relaxation, then you do not need a teacher ever. Learning it from a book, video, or workshop can be enough.

However, if you wish to go deeper with your practice, if your goal is spiritual advancement, then the access to a teacher may help you in cutting down the time required to make progress. Presence of a teacher is supposed to bring higher discipline and regularity in your practice. So, it is good to have access to a teacher to sort out your confusions or seeking clarifications but nothing beyond. Meditation requires one's own dedication and experimentation to make progress; it is too subtle to be learned or mastered in a classroom situation or by riding over the experience of others.

20. Technology can be used to perfect our meditation—In today's time and world, it is natural to look towards technologies to provide easy solution to our daily life problems. Even in the brain functioning field, there are scanning technologies that are able to detect how our mind operates at a given point of time. Such feedback can be very useful for exact analysis which were not possible just a couple of years earlier. But meditation is not about just knowing the thing; it is all about comprehension and realisation. Besides knowing, meditation involves too many right efforts and there is no possibility of inventing a magic pill that can direct us to our inside by directly cutting through all that goes in our body systems.

Some people take various kind of drugs to experience altered states of consciousness but that is closer to intoxication than meditation. On the other hand, you may come across various Apps available to take you through "how to meditate" using new age music and sounds to induce relaxed state of mind. Well, these can qualify just as alternative techniques rather than real help in meditation. No, unfortunately, technology has not found any solution to cut down on your efforts required to meditate. For thousands of years the ancient mystics, priests, monks, and yogis, all over the world, have been experimenting newer and newer methods for redemption from illusions or expanding consciousness but to no avail. True awakening, the main purpose of meditation, does not get served in any way by support from technology.

Fact remains that technology and sciences have only been successful in scratching outer surface of human mind. There are still no instruments to help understand working of many systems within us. Meditation is mostly about knowledge, awareness, serenity, one-pointedness, self-control and on that front technologies and sciences do not contribute much. Known drugs or intoxication only weakens these qualities. In higher states of meditation, the mind is in a state beyond all experience. In this state, any and every source of excitation, however subtle or wonderful, would be nothing but an unwanted distraction.

21. Meditation consumes so much of useful time—This is one of the most common myths surrounding meditation and scares many practitioners, particularly those who have not started as yet. As it is, they are under pressure of tight schedules and choked calendars. They wish to get few more hours every day to help them attend many critical initiatives which remain unattended due to paucity of time. Finding a full hour of quality time for meditation and that too on every day, no doubt, is a big call for many. Do not get scared as you can start meditation with as little as fifteen minutes a day and increase it slowly depending on your actual experience of real personal benefits. You can always stop it if meditation fails to compensate you well for your time invested. Feel free to demand best of 'Return on Investment' and give meditation chance only if you pocket your proportionate returns. That should sound as a good bargain.

Like every other activity, when meditation becomes a priority in your life, you find time for it. In reality, you find many high achievers from diverse professions as regular meditators. Positive attitude, higher acceptance, improved will power and such other skills improved through meditation actually bring unmatched efficiency thereby substantially improving productivity and improved quality of output. No wonder, every person successful in meditation is visibly more efficient, healthy, and happy than their counterparts not practising meditation.

Actually meditation works as a real time saver like no other method known to human kind. In normal life each one of us spend a lot of time going over stale thought process about our fears and anxieties which, in turn, bring confusions and sluggishness. Meditation does wonders by injecting clarity over thoughts and letting you work on right priorities. You gain clarity and focus on what is really important, and stop spending time on things that do not truly serve you well. Developed concentration allows finishing a job faster; focus on present reduces distractions; detachment cuts down association with results. Thus a meditation practitioner is far more efficient in discharging daily responsibilities saving hours on daily basis. Only a part of the saved time gets used back in sitting for meditation sessions.

22. Meditation is boring—Yes, it may be boring but only until such time that one is not into properly. If you try meditation expecting very quick results or to get some fun filled entertainment, you will certainly find it boring. In modern world, it is so easy to get instant fun and most people are seen spending all their spare time on fun as much as possible. On the contrary we still find millions of people throughout the world finding time for their meditation sessions. Here is a difference; you can opt for an entertaining option and kill your time without actually engaging yourself into it.

Meditation demands you to be focused, organised, consistent, and methodical. You cannot take it for granted or imagine anything about it. It does not allow you to multitask simply because it is far serious a business than entertainment, period. No, it is not like any other hobby, it is a tapasya and calls for sincere and genuine efforts. You are at wrong place if you are looking for fun in meditation. With only half hearted approach, your meditation is destined to become boring, for sure.

23. Meditation makes you emotionless—Emotions play important role in human life. Emotions differentiate us from machines and inspire us to learn, work hard and belong. Loss of emotions is a big sacrifice to make. You cannot be blamed to fear meditation if it really makes you emotionless. But it is not true at all. But meditation only reduces the degree and velocity of swings of emotions. It re-empowers your rational mind to gain control in reacting to situations. And rational mind acts rationally after considering bigger picture involved. To that extent, meditation makes us less of slaves to our emotions.

But on the other hand, meditation practice sharpens our perceptions of all our sense organs and helps us feel more deeply and clearly. It lets us feel many of those hints coming to surface, both from within or others being interacted with, that otherwise would have remain ignored. Yes, meditation helps us to be less reactive to emotional outbursts but only in a good way. It simply enables us to operate from a deeper place inside ourselves, a place that is larger than our emotions and concerns.

24. Meditation is just another artificial "feel good factor"— Many ignorant people do carry this impression that meditation is just another fashionable tag that modern hypocrites discuss about in drawing room talks to impress each other and, to that extent, it is just another thing similar to materialistic possessions or positions used to put one on a podium higher than others, a show off exercise. This is a harmless but very dangerous misconception. Such people do not realise that materialistic possessions, positions, titles are all factors that divide people by promoting separateness. Meditation, on the other hand, introduces its practitioners to oneness among all beings. A person proficient in meditation is able to cross over all perceived differences like levels of prosperity, education, social standing, caste, creed, religion, gender, language, regions, nationalities etc. Meditation helps beings to celebrate similarity, unity and interconnectivity of entire universe. It has no concern for 'feel good' or 'feel bad' factors at all.

In reality, meditation will generally show painful things about self that one was previously unaware of. It introduces us to our true nature and real response drivers of our actions and reactions and, at times, we never knew that darker side of ourselves. Meditation alone helps us to really know self as it exists without any ifs and buts, without any pre-existing image or false desire, without getting conditioned to what is socially correct or incorrect. In most cases, such knowledge is inversely reverse of 'feel good' factor. As your observation gets sharper, your mind gets more quiet, and you start looking more clear (due to colours from vision getting removed), you may comfortably see even parts of yourself that are not pretty.

Meditation is a very serious skill to acquire and people who wish to indulge into 'feel good' factors are in for a rude shock from initial sessions itself. No, meditation is not for people going after glitter but only for those gold diggers who do not mind removing tons of over burden in search of potential gold hidden somewhere deep down.

25. One need not do anything other than Meditation— You may come across some highly passionate people propagating meditation as an answer to all the problems of human life. They are seen supporting it as ultimate solution for all problems in areas such as health, wellness, growth, or enlightenment. But that will be exaggeration. Meditation should not be taken as the only aim of human life. You may call it a must have activity, one that is highly essential but not the only activity required for a complete and successful human life.

Generally speaking, meditation does dissipate some of your negative mental patterns, helps you manage your emotions better, helps you have better control over your thoughts, lets you see yourself as an entity beyond your body/mind and provide insight into the nature of your Self. But there are many other aspects of life that still need to be addressed with other tools and tackles. For example, you will still need to have good financial planning to meet your bills, you need to remain connected with ever evolving technologies to interact and respond socially, you need to increase your knowledge and wisdom about subjective world and its working, and beyond all of this, you need to make use of insight developed using meditation to make changes in your life, or in your surroundings.

In Buddhist tradition, meditation (*dhyana*) is only one of the three pillars of practice. The other two are wisdom (*prajna*) and ethics (*sila*). The second and third pillars remain equally important to grow in real stature of humanity. Meditation will help you keep healthy, but you still need to have good diet and exercise. It will help you have better relationships, but you still need to do self-reflection and tweak your behaviours. It will help you grow as a human being, but you will still be challenged, day after day, with the need of making the right choices. It will give you a peak into enlightenment but you will still need to be cautious such that ego does not bounce back if somebody steps on your foot. One better understand that this is why meditation is called a practice, a journey with no destination.

> (Some of the misconceptions listed above are appropriated from an article under the title "Live and Dare, Master Your Mind, Master Your Life, by Giovanni posted at https://liveanddare.com/myths-about-meditation)

While we still need to understand real meaning of meditation and its immediate benefits in modern days and lives, one must necessarily be able to put aside all these myths in the process of making right progress on meditation; these are real blind spots likely to meet us in our torturous journey called human life.

8

Role of Teachers in Meditation Journey

Teachers, preachers, instructors, guru, guide, coach or called with such other names, speaking generally, are believed to have critical role in imparting new skills to their wards. To that extent the role of a teacher should be obviously positive for learning meditation as well. But meditation is no common skill; it is by far the most significant and life changing skill with no other parallel. Yes, it is also an acquirable skill and presumably step by step instructions available to a beginner indeed may help advancing it. Historically also there are ample mentions of key role for a teacher for providing step-by-step directions to new learners while they unfold newer and deeper potentialities of their mind. But times have changed and entire process of dissemination of skills has undergone sea changes requiring a fresh view for importance of teachers for learning meditation.

Age at which meditation learning starts is one obvious difference from other skills. Normally it starts when the person is fully matured and has already experienced a great deal of things life has to offer. Secondly and even more importantly, the urge to learn meditation is entirely voluntary, optional and self-induced. It is unlike other skills pursued to follow some popular trend, under parental/peer pressures or for advancing career/profession. Wider sets of objectives and strong self desire make meditation learning something more than simply picking yet another new skill. The objectives sought are also generally ambiguous, non-measurable and numerous.

Acquiring normal skills like playing a musical instrument or excelling in game of cricket offers plenty of room for instructional dos and don'ts. Receiving and following instructions from experts for such ventures is indeed helpful and do influence speed and quality of learning achieved. Actually it is almost impossible to imagine mastery in such skills without the active support of qualified teachers/ coaches, etc. So much so that many people excelling in such fields are identified with the name of their teachers. And appreciation or recognition conferred on these performers is incomplete without mentioning the name of their Gurus.

On the other hand, we have performing arts like acting, singing, music or even cooking, representing different skills where teachers have limited role beyond introducing their wards to the basics or technical knowledge of respective subjects. Thus, scope and significance of teachers vary from skill to skill. Meditation is entirely a different practice where instructions and guidance have even smaller capacitance. To that extent, meditation is more like painting. The role of initial instructions and self efforts are highly disproportionate in this practice. Interestingly initial instructions for meditation are very general in nature and are easily available from plenty of sources on print, audio as well as video sources.

Success in meditation comes from self-sittings and self-experiencing. Mastering the map takes you nowhere in meditation because there is no map to begin with. For example, one of the most basic instructions for sitting is to 'continuously keep your attention on your breath and the moment you spot it getting distracted, bring it back on breath again'. This one line instruction sounds a very simple, clear and seemingly harmless instruction and one should have no problem in following it instantly. But people with experience confirm that it takes years and years to implement this single instruction. Any amount of repetition by the teacher to that effect invariably fails to make any further impact. Actually, this instruction by and large summarises the entire journey of meditation and perfection thereof because when you are already focused on your breath there is nothing left to do and no guidance needed anymore.

> "Meditation is one of the greatest arts in life—perhaps the greatest, and one cannot possibly learn it from anybody, that is the beauty of it."
>
> —*Jiddu Krishnamurti*

The real requirement for advancing meditation is to grow unique mental muscles which are trained to respond to your desire to ignore distractions and focus on conscious object selected for meditation. To that extent, it is quite an innate ability to be cultivated where outside guide is of not much use. Later, we will see in greater details that most common hindrances on the path of making progress in meditation are continued worldly desires, dislikes, laziness, lethargy and most importantly doubts. It may be sufficient, at this stage, to suggest that presence of a guide in no manner contributes to overcome these well known hindrances. Neither there are medications or vaccines available for that. Antidotes for these hindrances have to be developed by each person by their own efforts and in their own labs.

But this is not to say that teachers have no role at all. That will be utter injustice. Yes, you encounter typical obstacles in your long journey for cultivating the practice of mindfulness and an experienced guide may prove to be handy in making you understand such obstacles and help you overcome the same. An experienced teacher may also observe your practice and can provide useful inputs in terms of obvious things getting overlooked. But most part of churning happens inside your individual mind. It is impossible for anybody from outside to clearly understand correctly as it happens. Being a very subtle subject by nature meditation involves many nuances which are best perceived by you yourself.

Teaching as an activity involves different levels of obvious and descriptive methods while meditation demands more of subtle nuances. As a result of this difference, qualification and experience of an effective teacher is more critical as compared with other skills. A person best suited for this has to be an advance practitioner himself because meditation cannot be taught just as an occupation. Quest for such a teacher, therefore, becomes that much more complex. Another compelling reality is about the timing of your practice. The ideal time of practice is generally in the morning and at your own home. Sheer time and place makes accessing a right teacher beyond reach, unless affordability is not a matter of concern for you.

Traditionally, search for teachers was less complicated, especially with reference to Indian culture. Traditional teachers were imparting knowledge about techniques as much as principles, ethics, and morality of a particular tradition they belonged to. They also use to teach way of life of their respective traditions as well as shaping the entire world view of their students. Students used to remain with their teachers, mostly in forest academies, on 24/7 basis, for several years on exclusive basis. Acceptance to such academies was quite strict and only most qualified wards were taken in on residential basis. Students not having required maturity or lack of sincerity were refused entry or were kept on a slow pace. Teachers were basically priests, monks, yogis or acclaimed gurus and had full knowledge about their students, their families, orientations, social standing and such other issues. Those matured teachers knew tiniest nuances of their students even ahead of student himself. Just imagine the situation today and conclude how much help to expect from teachers available on hourly rates.

Today many Tom, Dick and Harry call themselves meditation teachers and admissions are based on capacity to pay rather than readiness or ability to learn. They do not have time, energy or interest to know internal make up of their students. This limits their ability to effectively guide such wards, especially on fine inner shadings. On the other side, majority of students also are unable to give their total time for learning like before. They have jobs, professions, careers and families to take care of at the same time.

Some teachers also go to the extent of exposing practitioners to manipulative techniques and promise them out of the world experiences. Please guard yourself against falling for such traps. Artificially modified state of consciousness (derived by all means including but not limited to use of banned substances) are just temporary thrills and nothing beyond.

Common *modus operandi* of many centres is to carve out some particular method (preferably named around some catchy phrases) that they can proudly claim to be their own copyright and promote the same as a brand to get more and more followers. Their drive is not their passion about spreading knowledge but simply a lucrative business proposition. All their initiatives are guided towards ballooning of their bank accounts. Most recent fashion is to conduct retreats where the teacher take multiple students on a residential basis and provides a sort of platform for helping you conduct your practice in a conducive environment. Even if the entire gamut of money is kept out of consideration, such endeavours, at best, qualify more as facilitation than teaching.

Qualities of a Good Meditation Teacher

To begin with, your ideal teacher is someone having his own meditational experience of years, if not decades. Guided exclusively by genuine desire to share his experience, he should not be greedy for money and increasing his following. He must be showing qualities of calmness, kindness, patience and compassion. He must exhibit living life with humility, sympathy, truthfulness and openness. He must have par excellence record of ethical and moral conduct. He must focus on your self sufficiency rather than continued dependence on his guidance. He should be giving credits to the process rather than personalities or taking self credit. Qualifications of such people are difficult to explain but they are easy to be identified. Unique stillness in their eyes and their own characteristic luminosity may hardly be missed even from a distance. Well, it certainly cannot be helped that search of such eligible meditation teachers sounds more like day dreaming than a genuine possibility.

Continuing with practicality being the focus of this book, the real solution lies in becoming your own teacher. The right example to follow is the famous character from Mahabharata named Eklavya, who installed a statue of his revered guru Dronacharya and learnt archery over the years with great sincerity and became better than royal princes trained by the legendry Guru himself. The compulsions and consequences of poor Eklavya may not be so relevant today as those were different times. But the central theme remains exploring possibilities of improving one's own skill through resolute hard work and sincerity.

Lastly, meditation is more about practice than learning. Let your inner state fill you with clarity, love and subtle awareness and guide you as your own shadow all through your journey of meditation. With these elements, you can very well be open to your inner expansion. The inner light is completely capable of illuminating your journey and bestowing you with its presence as an unseen guide for all times to come. No, you need not invoke a teacher just because others say so or as a measure of some superstitions or meeting some psychological need. For practising meditation you have a guide sitting well within and all you need is to activate your contact with it to enjoy its guidance at every moment.

9

Obstructions and Hindrances for Meditation

Starting any good habit is difficult. Initiating a fascinating habit like meditation may have its own attractions but sustaining this practice over months and years is certainly a daunting task. In general parlance, a work well begun is considered half done but not so for meditation. It is a lifelong practice with no end in sight. Sustaining desired levels of focus, interest and determination for such long times, in an uninterrupted manner, has its own mountains to cross. The challenges for beginners are even greater as they remain in thick and thin of real world for most part of their day and real world has its own pulls and pressures which are far severe today than any time in the past. But the stringency of requirements for sustaining meditation over time has not changed a bit. Thus the gulf between 'what is required' and 'what actually is' is much wider and deeper today. This calls for even greater guarding against all known challenges. Interestingly, the tendencies that create roadblocks in meditation are not much different than those causing difficulties in normal life. Meditation is supposed to be the Gym where the practitioner grows powerful new muscles of calm and insight which are used to find solutions for bringing happiness and success.

Sensory desires are other compelling combo of physical and mental obstacles to be dealt with every so often. The world of five senses offers variety of delights, interests and involvements. A lot has been said about these, but even at the cost of repetition, let us remember that the only way to abandon these attractions is little by little, step by step; with constant and regular realisation and reinforcement. Each one of us has to develop our own delay devices so that sensations are not allowed to reach the mind instantaneously. And sex is not the only thing to fight, there are plenty other disturbing sensations one goes through on daily basis.

To ensure continued practice over longer periods, you have to humbly remain committed against all obstructions. You have to navigate the practice through all types of resistances and hindrances and that too without getting angry. Becoming too hard on self only agitates the mind. That agitation will distract focus even when you resume your practice. The product of this situation will be failure which fuels your anger further. Calm mind is as much essential for success as finding the time, space and environment for meditation.

One must always remember that quality prevails over quantity and meditation is no exception. Simply sitting in posture for defined length of time is not enough. That does not take you anywhere. You have to have balanced inhaling and exhaling, you must have normal and stable heartbeats, blood pressure must be well regulated, and body must be free from any types of pains and pressures. The body is the equipment to be used by mind, hence, it must be at its performing best to ensure positive outcome. During your interaction with other practitioners, you surely will come across people who complain of not making much progress even after undertaking practice for reasonably long periods. If and when you are in that situation, be kind to remind yourself that one or the other expected obstruction is in action. A revisit to this section of the book and proper identification should lead you out of logjam.

Deeper understanding of well established obstacles can help a new practitioner in creating desired precautions so that progress is faster, stronger and steadier and unwanted detours are avoided or shortened. Deeper comprehension of these known roadblocks will certainly help him erect credible strong defense mechanism to make those hindrances powerless. Meditation is basically a new and strong mental skill that demands harnessing natural abilities as well as cultivating that skill similar to efforts deployed by high achievers in every other field. Progress in meditation is like growing an altogether new muscle within one's own mind.

Interestingly, these hindrances, psychological in basic character, are quite universal in nature. As such, irrespective of your physical or mental predisposition, you have to guard against these hindrances without exception. Normally, these hindrances are not obvious in early stages of your practice because your mind considers meditation as yet another fun toy. Initially the mind does not take meditation as capable of rocking its boat in any significant ways. Later, with some progress in place, mind's devious and evasive forces start feeling threatened and then alone mind starts throwing its tantrums like defiance and disruptions. Here we shall restrict our discussion for five major hindrances. All practitioners are required to develop their own effective antidotes to control these menaces so that progress in their practice continues on desired pace.

Let us first look a summarised Table. Later we can elaborate each one of these at suitable length:

Major Hindrances with Identity, Explanation and Antidotes

No.	*Hindrance*	*Identity Signs*	*Brief Explanation*	*Effective Antidote*
1.	Worldly Desires	"I need......." "I want......." "I must have.." "I deserve this..	- Pursue the pleasures and avoid the pains. - Enjoying fame and gain; cursing obscurity and loss of recognition.	- Unify the mind - Strong Moral and Ethical Codes - Practising Contentment
2.	Strong Likes and Dislikes	"This is wrong..." "How is it fair?" "What I think is the right way"	Mental negativity involving judging, rejection, denial. Non-acceptance including impatience and dissatisfaction.	- Accessing to inner happiness - Removal of negativity towards one and all
3.	Laziness and Lethargy	'It is too tiring' 'It is waste of time' 'Today it will not work' 'I don't feel well today'	- Cost of activity looks greater than benefits. - Loss of energy and fire - Reduced internal motivation.	- Evolve 'Just Do It' approach - Improve quality of your attention - Develop sense of importance

No.	*Hindrance*	*Identity Signs*	*Brief Explanation*	*Effective Antidote*
4.	Distractions from Worry and Repentance	'What if....' 'It looks difficult...' -'It is unlikely to work....'	- Repentance for unwise, immoral, illegal activity. - Anxiety of things happening in dreadful ways.	- Cherish joy from Meditation - Promote confidence and optimism - Stop preempting results in either ways
5.	Suspicions and Doubts	'Is it possible....' 'May be I am not up to it...' 'I may be missing something critical..' 'I may not have what it takes...'	- Biased and regular unconscious focus on possible negative outcomes. - Persistent hesitation stopping one to make strong efforts.	- Making Attention strong and unwavering - Making efforts consistently without thin-king about results - To become a pure Karma-yogi

Let us now look at each of these critical hindrances one by one in required details.

1. Persistent Worldly Desires

Insatiable desires of sense organs present the very first roadblock on way of practising meditation regularly. Both physical and mental senses are, by very design, always looking forward for every opportunity to continue enjoying likable experiences and disliking the opposite. Celebrating gains and mourning losses is considered being human. Maximising pleasures and minimising pains, seeking fame and avoiding obscurity, accepting praise while rejecting blames, are very natural to expect in normal life. Our current DNA is a result of our biological programming in this manner since the early evolution of humanity. In this physical/material world, these behaviours help us to survive and thrive. Human life will be so dull minus all these thrills.

Be it eating, watching, listening, thinking, imagining or even sexual activity, satiating these desires certainly results in continued over-consumption. Meditation sharpens our insight to see through these desires and prepares us to go against conditioned programming of the senses. Forget complete surrender, even moderation practised towards all these senses can result in so much of savings in terms of time and energy on a daily basis. Further, there are secondary senses which keep our mind busy. Itching in a part of body, attention moving towards every source of sound, eyes trying to see even when closed are all such desperate attempts made by our senses. Meditation lets us realise that all such indications originate from desires asking for excitement and stimulations.

Progress in meditation, in spite of these forces at work, will ultimately replace cravings with contentment. A well regulated mind, achieved after prolonged meditation, prevents such stimuli at the subconscious level itself. But to do that, the practitioner has to up his game and master all the moral and ethical values in desired proportions.

2. Strong Likes/Dislikes and Hatred

Known also by name of its other siblings like disgust, malice, resistance, we all are well aware about negative state of mind where we are constantly possessed by one or other these undesirable feelings, emotions or thoughts. For broad understanding and sake of brevity, let all these negative feelings collectively be named as 'aversion'. Its expanse operates in a wider range where a harmless 'less liking' or 'not liking' a thing lies on the lower end and 'readiness to harm' or 'actual harm' to others lies on the top end. Loss of interest, dissatisfaction, every type of fault finding, calling names, show of impatience or accusations (others as well as self included) are all nothing but different degrees of manifestation of 'aversion'. Some of these tendencies may appear normal but they are critical for meditation as they always keep the mind engaged around them resulting in total wash down of all possible advantages of meditation.

Agitation caused by 'aversions' create whirlpool of distractions holding back the mind from concentration, an absolute requirement for meditation. Negativity generated by these sensations work like holes in our little vessel of happiness. That is why every practitioner must make extra efforts to completely extinguish these sensations completely. These must be replaced by stronger positive vibrations through augmenting the skills such as acceptance, kindness and compassion.

One needs to be happy to see the world go by at its own pace and direction. As it is, world is so big and you are so small to make any difference. Thinking logically, there may be several wrongs taking place in front of your eyes but you are neither responsible nor capable for changing them. So why feel aversion for such happenings? How can you actually make the world move under your direction? Your likes, opinions, evaluations, judgements, sermons have relevance, if at all, only for you. Do not expect others to care for your views and desires at all. You are expected to behave like lotus leaf in muddy waters.

3. Laziness and Lethargy

Inventing and reinventing possible reasons to avoid sitting for meditation is a very casual and harmless but significant hindrance for maintaining regularity in practising meditation. All tactics used by our mind to delay or avoid practice get clubbed here. These tactics cajole our mental processes by one or the other compelling artificial reasons for not meditating on a day or for not letting the mind undertake serious contemplation. The most crucial form of this hindrance is creeping feeling of sleep within minutes of practice such that the mind withdraws from conscious awareness and drifts into dreamy cycles. Those practitioners having been in meditation for comparatively longer durations will vouch for it as how their sessions are rendered useless as sleepish feelings engulf their entire existence in a manner that even after sitting for full one hour, there is no effective contemplation gets achieved. Both body and mind may certainly feel fresh after such sessions but those are benefits of sleep. Effectiveness of your sessions is based only and only on condition and caliber of contemplation achieved.

Unfortunately, this hindrance works as seductive trap. Within minutes into practice, you start enjoying the dreamy sequences induced by this hindrance. It happens because dullness is inherently a pleasing phenomenon. Dullness leads to past recollections, typical visions or even pleasurable sensation creating a false impression as if something ultra important is happening due to success in your meditation. Anchoring attention on the in and out breath all through the meditation is recommended as most crucial element to counter this hindrance as constant attention on breathing does not provide space for this hindrance to set in. Constant attention of your conscious awareness on the object of choice is possible only when you are able to construct a strong wall against this tendency.

Overcoming this hindrance calls for comprehending full working of our mental processes. In its simplest explanation, sitting in meditation demands a mind that does not entertain random thoughts. Engaging in random thoughts always brings mental activities to a lower/slower level. Slower level of activity works as open invitation to sleep due to our original orientation. The moment our mind is asked to reduce its activity, it develops lack of interest and excitement and it immediately directs the body to go in recuperation mode, the sleep, body's default setting. Every untrained intelligent mind finds sleep as a better and fruitful use of time as *compared to* sitting idle in meditative pose. That is one precise reason, meditation is generally not recommended in the evening. After a good night rest, early morning time is preferred to not let the mind befool our physical body to opt for sleep all over again.

The only effective antidote in this situation is self motivation by letting your mind remain aware of the potentially great advantages out of meditation practice. You are best advised to keep a short list of direct benefits handy at each stage of your practice. Literally, you have to keep score of targets set, progress made and evaluate your progress on almost monthly basis. Evaluation tests are effective not only in school education, they are equally important for progressing on this most important path of human life. You have to literally work and review your intentions, intellect, and discrimination capability of the mind to recall the list of advantages every time you spot lethargy setting in. Opting for standing meditative pose is yet another tool to weaken the forces of this hindrance and may be found useful by beginners together with good splash of cold water as soon as a sleepy situation gets sensed.

4. Repentance or Worry

Our mind likes to go back to memories of events, situations, or persons to evoke shivers of pleasurable provocations, or the burns of anger or even soreness of grief, time and again. Pondering over imperfection of past or flings of future always leads to innumerable repentances and anxieties. In everyone's life there are plenty of past decisions to repent about which, if taken differently, may have resulted in a different and better present. It is but natural for mind to keep going back to the past episodes sitting in the window of present. Past wrongdoings keep haunting with direct repercussions on present. No surprise for that, as everyone is always more intelligent about past. But what is gone is gone and is never coming back. Thinking about past is simply a waste of time and energy. That is why, a well regulated mind remains focused only in present reality.

> "Untrained warriors are soon killed on the battlefield; so also persons untrained in the art of preserving their inner peace are quickly riddled by the bullets of worry and restlessness in active life". —*Paramahansa Yogananda*

Mind always enjoys recalls of emotional memories involving love, romance, excitements, pride and joy basically to recreate similar emotional experiences, even if it is through day dreaming. But recall is not a passive activity; all recalls derail you from your focus on activity in hand in present, especially activity demanding stillness of both body and mind like meditation. No wonder, when you ask your mind to withdraw from all its preoccupations and surrender to nothingness, it becomes rebellious and starts playing with all the dirty tricks at its command to avoid surrender.

Purifying your entire system from the burden of past or worry for future, therefore, becomes all the more critical. Forgetting past will keep getting highlighted in any discussion about meditation just because it is so critical a factor in ultimate success or failures. So please do not feel boring about it. Forgetting on everything other than present and living in moment by moment rooted in present is the only accepted, tried and tested antidote against this very hindrance.

5. Suspicions and Hesitance

Entertaining doubts about everything around has its own importance and cannot be brushed aside lightly. Taking doubts seriously and acting against them swiftly act as safeguard against unwanted failures. It is completely a natural and logical approach. Being just careless and throwing caution to winds makes us vulnerable and an easy prey for wretched situations. There is no harm so long as doubt operates only for abnormal and unexpected situations. The problem arises when doubt starts working on unconscious mental processes where it starts expecting negative situations or outcomes even under normal and positive situations. At such stage, doubt starts ruling our conscious mental space. And a mind entangled with doubt holds strong powers to reduce best of meditation sittings into useless episodes.

This problem becomes sinister for practitioners running low on self-motivation. Even harmless sounding doubts, in their case, start spoiling even better features of their practice. Under this condition mind is able to highlight short term pressures of meditation by relegating long-term benefits as unachievable goals. Impacted by this hindrance, poor practitioner starts invoking endless self doubts about techniques being used, methods deployed, priorities being set, success actually achieved and even intellectual ability to sustain the pressures of continued meditation. Experience suggests that many enthusiast beginners, captured under doubts and suspicions, end up giving up meditation even when actual progress made by them was on expected lines or even better than many others.

Difference between Hindrances and Obstacles

It may be noted that in this section we have dealt with only hindrances which create resistance in the initiation of meditation practice. These are smaller disturbances which can be solved by appropriate methods. The end impact of these hindrances is delay in progress. Hindrances are more like warning signals asking us to remain alert and persistent. Interestingly, with better understanding and preparation, all these preventive signs can be dealt with even before these actually come in our way. Obstacles, on the other hand, are bigger road blocks that can disrupt your practice altogether. Obstacles get experienced much after your learning phase is over, when you have made some significant progress in your practice.

Taking a simple example of a morning walker, an hindrance is like loosely tied shoelaces that can make your walk slower and a bit uncomfortable while obstacle is like finding a deep ditch in the center of the road resulting in disruption and stoppage of entire traffic of that road. Hindrances make continuing practice difficult but not impossible. Obstacles are major obstructions and result in stopping our entire practice for an unknown duration. Their end result may dramatically stop our practice or significantly reduce our progress. Obstacles can be faced only when you actually experience them. Any amount of advance preparation or understanding cannot equip you to overcome obstacles. Also, each obstacle has its own unique solution or technique to get past them. Obstacles generally come to surface during advance meditation practice. Accordingly, obstacles are to be explained only towards end of "Third Stage" of meditational journey.

Stage Two

The Beginner

Having settled the preparatory issues, there is no more struggle for finding time and energy for each session. The issues relating to what to expect and what not to expect from sittings are also well settled in the First Stage together with a good exposure to hindrances to be guarded against. However, mind is still not willingly ready to cooperate for surrendering its selfish designs and to look inward. Mind still remains preoccupied mostly with repetitive thoughts. Poor unregulated mind is unable to remain attentive on the object of meditation for any reasonable length of time. If Stage One was dedicated for preparatory issues and making the body ready for sessions, Stage Two is largely dedicated to making the mind willing and cooperative for meditation. Its challenges and milestones make this stage both tricky as well as interesting stage of the entire meditation journey.

If we consider meditation journey similar to building a super structure, the Stage One concluded earlier is similar to picking a site, soil testing, bedrock findings, studying wind and seismic activities. End result of Stage One is like ground breaking and arranging material for starting construction. In short, it was more about planning and arranging. The work on pilings and creation of load bearing capacity to start laying strong foundation is for discussion here under Stage Two. Now, we know that stability of all subsequent structures entirely depend on the strength of its foundations. Interestingly, planning stage does offer opportunities to make amend as many times as required but once the foundation is laid, major flaws cannot be rectified later. Issues discussed from now onwards, similarly, are like getting cast in concrete.

The entire objective of this stage is to ensure active willingness of the otherwise strolling mind to voluntarily withdraw from outside and focus towards inside all through the length of each meditation session. As we will learn in due course, there is no force to apply or trick to play for the mind to become willing and voluntary. Mind is said to have mind of its own and it loves to behave like a master every time you expect it to be a humble servant. Other important objectives for this stage include crossing over physical fatigue, boredom, declining motivation and frustrations (due to extreme nature of results from individual sessions). Identifying and retracting the mind from daydreaming is yet another unremitting challenge to be dealt with at this stage.

This stage of meditation is also comparable to Middle and High School stage of education system. At this stage you focus only on core course of study which typically includes language(s), basic mathematics, social studies and an option from science, humanities or commerce streams. The academic programmes are rather predetermined with a limited choice for electives or optional subjects. Focus is essentially on academic and cultural foundational knowledge and skill. Conformity is heavily rewarded. Testing is frequent but covers only small amounts of material. The markings are liberal where few students earn near perfect scores. Students operate in fairly known environment with many friends and guide available at back and call. Extra curriculum activities are largely for fun. As a guiding principle, you are expected to learn only from prescribed textbooks or material assigned by teachers.

In the beginning of this stage, attention span is very short due to frequent distractions and that is quite normal to expect. So much so that, at times, the practitioner even find difficult to recall what was the object of meditation seconds before. That is why ability to hold attention span over the selected subject or keeping a track of where the mind is engaged and quickly bringing it back to the meditation object is indeed a substantial success.

> "The thoughts resolve themselves. Just sit there with them. The reason they don't get resolved is because you're either running away or fighting them. If you sit there with something long enough, it will get resolved."-Naval Ravikant

Let us now deal with the real issue of mind's voluntary willingness to focus on the inverted view, and that too for full length of the session. Surrendering and willingness of the mind requires freedom from physical attractions of the visible world, absence of desires and opinions, and clean and clear heart. It demands practising and mastering skills of contentment, positivity and gratitude. And all these virtues must be firmly grounded on rock solid moral and ethical behaviour. Since the grip of these vices significantly differs from person to person, the time required for mastering this stage may widely vary from one another in proportion of clinching power of his attachments.

Towards the end of this stage, issues related to 'body' no more pose problems of any nature. You would become physically comfortable for the entire length of your session. Earlier pangs of sleep leading you to daydreaming should also have stopped. You will achieve success being in sync with your surroundings where earlier irritants like temperatures, noise, sounds, etc. have settled too. As the practitioner advances, his ability to keep attention on the chosen object gets stronger with distractions becoming less frequent and short-lived. Both the depth and steadiness of his attention get developed.

This stage is considered achieved once you start realising that mind is able to remain engaged on the object of your meditation for ten to fifteen minutes at a stretch. This becomes possible only when you are able to cross over the bond of your 'self' with real issues of normal life. In terms of example of space rocket launch, this stage is achieved only after successful separations of boosters and lift off engines. This is the stage where bulk of the distance is covered and where speed is gained to meet desired velocity to cross over the gravitational force.

One of the chapters of Stage Two deals with theoretical knowledge about major types and techniques of meditation. Exposure to multiple techniques is aimed towards exposing the reader with respect to most popular practices in vogue. Different types of meditation practice may suit particular types of practitioners at specific stage of their meditation journey. While there is no 'best way' or 'more suitable to me' recommendation, a general view of all popular techniques is expected to help the practitioners explore their own choices after proper navigation through the alternates available. In subsequent stages of this journey, practitioners must try out different techniques and use what works for them at specific halts. But until such time, you better continue with a neutral technique of focusing the attention on a single object during the whole meditation session. This object may be the breath, mantra, visual image, body organ, external object or whatever is disturbing to your mind including a nagging person or problem.

10

Uplifting Moral Standards

'Nothing grows in isolation' is the universal rule and progress in meditation is no exception. Real progress on the meditative journey requires support from strong moorings which get created from heightened morality and ethics. It is not practical to continue materialistic life laced with desires and hatred for 23 hours and expect changeover to a recluse for the duration of the 24th hour of the day. Normal human life is like stream of muddy water filling our overhead water tank from where the water is drawn for all our requirements. How can you expect clean water for cooking and muddy water only for flushing from a single overhead tank? The mud is nothing but mix of our desires, aversions, and attachments. Clearly, to ensure supply of neat water, we must clean the tank and more importantly must install well sized filters to prevent further muck entering our water tank. Any effort to allow those filters only for one hour a day will never result in a clean tank. Uplifting moral standards and ethical behaviour are those very filters that need to be in operation at all times.

Morality consists of values and norms taught by parents and society that become integral part of personality. Through repetitive internalisation of social interactions, morality becomes a well activated faculty and starts regulating person's internal as well as external behaviour. This faculty passes judgement on our inner impulses by repressing those considered unacceptable and vice versa. All this while, unfortunately, even undesired traits, some of which are indeed invasive and disturbing, continue to exist in our overall system. We continue to harbour inhibitions that prevent us from actually doing many acts considered immoral.

Living life normally, these negative traits as well as moral filters remain somewhat dormant. Presence of these filters, *per say*, does not scare us as we get used to their being around. This is a strong understanding and needs a bit of time to sink in completely. Because of this fact, many a time we end up not knowing ourselves in very clear light. Effective internal focus achieved on way of progress in meditation ends up spoiling this delicate ignorance. Because meditation brings all our internal contents in open with naked clarity, we no longer can keep eyes closed like earlier. Stark realities of our impulses of greed, desires, attachments, aggression, lust, envy, etc. which were hitherto buried, start spilling out in open surface opening the Pandora's Box of our unwanted reality.

Before achieving progress in meditation, we generally live in a make believe world of 'what should be' rather than true reality. Reality bites hard. For example, a reality check that your past actions were not as moral as you thought is a big burden to bear. Knowing about reality of self is indeed very depressing. To make the matter worse, meditation induces negative feelings with even higher intensity and deeper recognition. This makes the working of our moral faculties much more expressive and strong armed. As a result a wrong action accentuates the feeling of shame or guilt more acutely and fiercely than before. Your impulses might still succumb to temptations but the degree of repentance and pains will be more intense now that your meditation has widened your guilt perceptions. One can easily picture out the impact of such repentances on quality of his concentration and focus during meditation. No, guilt is quite overpowering and a guilty mind just cannot concentrate.

Enhanced morality standards practised over long periods of time develop new neurons in our brain helping in establishing improved moral behaviour. In addition, these neurons also induce conditioned positivity in thoughts and actions even under negative situations. This is no exaggeration as it happens to be the process responsible for evolution of human brain into its present condition – increased frequency of use of any muscle makes it stronger than before. Persistent moral and ethical behaviour shines self-awareness producing a very sweet by-product in form of enhanced long term happiness. This also enhances positive reflection of our character in self-view boosting self confidence as well. All this also helps in defending own perception held by people around with greater maturity.

Generally, all moral issues operate in invisible manner downplaying their results as rather insignificant. In reality, however, these issues hold superlative impact on our entire psyche. As a default setting, we are wired to feel pricking in inner core with every moral violation. It does not matter whether such violations get committed knowingly or under ignorance. You cannot imagine a human being not bitten by inner conscience after getting involved in any immoral or unethical activity. Even when some people keep a straight face, immoral action always leads to the pangs of pains, sufferings, regrets and self-tortures. Yes, an immoral act may provide a momentary excitation and stimulation but the guilt and disgust that follows is always dangerously powerful and last longer.

The basic idea of deciphering morality for meditation is to help readers and practitioner realise that success in meditation demands fundamental work on cementing morality without exception. It is a just belief that success in meditation depends not on what you think while sitting on the cushion but what you actually do while away from the cushion.

Hardships Involved in Improving Morality

We all wish our morality to shine as pure gold and be seen so by people around us. But gold does not come to its shining self just like that. Shining morality is assured only if we are ready to go through the process similar to gold refining. Beginning from the ore level, gold goes through series of tedious processes of smelting, refining, leaching, precipitation and filtration. Each of these processes is necessitated to get rid of obnoxious impurities surrounding the tiny particles of gold. To begin with, gold ore rocks have shades of black, green or metallic shades like normal rocks we see every day with no sparkle, glow or lustre. The yellow shine identified with gold arrives only at the end of all environmentally challenging processes mentioned above. Efforts involved in improving our morality and ethics, similarly, have to go through every step of arduous journey of refining over and over again. But ultimately, that very morality shall makes us 'one among equals' as gold becomes precious among so many other metals.

Purifying individual's moral and ethical self requires refinement for every word spoken, every thought and every action being moral and ethical. This process, no doubt, involves a lot of inevitable sufferings as one has to get rid of natural human weaknesses of anger, selfishness, envy, lust, greed and pride. Luckily, pursuing redundancy for these weaknesses is difficult only to begin with. There are some very sweet low hanging fruits that await you in the initial period of your efforts itself. Within no time of your sincere efforts you start seeing success in your endeavours; you start getting real inner encouragement for giving up these weaknesses progressively with increasing pace. Subsequent sufferings are not felt as insurmountable. As a passing reference, improved morality also helps dispersing clouds of doubts and ignorance hovering over our hearts and minds. This by itself is a unique respite on many occasions.

Interestingly, one may come across situations which, depending on tradition, philosophy or cultural background one comes from, may have been acceptable to pass the test of morality. But filters for morality for meditation are far beyond such differences. Meditation links you with your inner core and bypasses all manmade filters that you may have applied until now. The new you start viewing morality acceptable or otherwise based on your well contemplated reasoning rather than what was culturally inherited or viewed by others. That is why discussion here on morality is about an absolute virtue that has nothing to do with any particular religion or culture or customs one comes from. This disclaimer is made lest anyone gets hurt for reasons beyond our scope of interest. Morality used for meditation is to be assimilated based on individual's inner pure core and not by any external diktat.

Understanding Ethically Correct Behaviour

Unlike morality, understanding what is ethical or otherwise is rather simple. Our actions do impact other people in varying proportions. Ethical behaviour involves uncompromised respect for key moral principles of honesty, fairness, equality and dignity towards others at all times. Lack of such respect for impact of own actions on others is simply unethical behaviour. Dilution in ethical behaviour creates voids between the world and us. Ultimately, this void hits back on us by making us lonely and frustrated beings. Each unethical behaviour results like a hole in our pitcher holding nectar of spiritual earnings. All our actions must pass the test of being ethical without exception. Also, there exists no gap between ethical or not ethical; it is perfect black or white scenario with no room for grey in between.

Meditation being a spiritual practice solicits pure lifestyle, one that is morally and ethically immaculate and untainted. Being an introspective activity, meditation touches us at deeper levels. It calls for reorientation of our basic attitudes towards very existence. But this entire process of introspection creates a lot of churning which is bound to bring out most of our hidden guilt, regrets and scars. Right quality of attitude is to be expected only after completion of this churning process. But if, side by side of this process, our immoral or not so moral acts and ethical violations continue, how can we ever get to see freedom of that free mental attitude?

Tools for Uplifting Moral Behaviour

Having understood the significance of moral and ethical behaviour, we must look for proven practices for augmenting such behaviour on sustained basis. Actually, this is not a modern day challenge to humanity. This dichotomy continues all through the recorded history of humanity cutting across cultures and civilisations. For example, Indian system of Yoga Sutra compiled by Maharishi Patanjali lists out five distinct impulses keeping human mind their slave, namely, Ignorance, Ego, Passion, Disgust and Lure for transient life. These impulses are said to surface and resurface one after the other in inexhaustible manner attacking hold of morality. Yoga recognised these being part of human's fundamental nature where one cannot win over these impulses simply by study or understanding. Let us look at some of the most effective and proven practices available for mastering our behaviour in desired directions.

(A) Perfecting Recommended Yams and Niyams

Those familiar with Ashtanga Yoga, the eight limbs Yoga, also known as Raja Yoga, popularised by Yoga Sutras by Maharishi Patanjali, would know about importance of improving moral and ethical behaviour following prescribed Yams and Niyams. Ashtanga Yoga considers these as foundational steps and a seeker has to master these steps much before sitting for the very first posture of Yoga. Mastery over these worked like entry barrier to the Yoga arena. Subsequent Yoga steps are to be initiated by a practitioner only after mastery of Yams and Niyams. Irrespective of their antiquity, mastery over these still remain as relevant today albeit with modern day interpretations.

Yams are basically the 'do not' prescribed for every spiritual seeker. The very first Yam is about strictly practising nonviolence. Life is regarded as sacred and tendencies of fear or weakness are said to cause violence in behaviour. Non-violence includes shunning away from every action, word or thought that directly or indirectly harms others. Just for clarification, Ahimsa means much more than abstaining from violence in action. To the very least, it is the ethical and moral principle of not causing any harm to all living beings. Showing mercy for all creatures, practising forgiveness, abstaining from act of cruelty are all logical extensions of this very Yam.

Second Yam prohibits desire to possess anything in excess of minimum required. This desire is equated with stealing which also includes holding an item that is not given to you or accepting a thing that you do not need. Under this concept, plucking a fruit from the tree violates the principle while picking a ripe fruit from the ground is acceptable. Life of a materialist is diametrically opposite to this law. This self-restraint indirectly asks us to cultivate sense of self-sufficiency in whatever we got. This calls for living a simple life with contentment while maintaining a sense of gratitude. The principle behind this Yam is about avoidable pain that is inevitably experienced during acquiring the things in excess, in efforts required for maintaining its possession, pains of allurement of its glow, pains due to sense of attachment, desire for having more, and inevitable fear of losing that very thing. Each of these activities leads to nagging excitations and mental disturbances making our mind distracted and throwing our meditation success out of the window.

Third Yam calls for total truthfulness for every word spoken. 'Satyam Vada' is one of the strongest mantras from the Upanishads. Sticking to truth in speech has to stand true without any exception. Truth alone is considered vital. Besides being true, every word spoken must pass twin test of being essential and kind. It requires you to first weigh the very need of uttering every single word. Verbal diarrhea is a contagious disease and needs to be treated with proper medication.

When necessary, you can speak but your words should convey only truth and nothing but truth without any shade of distortion or deception. Besides speech, it asks to maintain purity of mind and honesty with self. Its theoretical meaning may be speaking truth but real meaning in action is living life in balance of principles and reality. Each one of us may have failed this principle at vulnerable moments and can well realise that every lie is a burden on our soul and a constant irritation leading to disturbed mental states.

Fourth Yam demands abstinence from sex and intoxication in order to preserve vital energies called 'Ojas', the power of Chastity. Ojas means vitality, vigour and virility. Ayurveda calls it special substance in body that governs radiance, aging, immunity, vigour as well as spirituality. Ojas is the oil that brightens our lamp of life; this is what upgrades illumination to brightness. Depleted level of Ojas only means low brightness in entire existence and vice versa. Besides obvious impact on physical appearance and aura, it also impacts the intellect and spirituality of every person. Sexual intercourse is said to be the quickest way of losing Ojas. Some people cite that marrying necessarily involves sexual proximity among partners but that is not a solid argument. Sex has been designed only and for procreation and we see most other primates still practising this principle. Married life has so many other factors to express loyalty and dedication to spouse beyond procreation.

Chastity, without any argument, has always been considered a higher human virtue under all religions and cultures. Ojas gets created in a very long drawn process and taking special diets filled with tonics, vitamins or any amount of proteins do not help in restoring levels of Ojas wasted in sexual encounters. Even modern day psychologists have reported results of scientific researches that people with the highest IQs are actually the least sexually active. Intoxication, on the other hand, weakens the power of judgement leading to depleted will power. Fifth and last Yam suggests growing detachment which has already been discussed under a previous chapter.

Coming to Niyams, the recommended 'Dos', where the first principle is purity of body and mind. Keeping physical body and surrounding environment clean, one achieves clarity of thoughts. The importance of personal hygiene does not require too much explanation. Second Niyam talks about practising contentment. Idea is not to indulge in satisfying desires but to accept life as it exists and cherish each moment by remaining grateful in whatever comes your way. Third Niyam deals with austerity. This means developing perseverance, passion and discipline by opting for fasting and penance. Next Niyam asks for becoming self-aware with self-study. Idea is to learn about our basic drivers for desires, study our inherent intentions, and coming face to face with our deepest fears which otherwise prevent us from feeling free in our thoughts, words and actions. The last of Niyam calls for complete surrender of individuality by developing trust and accepting each situation with open mind and heart.

Yams and Niyams are originally prescribed as step one and two of Yoga but are equally applicable for getting ready for undertaking serious meditation. Dhyana, the seventh step of Yoga is nothing but meditation itself. Continued and un-wavered practice of these principles, without any exception or compromise, alone leads to assured success. Every aspirant has to show deep dedication in following these preparatory conditions before expecting progress in meditational journey.

(B) Propagate Virtue of Compassion

Modern day life generates and inflates many undesirable vices like stress, sense of comparison, anger, envy and greed. While people are busier than ever to achieve more and enjoy more, increasing focus on materialism leads to conflicts with others around. Most technological developments and internet based human connectivity have resulted in a deep void for real social interactions like never before. Basic human virtues like compassion and gentleness that used to be regarded as underlying natural human instincts today sounds like words from some preacher. But deep down human beings continue to remain social animals where other people play defining role in our happiness and celebrations. Company and positive vibrations from people, from family, social circles, work environments and society at large, still mean a lot for our very existence. This loaded imperative on people around calls for advancing the virtue of compassion to continue our social relevance more than any time in the past.

Compassion refers to extending your support to mitigate sorrows and miseries of others; to feel their sorrows as your own. Compassion has the power to connect all human beings by breaking all known boundaries. Compassion is also a state of mind where there is only peace, for self as well all others around. It involves giving up aggression of every shade and genuinely desiring freedom from pains for everybody around. Compassion originates from the realisation that all beings are connected and deserve to be free from all miseries and sufferings. It promotes sense of belonging as if we all are one large family. Compassion, once fully developed, brings down all walls between friends as much as enemies. Forgiving is important part of compassion as it makes you free from grudges against others. Compassion, in some ways, is Ahimsa plus doing something meaningful for the welfare of others. The best of all description of compassion is quoted in 'Voice from the Heart' by Eddie Shapira, and it goes as:

> "A mind committed to compassion is like an overflowing reservoir – a constant source of energy, determination and kindness. Or this mind can be likened to a seed; when cultivated, it gives rise to many other qualities, such as, tolerance, inner strength, and confidence to overcome fear and insecurity." — *His Highness, the Dalai Lama*

The real compassion emerges out of the understanding that every one shares the world and has equal right to live life like we ourselves do. Sense of equality and commonality allows the affinity to permeate in interactions with others around. In a way, well developed compassion injects positivity in our attitude and changed attitude starts chain reactions where many of the earlier interpersonal tensions like rivalry, envy, and competition vanish giving way for tolerance, acceptance and oneness, in the same order. Besides this, compassion works for enhancing kindness and generosity, which contributes significantly for our moral and ethical cleansing.

Our mental state in compassion is entirely different from what we have when we are down with our sufferings. Own sufferings make us feel the burden of anguish and distress. But compassion encourages us to do our best for others even when we are burdened with discomforts. This is exactly what 'Nishkam Seva' of Gita, the principle of selfless service to others, means in reality.

People having compassionate attitude enjoy better psychological and emotional health as it induces a calmer mind, enhances joy and eliminates stress and depressions. Those of us who actually extend help to others can directly relate with unique sense of satisfaction coming from reducing hardships of others; no amount of money can buy that feeling ever. And this very sense works on our mind to make it calm and still, away from being flighty and excited.

Most importantly, virtue of compassion can actually be fostered. As baby steps, you can start with people in your close circle and slowly increase the net to include total strangers. However, you are also advised to practise some caution as it has serious side effects if not practised properly. Idea is to feel obliged after actually doing your bit in ensuring that smiles return to the faces of people in distress. Merely feeling pity for them is of no help. Also, always remember that you are not doing a thing to get any merit in return. You have to practise compassion for goodwill and never for good feelings. Self-seeking in any way make it a tainted effort and, hence, abundant care is suggested for working on compassion beyond the obvious generosity. Size of your activities is less important. Real intent and efforts determine potential progress of your compassion.

(C) Augment Quotient of Empathy

By nature empathy, the ability to experience situation of other person, is selfless and focuses on others. Going beyond sympathy, empathy requires experiencing emotional state of the other person. In a way, empathy highlights all human beings being born similar and destined for similar end. Empathy finds common grounds on similarities rather than harping on differences. It helps us find space for establishing trust and faith every time we interact with other beings. This approach yields result in the worst of political, social or historical stalemates.

This interlinking with others bridges all differences among human beings like education, money, power, positions or social status. A person with augmented empathy does not let these superficial differences spoil the all important level playing field while dealing with other human beings. Modern day life is full of stress which unfortunately weakens empathy. So-called comforts and luxuries make us agreeable and comfortable making it increasingly difficult to empathise with sufferings of others. Generally, empathy can be used as an extension of compassion itself but there is a subtle difference between these two virtues that especially matter for morality and that is why empathy deserve discussions as a separate virtue. And it is not that we do not come across situations where empathetic behaviour is expected of us. No one needs to look too far to spot situations in daily life where empathy is required. Someone getting bullied, a known person facing defeat in exams/tests or games, a overwhelmed colleague at work place, an associate incurring financial losses, a friend going through tough relationship issues or cases of gender-biased behaviours are some such everyday situations that we regularly come across in our immediate circles.

Soon after starting meditation we begin to realise that a big chunk of our thoughts pertain to relationships with others. Virtuous capacity of empathy allows us to understand actions, responses, outbursts from both sides and help us resonate emotionally with each other. Being at peace with others plays very critical role in advancing our meditational practice. Poor empathy will stand in the way and prevent us from understanding and appreciating issues and reactions of others. Peace with others facilitates our efforts of achieving still state of mind enabling faster progress on meditative journey. While other people are source of agony and anxieties in normal state, with improved empathy those very people become our support system for helping us enjoy human life to its full potential.

It is interesting to know how empathy helps in improving morality and ethics and finally aid improving meditation. Actually, empathy is a fundamental building block for strong morality and key to all successful human relationship. Speaking broadly, there are two aspects in which link between empathy and morality impact our actions and behaviours. First of all, empathy is considered necessary for making moral judgements. Empathetic responses indeed allow us to see actions or thoughts as being good or bad. As we may realise, every virtuous action ignites streams of pleasures while a vicious action only triggers pains. Actually, you may not judge an event as good, bad or neutral unless you have empathy for the person impacted. To that extent, empathy is considered a precondition for arriving at moral judgement of an action or event.

Secondly, empathy motivates moral conduct by becoming an igniting force for our conduct. It strongly prevents us from acting indifferently under many situations. Thus, empathy converts our judgements into real actions. In short, empathy first induces our moral judgement, later it also facilitates increased motivation for desired action.

How to improve empathy levels? Technically it should be easy as we have some common neurons in all human minds that communicate with each other. All it requires is an active Wi-Fi. This activation starts when we pay full attention to and observe others like the metaphor of "stepping into other's shoes". To be effective, this connection with others must be made via emotional brain. Feelings from such attentive observation start assigning vigorous force initiating our actions or reactions, as the case may be. Putting simply, please try to look at things from perspective of others and you will come to appreciate why they do things in the manner they do. And all this starts coming cleanly the moment we start putting others first. It might be a good idea to start focusing on actions of people from our inner circle to begin with. Later we can always include more and more people. Once fully developed, this trait enables us to consider miseries of people impacted by earthquake in Japan or Indonesia as much as people living in our next cluster.

Also, give chances and back your actions based on your instincts about others because instincts are nothing but feedback from those common neurons received over Wi-Fi and are seldom wrong. As a practice, you should also cultivate your sense of curiosity about others. Lastly and more importantly, abstain from letting your empathy work on selective basis. Being selective about your feelings limits you as a person. To be empathetic you have to feel the universal equality among entire humanity.

(D) Regular Practice of Yogic Asanas

With the popularity gained by Yoga the world over, it is a common knowledge now that practising Asanas on regular basis enhances flexibility, improves strength, reduces stress level, improves blood and oxygen circulation, bringing in innumerable physical health benefits. Scientific studies carried out in recent decades also establish specific benefits like strengthening of immune system, boost to improved focus, remarkable improvement in metabolism, longer hydration of spinal fluids and clearing of many unwanted body toxins among others. But people with Indian roots cannot miss the bigger picture that all physical advantages of Yoga are just incidental and that fundamentally Yoga is practised for its psychological, philosophical and spiritual advantages.

Meditation (Samadhi) happens to be sixth step of the famous Astanga (eight limbs) Yoga while sitting in Asanas is step number three. Pranayam is fourth step and Pratyahara (restraint of senses from their objects) being fifth. This sequence clearly establishes the important role of Asanas and Pranayam before seeking success in Meditation. We may also recall that the original system mandated the practitioner to master previous stage before qualifying for starting the next. Perfection in Asanas, therefore, comes much before initiating meditation. In the Yoga Sutra, Maharishi Patanjali gives instruction on how to meditate and describes what factors constitute a meditation practice. The second sutra in the first chapter states that yoga happens when the mind achieves its stillness. This mental stillness is created by bringing the body, mind, and senses into balance which, in turn, relaxes the nervous system. Asanas help in achieving stilling the body while pranayam contributed towards stilling the mind.

It is sufficient to say that if Yamas and Niyams are like desired quality of soil critical for germinating seeds of our meditational tree; practice of Asanas is like right watering for ensuring desired growth of that plant into a strong tree. Best of soil cannot support growth of the plant in isolation just as merely right watering on a bad soil do not help the tree to grow any faster.

Finally, let us look at how Yoga helps strengthening morality and ethics. Yoga and ethics need to be taken as intrinsic rather than mere complimentary to each other. Let us also remember that ethics and morality are not issues of reason or intellect but a matter of practice, an understanding that comes only to actual practitioners. Practising yoga encourages strict discipline in what is being eaten, how sleep is regulated, and such other activities involved in living normal life. Thus entire way of life gains traction for the better. All this helps in magnifying good quality of the states of body, senses and mind.

While Yoga is very well known, it may not be out of place to understand that right method for conducting Pranayam continues to be a grey area. So, there are several different types of Pranayam but one such programme is the standard 'four times four' method which requires breathing in counting up to four, holding the breath for full four seconds, exhaling slowly spread over four seconds, and finally holding on empty again for four seconds. Few cycles of this routine is an established method for regulating breathing, balancing the moods and pacifying the body at all times.

Every session of Pranayam conditions mind and body for undertaking fruitful meditation. The routine popularised by Swami Ramdev of Patanjali Yogapeeth is also accepted as an excellent starting point for the beginners. The most popular eight breathing exercises emphasised by him include Bhastrika, Kapalbhati, Bahaya, Ujjai, Anulom Vilom, Bharamari, Udgeetha and Pranav. The sequencing, intensity, total time used for practice for all these can be periodically varied to avoid monotony as also to know what works better. The whole process may take around thirty minutes in the beginning and be increased later as practice advances to higher levels.

Morning time is always ideal for its practice but any other time suitable may prove to be second best option. It is advisable to take bath and obtain relaxed state of physical body before sitting for Pranayam session. Over months of regular practice, you will be able to evolve your own right routine based on comfort level and stage of practice. But the golden rule is to keenly participate in your routine with complete focus as if you are having meditation session itself with object of focus being your breathing. In a way Pranayam is precursor for final meditation session. Regular practice of pranayam keeps temptations at bay and keeps the negativity and impulsive responses out of system.

Morality induced by practising Yoga is indeed true morality as it arrives from purification of consciousness. Morality originated from inside, under guidance of pure consciousness, certainly is foundational in nature and unwavering in character. True that results from Yoga induced moral upliftment are not immediate or visible but as and when these accrue, they are rock solid and bring transformational support to our practice of meditation. So giving it a few minutes daily is many times worth the time invested in practising Yoga and Pranayam exercises.

11

Developing Positivity in Attitude

"Your attitude, not your aptitude, will determine your altitude."

Thinkers and philosophers agree on the fact that this entire world is nothing but a complex game of energies. One may look at energy as active or passive, real or potential, subtle or solid. Quality of energy is also open to be classified into negative, neutral or positive. But everything in human life is explained as energy in one form or another. It is also said that our every thought, word or action gives rise to one or the other form of this very energy. Secondly, energy we create later echoes back to us in form of different kinds of vibrations which return to us without losing its character; good energy brings good vibrations and vice versa. So even when we do not realise it directly, creating positive energy through our actions, words and thoughts is generally our own creation. The final outcome of this solid understanding and conviction in these fundamental principles is what we call an 'attitude filled with positivity'.

In our normal life, we see individual colours getting associated with things bad, good and everything in between. For example, grey is epitome of confusion and sadness, while red colour represents passion and so on. Our life is also like a big canvass where attitudes are like different colour crayons in the box. Entertaining confusions and sadness means too much use of grey and black crayons while sporting passion, happiness and energy means use of red, yellow and orange colours respectively. It is not hard to think that we surely want our own reflection to get projected in lively colours by completely avoiding gloom or doom contours. Positivity is like combining all bright colours adding shine, humour and brightness to our background. It is actually that very simple.

Interestingly, positivity is said to be the original, natural and likeable state of our self. Our mind and body is always at ease within positivity while we genuinely detest negativity at all times. We are also advised to shy away from complexities and adopt simplicity in whatever we do as these two concepts do not ever fit together. A positive approach is undoubtedly simpler, if not easier. So every time we move away from positivity, it is like swimming against the current with its own risks and hazards.

Vibrations emanating from positivity have power of improving chemistry even among people not known to each other. How many times we see situations filled with anger and overflowing egos ready to strike each other and there enters a person with positivity-filled aura and the entire situation get diffused. Yes, positivity is that much powerful and works under most testing situations. Having positivity does not mean there will be no bumps on the road but a person with positive attitude will not stop or fall and will keep going on even after setbacks and bad encounters. Similarly, positivity may not ensure a sound and healthy body by itself but it can very well motivate you to be careful of what you eat and how you regulate your exercise regime so as to remain fit and fine.

Positivity Being Different from Hope

Suffering from cold with all symptoms loud and clear but repeating that 'all is well' qualifies as 'hope'. Continuing suffering from running nose but telling your system that all is well is sending confusing signals to your own subconscious system. This will certainly disturb the internal communication among various systems at work and surely impact the process of recovery. Being positive, thus, is much more than hoping or wishing. It is about building a better and stronger future even on the debris of painful past. Let us repeat that it is a skill which comes to you only if you work for it. It is not like waiting to grow older in the hope that aging will make one wiser. Yes, few traits on physical, psychological and social fronts do get improved with aging but there are so much more wisdom that get earned by a person with his own learning and relearning alone. Similarly, positivity has nothing to do with age, gender, religion, or race because it is completely a neutral skill.

Can Positivity be Acquired?

Yes, positivity in attitude can be acquired because it is not a trait or talent which is either there or not there. Cultivating positivity is a skill to be honed with practice and dedication. Positivity is actually not about what is a 'given situation' but how do we 'respond to that situation'. Thus, there is nothing 'passive' about it. Some person may argue that it is good to be a realist and hence there is no need to acquire this critical skill. But being realist may be called, under this situation, a poor disguise or a lame excuse or just an escape to avoid working hard to acquire positivity by putting concerted efforts.

Practical Tips to Grow Positivity

After accepting positivity as a skill, let us look at ways and means helping a willing person towards cultivating it in a practical manner.

- **Make action plan listing several smaller goals**—Success, big or small, is always a generator for positivity while failures makes positivity at least two times more difficult. You better stop looking success only in big ticket events which are always far and few. You should be able to evolve a detailed action plan for your immediate objectives with many simple and achievable goals duly listed. Success of each of the smaller goals offers chances to celebrate your achievements. This success breeds more success, which means more positivity. Failure has dampening effect similar to a bucket of water thrown for quenching the fire. The magic lies in fixing goals that are challenging enough to motivate and achievable enough to ignite positivity.
- **Get Surrounded by people having positive approach**—Actually, both positivity and negativity are completely contagious and have capacity to engulf you if exposed for longer time. People surrounding you may either help you cultivate positivity or destroy the same depending on their own attitude. So, please spot people in your vicinity displaying negativity in attitude and just run away from them as quickly as possible. The proverb that 'you are known

by the company you keep' gets applied for positivity quite strongly because ultimately you will start behaving like them. Further, identifying people captured with negativity is no brainer. You can spot them from a safe distance. Make efforts to keep company of people displaying positivity in actions and thoughts as much as feasible.

- **Practice Gratitude**—Perpetuating attitude of gratitude brings most effective transformation in many aspects of human life. The art of being thankful for every little thing is potent belief keeping you overwhelmed with abundances on offer. It redirects you from seeing the glass as half full rather than half empty. Considering everything gained as a bonus, ignites a sense of happiness and improves relationships, health quotients, reduction in stress and most importantly insulate you against the feeling of envy.
- **Remain Physically Active**—Remaining engaged in one or the other physical activity is the simplest way of cultivating positivity. Look around and you see all happy people have a thing in common that they always remain engaged in something or the other. It is difficult to visualise a happy man sitting idle. One must develop a habit of being on the move at all times. In order to remain positively engaged, our body needs constant supply of endorphins (a group of hormones secreted within the brain and nervous system and having a number of physiological functions) which is best supplied by right doses of physical activities/exercises. You must have a schedule where next activity awaits you eagerly before the last one gets completed. Our body needs a kick to remain active and healthy. Positivity detests living in an unhealthy body.
- **Always strive to remain in the Driving Seat**—People with higher positivity are eager to hold and maintain the pole position in everything they do. Assuming charge of an issue forces you to feel more committed, more responsible. Being in charge, you keep working to take the situation to its logical conclusion. As against this, the moment you allow others to take charge, you automatically opt to become a follower. Now, followers also do contribute but only in a limited

manner, more as a foot soldier and not like the general who commands. This is also a sure way of earning respect for your competence which enhances your acceptability among peers as well.

- **Live in Present**—Mental outlook of positivity oozes optimism expecting good things to happen here and now. Let the past not dictate your actions of today. Aspirations for a better future demand replacing all negative or neutral thoughts with positive ones. Success and happiness are destined for a person living in present moment. Fluidity of present helps in grounding of positivity without resistance. Positivity grounded in present helps develop only superior emotions like courage and adventure. Such a person is destined to bask in glory without fail.
- **Maintain 'never-say-die' Approach** – Yes, life will keep throwing challenges, day in and day out, and challenges never end. Each one of us has to keep facing these tests and it better be like that. Winners stick around no matter what. Never give up or get discouraged. A soldier with never-say-die approach keeps fighting even when situation may appear scary or dangerous with little chances of victory. Strengthen your spirit of not giving up. Punches received from life can also be taken as a sport but only so long you are game for it. Look around and see that people expecting smooth ride are always stuck at the bottom of the ladder of success while those who were open for taking on challenges, move up and far.

Positivity must remain high every time we interpret the perception of reality. Let your attitude determine your direction of entire life. Believe that you can change your approach to live through situations. Make your imaginations strong and let it help you create image of your future founded on your own initiatives. Do not waste time on opinion of others as opinions are reflections of their personal attitude rather than your assessment. Cultivating positivity goes a great distance in helping you pick up new skills and making progress on meditation is no exception. Most often one reads that meditation helps developing and maintaining positive thinking capability but experience suggests that positive approach is a prerequisite to get attracted to meditation.

Positivity essentially paves way for a beginner to cross initial hiccups on way to enjoy his daily meditation.

Positivity and Meditation

Most published material and blogs talk in detail about how meditation helps in gaining positivity. This is precisely where a big fallacy lies. It is like that unresolved issue of what came first, the chicken or egg? Yes, a well progressed meditation practice generates abundant positivity helping the practitioner in all spheres of life but basic question is how to reach to that level in the first place. Meditation is like that creeper (for example Philodendron) which, once strongly rooted, protected and nurtured during its infancy, keeps growing and blossoming with bigger leaves and stronger stems by taking nutrition support from every type of surface it finds on its way of growing. Such creeper draws only a fraction of its total nutrition through its roots as majority of intake is through sub roots coming out of stem. Positivity is one such surface that meditation draws on during its infancy stages.

Calmer approach rooted in positivity helps practitioner to continue his practice in spite of whatever life throws at him. Positivity reduces anxiety levels which help in preparing mind ready for meditation to begin with. Positivity also results in enhanced creative abilities which are so critical in choosing and perfecting various meditative techniques at different stages of the journey. Positivity provides better tools to manage problems that keep arising with respect to one or the other aspect of meditative practice and keep it going by keeping perplexities at bay. In the absence of positivity, even the intelligent practitioner remains surrounded by self doubts.

It is safe to conclude based on personal experience that positivity plays a very crucial role for bringing consistency and steadiness in our meditation practice. Later, much later, once meditation becomes a habit and the practitioner starts reaping its benefits, meditation helps a great deal in firing up the flame of positivity even higher. Meditation at that stage starts manifesting positive experiences in your life right until it turns to form a thick layer at the subconscious level. Those layers alone push away negative forces of worry, anxiety, anger, depression from your thought process for good.

12

Magnifying Self-Awareness

> "Knowing others is intelligence; knowing yourself is true wisdom. Mastering others is strength; mastering yourself is true power."
> — *Lao Tzu*

Being self-aware seems to be a very natural thing we have been doing all along. Sudden urgency to enhance awareness about self may, therefore, likely to raise a valid question about why is it so essential for our discussion. Well, enhanced self-awareness is the key for all subsequent initiatives intended towards bringing transformations in one's life through spiritual advancements. Meditation works as an established technique for practising that very spiritual evolution. Soon we are going to realise that actions of a self-aware person are always better aligned with his personal standards. This alignment helps in evaporating stress from this person's life and allows the freedom to live in present.

Reference to self-awareness keeps coming all through discussions on meditation or any other spiritual practice, and as such, it needs to be dealt with in desired details. It all starts with a detailed journey of self-discovery, defined by American English Dictionary, as becoming aware of one's true potential, character, motives, etc. This journey is full of tedious path demanding confrontation and combating with own fears, confusions, misunderstandings, etc. Discovery of self is truly comparable to an expert explorer studying the mountain to be conquered from all its slopes from all directions, all its peaks and valleys, etc. Self-awareness is nothing smaller than your own Mount Everest that has to be climbed and conquered. A novice climber better prepare hard before initiating his climb else perishing is destined sooner than later. Interestingly, this climbing expedition is known to revel many wow moments on the way to the peak making it highly exciting and rewarding.

Understanding Self

To begin with, self can be classified as Physical self and Spiritual self. Physical self is well known to each one of us as we live together. Second part of Spiritual self is also called by other names like Conscious Awareness and, considering the complexities involved in its realistic perception, is postponed for advance stage of this book. Under present Chapter, the focus is only on Physical self. It is like first preparing for only issues involved in reaching up to Base Camp of your expedition leaving the exposure to bigger issues like avalanches, crevasses and oxygen deprivation for Advance Stage.

To begin with, we have five elements joining to make the physical body and later mind, intelligence and ego get added to it. Together, all these eight make a unique 'me'. This 'me' is very obvious and visible and it operates with plethora of other sub-systems like emotions, likes-dislikes, thoughts, desires, perceptions, memories, and every other thing that can be identified with the word 'my'. 'Me' is the main motive behind everything in life and quality of this very 'me' determines who we are at the end of the day. The evolution of this 'me' is a slow process that starts right from early days of an infant. With every passing day, this 'me' comes in contact with other plural 'me' and external world and starts absorbing some of their impressions on itself also. This snowball effect continues all through our growing life.

To begin with, this 'me' is just like a fresh canvas. Every interaction and experience of real life leaves its coloured imprints on some part of that canvas in very subtle manner. Slowly, all through the growing period, the entire canvas gets coloured where further brush strokes continue shading over the existing colours as an additional layer. This all happens in very slow but steady manner. Over years the entire canvas gets deeply divided in endless fragmentations of different hues and shades, in layers after layers. This evolutionary process continues unabated in several directions, gradually growing more and more complex where demands and desires keep moving over from basics to superficial levels without any end in sight.

This part of self also includes a person's essential being, his core; specially considered as the object of introspection or reflexive actions. This part of the self is beyond ego syndrome and starts from the place where ego ends. Over the years of a person's life, all his traits, goals, aspirations, experiences, interests and every such other quality that go to differentiate him from others keep evolving and cementing this 'me' in more and more individualistic form. Also, this 'me' keep enjoying that separateness and keep fuelling it more and more. This self is so clearly visible in most adults that you talk to them for a few minutes and you get examples after examples of they being very proud of their 'me' to the exclusion of other plural 'me' around. This 'me', however, is not something to be despised or detested. In fact, this 'me' needs to be revered by us as much as possible because this 'me' alone is our entire existence. 'Me' is our closest friend, admirer, supporter and undoubtedly our greatest well-wisher. 'Me' does not care more for anyone else in the entire universe.

'Me' is our senses, our perceptions, our impressions, our memories, our desires, our attachments and every other such thing that normally we try our best to acquire, use and preserve. We use all these elements over and over again for repeating pleasures and avoiding pains. Due to its never-ending attention on us, it is normal to fall completely in love with this 'me'. And you often come across many people in your vicinity boasting loudly about their love with their 'me'.' It is this 'me' part of self that makes us think and believe that we are doers of all our actions.

This very 'me' guides us to discriminate rights from wrongs. Being our discretion, it brings a lot of understanding as to why our personal and social behaviour should be of particular kind. Imagine there was no dissuasion by internal discretion cautioning us against indulging in sense pleasures. Each one of us would have been certainly worse off. The problem starts when, in ignorance, one starts pampering his 'me' too much. Such a 'me' starts behaving in dictatorial manner with self-centered arrogance and starts actually believing that his 'me' is far superior from others and must be respected, feared and worshipped by one and all. This person starts feeling humiliated and insulted with tiniest pricking.

> "Meditation practice isn't about trying to throw ourselves away and become something better. It's about befriending who we are already." — *Pema Chödrön*

How Does Self-awareness Helps?

Enhancing self-awareness protects against all ills arising from too much focus on your 'me'. Putting simply, self-awareness is about learning to better understand why you feel what you feel, why you act the way you act, why you think the way you think and why you behave the way you behave. Once you begin to understand this concept you get the opportunity to differentiate right from wrong and finally get freedom to change things about yourself. This process alone enables you to live a life where your feelings, thoughts, actions and reactions are aligned to your own reality. It is almost impossible to change and become self-accepting if you are not well aware about yourself to begin with.

Having clarity about who you really are and what you really want can be empowering. It boosts your confidence to make changes and succeed in making changes happen. Increased self-awareness brings clarity on everything around including thoughts. That in turn increases creativity and spontaneity. It sharpens the sensing capability of our sense organs. Improved awareness also fuels the desire to get

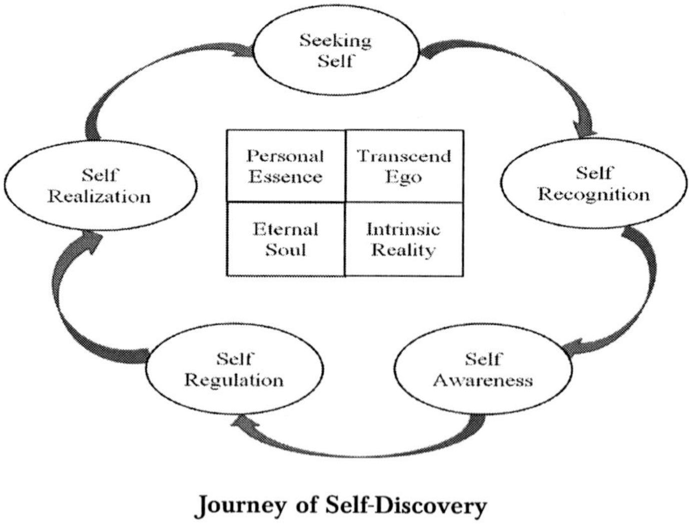

Journey of Self-Discovery

high, a desire that is found as common phenomena with most high performing individuals. Needless to say that the desire to get high must be satiated by heightened output of creative process rather than use of chemically induced banned substances. The state of high feeds to creativity. The importance of self-awareness is similar to pathological tests for the internist to identify proper diagnostic conditions before prescribing right medications. But its comparison with medical treatment ends at this stage itself because there are no drugs for cure or fast recovery. Improving self-awareness succeeds only when administered like a long drawn therapy.

How to Sharpen Self-Observation?

Simple statement as 'my hand' is enough proof that 'me' and my hand are two different entities involved out here. One of these is an observer and the other that is being observed; one takes action and the other which is subject of that action. For the sake of understanding, we can assume that the one being observed is the 'material part' and the one observing is named 'The Observing self'. For brevity, let us call the second one as the 'Seer'. On functional level, the 'seer' keeps witnessing everything happening at the other level and continues its constant feedback to 'me' irrespective of 'me' listening to its advice or otherwise.

As and when an individual is able to detach his 'seer', from body, mind and the ego, the perception for everything around becomes clear, deeper and complete. Such a person is able to perceive underlying motives for actions and true intentions of self and others without any attachment. This ability to separate the seer from the subjective duality (me) is the art to be mastered by learning and practising all the tools available and for as long as required.

This is where meditation and exploration of self converge together and help each other. The person who could achieve this convergence may rightly be called Enlightened or with such other similar names. One could bring in tons of material on this topic with heavy sounding words and loaded meanings but our purpose is to understand and appreciate rather than explore intellectual part of self. The idea is just to experience that yes any normal person can also realise the duality of its own self with ease and clarity before he starts working on ways and means to achieve transformations of his own self.

> "Every human has four endowments—self-awareness, conscience, independent will and creative imagination. These give us the ultimate human freedom… The power to choose, to respond, to change." — *Stephen R. Covey*

Difficulties in Being Self-Aware

Apparently, being aware about self should not be difficult as nobody else is involved in the process. However, just the opposite is true. Very serious efforts are required to access the depths of our own personality and even more to bring about the transformation required right down to our attitude level. It involves whole lot of reverse process for de-layering all those strokes from the person's canvas discussed in the beginning. Actually, it is much more than that because Self cannot ever be bracketed as 'has been' phenomena as identity of an individual has many different aspects at the same time and these identities keep changing all the time.

The reference to self is always open-ended to include ongoing experiences at present, this very moment, before it turns over to past. Comprehending about the pointlessness of past and futility of future has immense power of unshackling human beings from chains of unwanted prisons. Living our life in present is like fresh flower with all its smell intact and all its love and bliss flowing all around.

Interestingly, the only instrument available to awaken self is our mind alone. In normal state, this very mind is seen as captured by the superficial ego with all its allurements and false trappings. This is where the complexities arise as a single mind is required to divide itself into different parts; one part to work as 'observer' and another part to be 'observed' at the same point of time. One part of the mind has to work as a doer and other part to become witness of all doings. One part of the mind has to initiate an action while another part is supposed to evaluate that very action. It is indeed as difficult as asking the tongue to check its own taste or asking eye to see itself. Enormous difficulties in bringing this clarity invite seekers to try their own methods where some methods may succeed while many fail. Since 'me' and 'seer' for each individual is different from others so what works for one may not work for others.

Self is also an object by itself, the one that is witnessed or observed as an aspect present. Here it remains the basic form of consciousness, something that becomes obvious and recognisable only when maturity transcendence. This duality requires great efforts to see through. Actually, a major part of our entire journey of prolonged meditation gets devoted to develop the ability to crack this duality. But once this wall develops a crack, we are able to see everything on the other side with absolute clarity.

How to Refine 'Me' Part

The 'me' part is to be awakened by going beyond the gaze of the observer. This awakening gets facilitated by sinking or dispensing with the accumulated colouring agents such as useless memories, tardy traditions, rubbish rituals, stale teachings, endured experiences, borrowed perceptions, and everything else that prevents the right access to the genuine truth. It is here that the proverb of 'unlearning required for new learning' gets applied in its purest form. The personal identification with all negative forces like despair, conflicts, competitions, comparisons, aggressions, violence, attachments, failures, views need to be completely ended by seeing through these as transient. Taking all these dilemma issues one by one, and focusing attention as an external observer, each practitioner will have to revisit his existing knowledge and be ready to replace the same with new revised neutral knowledge. Using meditation sessions for processing this programme and its rerun is by far the best possible use of your time on the mat.

What needs to be observed? Well it roughly includes everything, like what we talk, think, react to, read, watch, and listen, etc. Also need to be observed are each word selected in all types of communications, tapping on intentions going through the mind, motives coming out of mental processes, fears, dreams, aspirations, people and feelings igniting hate and love, indifferences and reasons thereof, what you wish to acquire, what you wish to hold on, what you wish to give away, what would you die for. It includes all aspects of life including but not limited to greed, envy, ambitions, work environment, colleagues, successes, failures. Basically this list includes all issues normally passing through mental space in normal living. We must cover everything flashing through our mind without differentiating anything as big or small, significant or otherwise, important or insignificant alike. Idea is to develop sharper but neutral view to observe and understand the result as it appears, without any colouring or justification or conclusion. This process also answers the question as to why meditation practice spans over years before making real progress.

Sinking of this baggage of colouring agents creates freedom for the self. This sinking allows self to regain its original nature filled with innocence, love and peace. In a way, the entire communication narrated in the Bhagwad Gita is extension of this very process where Arjuna is 'me' sitting down and faced with dilemma and Lord Krishna is the ultimate aim of human life. All the methods and approaches discussed in the Bhagwad Gita are processes for facilitating evolution of 'me', the Arjuna, to unite with the very source of all existence, pure Soul, the Krishna. It did require very many steps and necessitated taking multiple efforts spanning over 18 long chapters but Bhagwad Gita paved way for removing all ignorance from the mind of Arjuna and prepared him to undertake his own right-full obligation without losing his access to superior aim. Yes, it took, even for Lord Krishna, many efforts but ultimately all the suspicions, hesitations and doubts of Arjuna got sorted out completely. Every aspirant has to regain the same Arjuna nature through study, practice, contemplation and more practice.

Developing Key Observation

Observing self involves recording everything happening from a distance so that every activity, reaction, thought or desires get captured. The next step is to absorb the essence of things recorded. This calls for clear differentiation between seeing and observing; while one is mechanical activity the other is qualitative. Keen observation is significantly different than fixing a gaze. More than open eyes, real seeing involves a loving heart and a mind filled with peace and tranquility. And in order to become peaceful, the mind should be ready to shed its existing inhibitions, its attachments, its existing knowledge and above all, its judgemental nature. All you need to have is a fresh approach, full attention, and pure perspective. Once you acquire such a mind everything you see will be like seeing it the first time. In short, the lenses used for observing must be cleaned of every particle of shade, dust or dirt. Such pure observation alone provides access to reality of our existence.

> "The moment one gives close attention to anything, even a blade of grass, it becomes a mysterious, awesome, indescribably magnificent world in itself." —*Henry Miller*

The very first step is to develop a focused vision to clearly observe every big and small activity going on within our mind. Cutting across normal process of scratching around the surface, we have to dig deep and observe the complete chain of our thoughts, behaviours, feelings, emotions and motivations. Being always on the go, preoccupied with some urgent work, we remain ignorant about these basic processes running through our mind. Every person maintains a long 'To Do' list such that mind is unable to be at ease for any length of time. And until we exhaust our pending job list, our mind is not ready to look deeper.

The challenge in developing such an observation is our willingness to rise above our divided existence. Keen observation brings us in direct confrontation with ongoing cluttering in the mind. Caution, however, is required to not get scared by results of such observations. Good or ugly, whatever we observe is already a part of our life and it need be faced squarely. Reality does not change or vanish simply because we overlook it or decide to look aside. Good and bad, we need to observe every part of actual thing happening in our life on ongoing basis, no less and no more. Train yourself as the video camera that captures everything happening irrespective of qualitative aspect of the event. A camera does its work irrespective of the event being birth or death; event being accidental or planned perfectly.

This observation is not one time activity. The observation for self continues for days and months or even years. It is only over long periods that pure observation becomes a habit. It needs to become one's second nature. One has to keep trying until such time that the real intention behind every action and thought comes out as clear as water. No, you do not have to fix anything at this stage. You do not even have to draw any conclusion at all. Improving observation is exactly like playing golf. Basically you play with yourself, you have the entire course open to you and you have bag full of clubs to choose from. You start with a stationary ball that needs to be hit and put in different holes. Pure observation, similarly, has the final goal of getting desired actions and thoughts; various techniques available are the clubs to be used; entire psychological space is the golf course one uses; number of shots taken to reach the destination is the period required to reach to final goal. Finally, the role of a teacher or guide is no different than that of an experienced caddy.

Stopping all tendencies involving imaginations and speculations is also very important part of the process. You will have to remind yourself that you are here to observe the reality rooted in self-experience by completely shunning all the borrowed knowledge or tutoring from others. Forget completely what has been read, known or believed until now. That was past and past does not help in developing awareness. Awareness requires the functioning of our conscious focus on present unfolding here and now. It should be like first time watching live stream of an unknown sport where there is neither any recording nor any commentary. Ability to blank out both past and future and holding on to present alone is the key to become aware.

Let us try being aware in a practical way.

Exercise for Observing Contents of Own Mind

- Take your meditation position and breathe deeply for a couple of minutes.
- Imagine yourself sitting alone in a movie theatre with a blank 70 mm screen in the front.
- Feel relaxed and wait for the movie to start and continue focusing on the imagined screen in keen anticipation.
- In due course, you start feeling some live video playing involving situations going through your mind and your feelings at that moment of time.
- Pay attention to the images; to sound of words being spoken, smell of the scenes, sensations aroused by the images getting flashed.
- Refrain from any desire to intervene in the happenings, just watch.

- Withhold any judgement and allow things to happen of its own.
- Take notice of change of scenes, events and actors, let them play out cool.
- After a few minutes, please come out of your experience and try recollecting what all was happening.
- Realise that things displayed were contents of your own conscious mind itself at that very moment.
- Take note of the contents and conclude what all were desirable and not so desirable.
- Direct your mind to ignore issues that you conclude as undesirable.
- Repeat this exercise over several sittings to get acquainted with your contents with clarity and purpose.

How to Grow Self-Awareness?

> "He who knows others is wise. He who knows himself is enlightened." — *Lao Tzu, Ancient Chinese Philosopher*

For sure, each person is a complex sum of many smaller parts where some are good, some bad and some even very bad. Some of these parts are of a peaceful loving soul while a few parts are cruel, violent or wicked. While one part of a person is educated and sophisticated, his other parts may be just of a rogue animal. These fragmentations exist on all levels, be it inward/outward or individual/social. Exploring self involves taking on all these parts and subparts in totality irrespective of pains while observing these parts. An explorative keenness to observe entire spectrum of existence becomes essential for this exercise.

How to develop the penetration of pure observation? We need to send our observing self out of our body to focus on self from a distance to make it work as an invisible drone fitted with camera and mind reader equipment moving at some distance in front to capture each one of our impulse. Its feedback to us, as an unattached, independent and unbiased third umpire on a cricket field with access to replay, will be the best technique for exploring self. Meditation sessions are indeed handy in practising this pure observation on self. Analysis of this pure reality happens best with eyes closed and concentration penetrated deep within. Once you focus your search at the right place, with right intent and unbiased attitude, your own intentions and underlying responses and reactions are destined to get decoded as an open book.

Now is the time to go over the contents of pure observation. Why do I like this and dislike that? Why I fail in maintaining discipline? Why do I succumb to morally unacceptable behaviour? Why my ethics are not solid like rocks? Am I really jealous of other persons? Do I really mean what I said? Why do I get so much angry with that particular individual? Why do I want so and so to use such and such words while talking to me? The list of such questions can be as long as our patience. Ability to find real and accurate answers to these questions is yet another stage to be self-aware. Right answers will remove the opaqueness from the surroundings and allow right access to inner space for living with clarity and purity. Knowing everything about self and knowing it accurately, is the purpose of entire self-awareness drive.

Embrace Reality Without Fear

Pure observation on all scattered parts of life can generally be classified into two important aspects, that is, fears and pleasures. With improved self-exploration and focused observation, we are able to see these pleasures and fears along with underlying reasons. For example, awareness about fears forces us to escape from situations and also increases our dependence on others. Some of those are in our close relation part of our own existence while many others are from external world. Some of these people come to us and many others that we go to. Soon this list of people we depend becomes long enough. But this dependence, like every other dependence, starts inhibiting our freedom and we do not even realise it in normal life situations. The real physical or psychological fears are far and few. Most of these are based on repetitive thoughts relating to 'what will happen if….' syndrome.

Similar thing also happens to pleasures. Every time we experience some exciting scenery or a work of art, our brain records those events on its hard disc. As a natural tendency, thoughts keep going back to those experiences and we continue desiring for their repeat as many times as possible. That desire also originates from our thoughts alone. Thus, both fears and pleasures are seen dependent on thoughts. Now, thoughts are also used for almost every other human activity we do including speaking languages, making scientific discoveries, managing all our past impressions. We cannot do without strong thinking process in functioning rationally, logically and objectively.

Before dealing about the management part, however, it is advisable to look at thoughts in some detail. In a way, thoughts are like vapours coming out of a big block of frozen ice. The frozen ice here is the bunch of memories, knowledge and experiences stored and compacted in our brain. On physical level, thoughts get generated based on inputs from body's sense organs and characterisation of that feedback by the mind. Now we know that our body has many marvelous sensing devices capable of sensing even subtle variations. But characterisation of all such inputs is done by mind under influence of past knowledge and experiences. Letting the mind to break such characterisation is called creative imagination, which is largely operated by intuitive guidance. Old experiences seldom lead to creative imagination, a faculty so critical for bringing unique solutions and results.

Intuitive guidance incidentally is understood as ability to acquire knowledge without inference or use of reason. Intuition gets strengthened in proportion of our spiritual progress. Intuition is supposed to help us know the reality in a flash. Ideas out of intuition are actually rated above ideas using intellect. In this entire scenario our mind works like a radio that can pickup signals only for the frequency that is tuned in. Signals out of frequency get clubbed as interference or noise beyond comprehension. But the beauty of human mind (when used as a servant) is that it honours any request made to it by intuitive guidance. In this mode, the mind is willingly engaged in learning. That is how all inventions and creations come into existence.

Management of Thoughts

The next key point is how to manage our thoughts. Incidentally, this should not be a big issue after developing intuitive guidance to desired levels. We know very well that once the same mind gets occupied with learning, it is known to quickly replace its earlier impressions. So engaging the mind in continuous learning, both voluntary and induced, is the most effective process for managing thoughts.

> "The mind is by nature restless. Begin liberating it from its restlessness; give it peace; make it free from distractedness; make this a habit. This can be done by ignoring the external world and removing the obstacles to peace of mind."
>
> — *Ramana Maharishi*

After developing keen observation our intelligence is tuned to apply findings in a neutral way. Soon, thoughts motivated by intuitive guidance react with our intelligence and motivate the mind to learn something it was not doing before. Beyond this stage, ours 'being human' helps as the logical reasoning prompts human brain to set right anything it finds problem with. We are programmed like that and no special efforts are required to activate this impulse. The resistance to change stands only until we are not convinced that something is wrong in the first place. Finally a mind that starts learning is destined to enhance its own intelligence. This is the turning point for all subsequent improvements in entire spiritual journey.

Once we are well aware of our actions in real life we take control of all our initiatives and reactions by making logical choices based on unbiased, unconditioned and un-fragmented new learning in place of our emotions and feelings used earlier. When clear observation and enhanced awareness ignite the generation of creative thoughts, the same mind is directed to learn and take well-informed action. Right actions in turn result in right emotions and feelings as well.

Events and people from external world still remain active and impact life as before but our response to such actions improves qualitatively. Actions by others no longer trigger our emotions. Emotions are chemical molecules that act as command circuits in our body. Emotions also work as bundle of energies that organise and shape our beliefs and behaviours over longer periods. But once our newfound skill of being self-aware is able to put stop to activation of the said circuits, emotions get no role to initiate our actions. Now we see every tiny development with a fresh pair of eyes. That in turn stops igniting our fears or pleasures. The new mind now looks at fear or pleasure as if it is looking at it for the very first time. Now there is no set reaction based on stored impressions. What happens now is fresh processing of keen observation conveyed to mind without any connectivity with the old baggage.

Replacing Knowledge with Learning

Please remember that every time we wish to learn something new, it necessarily involves unlearning of something old and open willingness to accept something new. In case of minds conditioned by years of routine live issues with set patterns, the most difficult thing is to unlearn. Ability to keenly observe our own things and conveying the pure observation to the mind without the reflexes of past memories and without the attachment with any particular outcome is the key however difficult it is to get acquired.

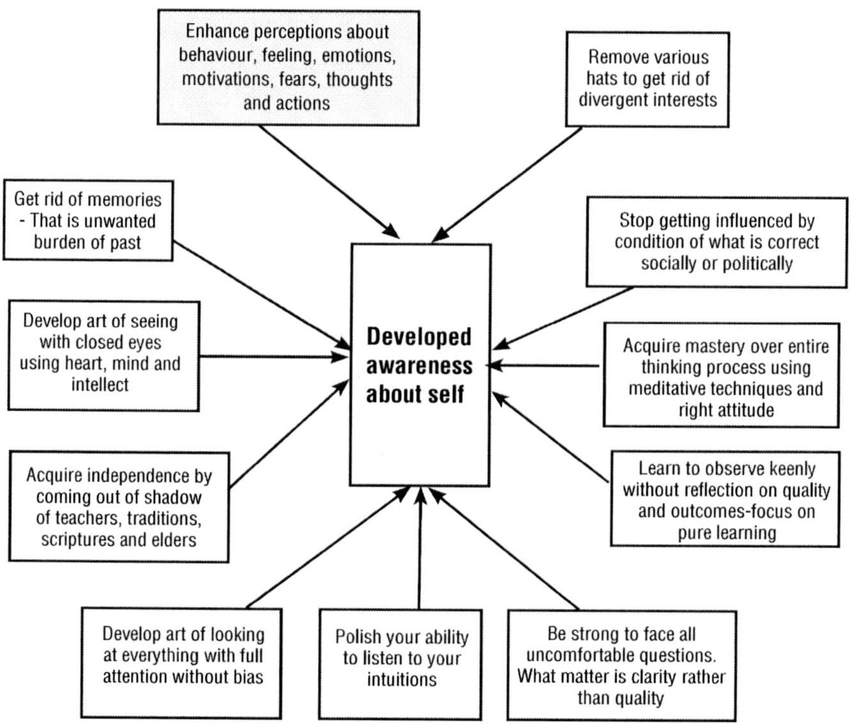

Managing Self-Awareness

Improved self-Awareness and Meditation

Becoming self-aware is a precondition to start real meditation. Being self-aware in itself is preliminary stage of meditation journey. In its essence self-awareness is a quite inner exploration and internal reflection for knowing our true nature. It is through meditation that we access our spiritual self and realise that we are connected to everyone and everything in the universe. Such an effort is unthinkable if we are not fully aware about own inner core. Building on the foundation of awakened self-awareness, one starts making progress to access his inner silence and stillness.

Awakened self-awareness allows genuine contemplation during meditation. And final objective of these contemplations is to let the mind make desired changes in activities, thinking process and behaviour. These are big ticket changes and that is why these are called real transformations. Yes, this transformation does not happen in an instant as series of observations on our core issues, both big and small, and cementing of those issues in fresh reality, is a long drawn process. It is only over long periods, these very changes make impact to the very source of origin of your thoughts resulting in changed attitude.

Interestingly, the strong grip of barriers in the process of enhancing self-awareness is unyielding only in the beginning of practice. The grip loses its resistance progressively with growth of meditation practice. Assuming resolve to keep courage and conviction for your practice remains firm in place, the process becomes smooth. Lack of gaining tangible benefits in initial period should not result in suspension of daily sittings. This being the most fulfilling trait to be acquired, one should be ready to work harder because success achieved against greater odds ultimately tastes sweeter.

Self-awareness is a live and dynamic process. Practice is most important for advancing both meditation and self-awareness. A finely tuned radio station always improves the audio quality. It is normal to come across lot of rattling from your mind but do not give up. Sessions and sessions of sittings will help in getting success in silencing the mind. Feel free to play around your practice as idea is to sit calmly and direct attention on live issues. Later, you can always be selective and innovative with specific practices.

13

Invigorate Willpower for Self-Control

> "Strength does not come from physical capacity. It comes from an indomitable will." — *Mahatma Gandhi*

Higher score on self-control is a sure sign of better behaviour, stronger emotional balance, improved attention, and controlled impulses. All these traits are essential to achieve faster progress on life's superior goals. Next issue capable of being a great facilitator towards successful progress of meditation practice is self-control. Self-control is not an innate trait that one is born with but an acquired skill that needs to be acquired with proper training. Good intentions alone help us get self-discipline but self-control demands much more. Developing stronger resistance from caving in to multiple temptations and cravings is most critical for sustained self-control.

Self-Control arises from Sanskrit word 'Atma-Sanyam' where Atma means self and Sanyam collectively describes three distinct virtues of control, integration as well as restraint. The basic purpose of this explanation is to highlight the fact that the word Control used in this chapter is much wider from its dictionary meaning and includes virtues of wider meaning of Sanyam. Success in self-control depends on detailed action plans and rigorous efforts for erecting stronger perseverance to act against temptations. One has to avoid being ambivalent about changes in habits. For example, you cannot continue eating food rich in carbohydrates once you desire to drastically improve your BMI. Needless to say that abundant self-motivation is required to continue this drive. You need to evolve and use effective self-monitoring techniques to stay on course. Willpower, the greatest human strength of all times, singularly plays most critical role in this entire bunch of initiatives.

Understanding Willpower and its Importance

Out of many explanations about Willpower, the one provided by Dr. Kelly McGonigal, Ph.D. who teaches 'Science of Willpower' class at Stanford comes out as most exhaustive as well as easy to comprehend. According to her, willpower goes as under:

> 'it is the ability to do what you really want to do when part of you really does not want to do it'.

As human, we daily come across the conflict between impulse and self-control. Willpower is the strength helping us decide in favour of what is best for us by resisting the thrill expected in the immediate term. For our subject matter of Meditation, the meaning of "Willpower" tilts more towards collective spirit of words like discretion, prudence and discrimination to the least. So all future reference to it must be taken accordingly. The Sanskrit word that truly encompasses the essence of willpower is "Vivek" which actually include wisdom, intelligence and judgement of right or wrong. Taken as a unique quality differentiating human beings from animals, Willpower being discussed here is much stronger than its common parlance and is actually at the root of our entire social behaviour.

Willpower is like a muscle present in our mind. Some people work on it and make it strong while many others ignore it and allow it to go weak. The importance of such optional muscle increases further for participating with perseverance in voluntary activities like self improvement and meditation alike. Stronger is this muscle, faster are our strides towards excelling in whatever we do. Strengthening this muscle demands determination and involves setting stretched targets. Practising for improving willpower involves doing a few things and, more importantly, not to do many others. Interestingly, we must use this critical weapon very selectively as it loses its potency if used too often. Hence, caution is required to use it very responsibly and judiciously for bigger aims rather than insignificant and frivolous minor slippages.

Willpower is also a limited resource. It depletes with every use irrespective of the issue being small or big. So, please do not waste it on smaller issues. If it gets wasted on trivial issues revolving around satiating the insatiable, you are not left with any more willpower when it comes to superior human goals. People with wisdom, on the other hand, preserve this scarce resource only to deal with stringent situations.

So please pick up your willpower projects very discreetly. Willpower is similar to missiles power of an army. One must exhaust possibility of firing bullets, grenades and mortars before going for missiles.

Judicious Rationing of Willpower

Dr. McGonigal is also credited to explain willpower as a sum total of three different aspects listed below:

- "I won't" power—the ability to resist temptations.
- "I will" power—the ability to do what needs to be done.
- "I want" power—the awareness of one's long term goals.

According to her, willpower is harnessing all these three distinct powers to stay out of potential troubles. Failures on the very first aspect are visible in terms of declining moral and ethical standards in general and social curses like addictions, crimes, violence, sexual assaults, etc. in particular. Interestingly, majority of human beings exhaust most of their limited willpower on the first aspect itself. The second aspect contributes to individual's better health, secured relationships, financial value creation, secure higher positions and most importantly, remaining happier. Third aspect of focus on long term provides the inspiration to show patience and not settle for small chips at the cost of big coins later. Just like school exams, the achiever needs to do well in all three areas to be at the top of the class.

Enemies of Willpower

Harmless instances like eating that extra portion, drinking that extra peg, skipping exercises on smallest pretext, wasting that extra hour on TV, leaving that book in between, over sleeping on Sunday morning, are all common enemies of willpower. We generally overlook such instances as minor aberrations without realising the strikes such instances make on our self discipline Most of these look small issues but if you want a big tree, you have to take care of the seed and roots first. Self discipline is indeed the very root that eventually helps grow the tree of our willpower to desired size and strength.

Willpower basically involves supremacy of rational mind over emotional mind. Emotional mind comes under easy influence of impulses purely because it initiates responses at a speed faster than that of rational mind. Faster responses by emotional mind enable it to hijack many issues even before they attract attention of the rational mind. The speed is so fast that many responses are followed by repentance. Let us briefly look at a few causes that make our willpower weak.

1. Wrong eating habits, interestingly, can be identified as the very first enemy of willpower, and one with having simpler solution. Food we eat must provide energy to the body and mind to help them work at full efficiency during waking hours. Reduced energy leads to mental exhaustion as much as physical tiredness. Exhausted mind is certainly less receptive for commands or propriety. This is precisely why fatigue has been traditionally used for torture. Please eat balanced food, food that releases energy over entire gap between two meals. It requires combining ingredients that release energy quickly with those known for delayed release. Frequent eating in small portions is even a better solution for maintaining energy levels for optimal working of both body and mind.
2. Sleep deprivation is next common enemy of willpower. Sleep deprivation basically dumbs you down. Loss of sleep also hurts your concentration, it makes your reasoning difficult, it brings mood swings, and it disrupts working of your central nervous system. It is unfortunate that many young people and adults alike try avoiding sleep with the objective of achieving more in less time. That is a myth and a bad bargain. Not sleeping properly makes you dull and pulls down your performance at all levels. Exercising willpower requires your agility at top levels. You have to fire on all cylinders; do not count the hours on wheel but the miles covered. So sleep smart.
3. Third most common enemy for willpower is stress. Stress is known to lead to rapid breathing, tension in muscles and pounding of heart. All these physical signs bring entire attention to immediate at the cost of long term.
4. Indulging in vices comes as next enemy of willpower. To remain away from all types of vices and at all times is too big a claim for a normal human being. But irresponsible indulgence in even harmless looking vices, like addiction to check updates on social media, keeps you stimulated. Later this state of overstimulation, unknowingly, manifests itself in the

form of strong feelings, desperate thoughts, physical, mental, and emotional tension, and inner restlessness. Under that influence, you do not even feel the urge to apply willpower.

5. Procrastination is yet another big enemy of weaker willpower. No one can deny being guilty of procrastination at some point or the other. Reasons of getting trapped in it may vary from person to person-it may be due to hidden fear for failures, lack of clarity about results, loss of courage to take initiative, sense of inferiority, or just a genuine dilemma. Most obvious reason for procrastination is lack of motivation to take quick and decisive actions. Under all situations, it robs us of precious time and weakens the control of conscious mind over the situation. It certainly leads to feeling of low-esteem and depression which, in turn, affect other critical areas of life resulting in empowering unwanted fears and anxieties.
6. Getting used to reoccurring failures, accepting sub-optimal performance standards, losing faith in what is fundamental, losing balance in too little or too much, over-dependence on other individuals and lack of firm belief in own judgements are few other factors weakening will power.

An extra bit of care and determination go a long way in avoiding too many damages to your self-discipline. Unfortunately, the very need of invoking willpower happens under pressure situations only. And study of behaviours of people displaying strong self-controls shows that staying out of troubles and minimising problems is better than doing many right things.

How to Improve Willpower

Willpower thrives on determination to direct all our conscious and subconscious energy towards achieving our set goals. Having learned about how these two types of minds work, building willpower requires presence of continued determination in the conscious mind so that subconscious is unable to let it slip from its attention. However, it is advisable to start improving willpower with smaller and simpler targets. As a simple rule increased self-discipline takes over many situations where willpower may have to be used. And improving self-discipline is comparatively easier. You may like to start with your normal routine activities, one at a time, like getting out of bed within three rings of your set alarm and work on it as a project for, say, one week. The split second decision to remain in the bed for few extra seconds does all the damage. Success achieved on smaller targets helps raise the bar progressively. A bigger problem be broken down in smaller parts and each sub-part may be worked one by one until the entire old habit gets kicked out of the system. This entire process must remain rooted on positive motivation and not on suppression or deprivation. For example, avoiding adding sugar to your tea/coffee must be done by respecting the taste without sugar rather than taking it as a punishment.

Once you start working on your habits, you are due for a big shock as to how many short-term temptations and petty desires for gratification exist within your system. You need not shy away from taking all such desires head on. Success tasted in strengthening willpower soon helps you to have better handle on your cycles of thoughts.

Another successful tip is to raise your red flag just when the very first thought about a temptation entres your mental space. The famous saying *"It is easy to avoid temptation than resisting the same"* becomes useful here. Winners do not go to unlit corners if they fear darkness; they avoid the very situation in the first place where temptation is expected to arise. So if you wish to avoid fast food, please eat at home before you step out for mall which is full with fast food counters.

Willpower and Meditation

Strong self-discipline backed up by determined willpower plays most critical role in ensuring progress in meditation. Meditation journey is long and boring where major benefits are obscure and very inconspicuous. Continuing efforts for such a practice demands tons of patience and discipline just to continue making efforts. On the other hand, daily life keeps throwing endless challenges in our way where meditation risks gets lower priority. In the process, people having fragile willpower are prone to drop the practice midway. That is why you need to have regular self talk and repeated self-reassurance for not giving in to pressures of the present and desires for immediate gratifications. Fortunately, issues of self-control trouble practitioners much more in the beginning months. Once the practitioners are able to make progress on concepts like contentment, detachment, and acceptance, the situations testing self-control subside progressively.

Besides, willpower impacts all normal daily routines like eating, exercising, sleeping and thinking. Here again, both willpower and meditation contribute towards growth of each other. Willpower brings the participant to the cushion while meditation nourishes willpower to become more strong and resilient. Actually, latest scientific researchers are increasingly finding meditation as best possible technique to boost willpower.

Let us look at technique of "Focus on Breath" suggested particularly for positive results in enhancing self-control.

- Sitting in a comfortable pose with eyes closed, one should practise focusing on breath daily for 10-20 minutes.
- Let the mind focus not on the nostrils but somewhere near the end of nose, around the nasal area.
- The flow of the breath, both at inhaling and exhaling, is to be regulated in conscious manner by bringing the mind to concentrate on the nose end point. The mind will keep going to other thoughts but the practice requires bringing it back to focus on the breath. t
- You can also practise to locate some other point of attention with the sole purpose of engaging the mind on breathing sequence all the time so that it does not get opportunity to fly away.
- In baby steps, let your mind observe sensations while inhaling and their changes at the exhaling; it can be change in temperature of the air breathed, the pressure of breath felt, the rhythm and flow of breaths, the smell of the air, the feel of breath at the throat glands, soreness in throat with change in climatic conditions, the feel at thyroid gland and so on.
- These variations are critical to keep the mind engaged without feeling monotony. Later these variations can be linked to kind of food or drinks you had the previous day, the impact of quality of sleep at night, impact of physical exercises etc. All these points need to be observed by the mind while breathing under keen observation every day.
- This practice will lead you to the habit of observing without judgement.
- Well-developed pure observation shall prove to be the tipping point for the silencing of craving centres of the brain.

14

Making Efforts for Unlocking Success in Meditation

Many people believe that special grace from Almighty, some sort of gift from God, is essential to make it big in life. Alas, these people are missing something rather important for success in life. In general, success in life depends partially on individual's talent and significantly on efforts made by that very person while role of blessings or grace may be found only by using microscope. Those familiar with achievements of batting maestro Sachin Tendulkar know very well that his childhood friend Vinod Kambli was equally talented, if not more. Sachin became 'The Sachin' due to 'efforts' he sustained all through his playing years, both on and off the cricket grounds. The difference in success achieved by two people operating roughly in similar conditions, and gifted with similar talents, coached by a single person, is a clear proof of the importance of 'Efforts' as a bedrock for success in life.

In particular, discussions about importance of efforts need to be highlighted to younger generation. Unfortunately, they lack appreciation for stronger efforts as compared with their earlier generations. We may keep talking about talent, knowledge or connections in any other forms but effective and multi-dimensional success in all spheres of life, be it education, professions, physicals, sports, mental, emotional, communal, political, religious, familial, or spiritual areas, depends substantially on right 'efforts'. One may also argue both knowledge (wisdom) and efforts to be essential for success but importance of efforts outweigh knowledge by miles and it should not be difficult to understand why. Well, you may gain knowledge with efforts but can never gain efforts with knowledge.

Right efforts are the foundation for acquiring mastery in every such activity where human potential is tested at extreme level.

The overriding share of efforts over other factors in success is well supported by modern day researchers also. Ms. Angela Duckworth, Professor of Psychology at the University of Pennsylvania, where she teaches courses on grit and self-control, also highlights importance of efforts. She opines in the matter under discussions saying "Perseverance—hard work and resilience in the face of adversity—is the single most predictive characteristic of grit. But it is only half of the equation. You also need your work to be meaningful, important and interesting." This statement pretty much reflects all critical issues to make good progress on your meditative journey as well.

Generally speaking, success in every sphere in life is not legacy for selected few. Well within overwhelming and chaotic modern day life, success is still a feasible goal for us as much as approximately eight billion other people we share this world with. But it does not mean that ultimately every person gets success. In reality, majority of people fail to achieve success that they deserve or desire and there is no mystery about this conclusion. The most common missing factor is lack of just and right directional efforts. Success never embraces anyone simply because they dream. It fundamentally requires one to obey the golden rule of 'Pay now and Play later' instead of 'Play now and Pay later'. Similar to all other spheres in life, success in meditation also demands hard work and determination.

> "One, who believes that God can be accessed with talent, only suffers. Similarly, one who thinks God can be accessed without doing anything, is only day dreaming." — *Anonymous*

Above two sentences very much highlight the importance of making serious, sincere and concerted efforts to realise progress on our meditative journey as well.

Words like caution, discretion, prudence and thoughtfulness are all here to highlight one or the other true aspects of 'efforts' required for proper meditation. Probably, meditation will qualify as the most important and forceful self-advancing or self-emphatic project you ever undertook. This entire process calls for one hundred per cent willingness and readiness of your heart, mind and intelligence. Understanding the deepest aspects and working hard to acquiring expertise, apply equally to a master sportsman/artist/craftsman and a master meditator. Masters from all spheres require superb self-control, patience in bulk, self-restraint, deep understanding, exceptional focus and single-minded dedication. The endeavour for Meditation has to continue with the same vigour right up to the point where your heart accepts complete surrender to the divine forces governing humanity, where there is complete oneness and all aspects of separateness disappear forever. Right surrender opens door for 'acceptance' and 'gratitude'. When this happens, all our efforts get automatically concentrated on our central goal.

Importance of Efforts for Meditation

New generation in general and millennial generation in particular are going for fast food, fast speed, fast relationships which indicate common desires for quick results, shortcuts, and easy paths. As a natural extension, people are generally attracted to an appealing tagline that meditation is easy to learn and effortless to continue. Such propaganda can gain popularity and encourage stressed out and exasperated householders to take meditation as a prevailing fashion under lure of quick and assured results. Ultimate results of effortless and casual approach to meditation shall always be shallow and superficial. Meditation was never a casual exercise and will never be, period. So it is absolutely wrong to subscribe to the impression that meditation can be initiated or continued without highest quality of efforts.

An effortless approach to meditation tells you to not to try anything with your attention, or use your concentration but just entertain the thoughts that naturally occur to you. Techniques like these generally suggest you to make use of mantras, audio/video support or guided meditation, aimed at bringing your mental processes under regulation. But any experienced meditator will easily identify such techniques with relaxation rather than meditation. Let us be clear that serious meditation has nothing in common with relaxation and that practising meditation involves increasingly harder efforts and nothing short.

Let us look at comparison of effortless meditation and efforts led meditation with the help of a simple example. Hunger is one of the most basic requirements that we attend to daily. On the one side, we have fast foods available across the counters, multiple choices, good to look at, attractive packaging, very well advertised, easy to serve and appealing to taste buds. Well, what we also know for sure is of its bad effects on health and pockets alike. On the other hand, we have self-cooked food where the ingredients are picked very selectively, cutting and chopping carried out personally, the process of frying (adding spices, heat level, synchronisation of adding each item) and cooking are all carried out with full heart and soul knowing its importance for loved ones. Well, both fast foods and self-cooked foods are used as food but which food is expected to prove better considering your satisfaction level, ease in digestion, general health, burden on pocket and total well being? Effortless meditation is that very fast food; good on eye and tongue but bad for pocket and stomach.

Carrying on this example a little further, self-cooked food greatly activates timely release of required enzymes within our digestive system such that the moment food gets received, our digestion system sets in motion. This is how home-cooked food is better for digestion. This very affinity also helps avoiding allergies and undesired side effects. Advice for proper chewing and eating slowly also aids in secretion of those digestive enzymes only. As against this, the fast food is like a black box where digestive process starts working only after the food gets dumped in the stomach. Progress on meditative path also takes longer similar to arranging things for selfcooking. Thankfully, its results are also as worthy and effective as self-cooked food for our physical well being.

Quality of efforts for meditation also demands extremes on both sides to be avoided. You have to train yourself just like an expert swordsman who is ever watchful of every sensation of self and opponent and always ready to make a strike because he knows well that one small mistake and his head may get severed by his opponent. Similarly, for meditation world remain active as usual, breaths continue as usual but the heart and mind remain concentrated only on the subject of choice. Efforts for success in meditation must also be egoless, that is, without having interference of 'me' or 'I'. Meditation requires deep concentration on consciousness but without expecting miracles or being too anxious for ground being covered.

There is yet another significant factor making Efforts so critical for meditation. Significance in life has a unique equation about ratio between efforts and rewards-anything received without efforts or with fewer efforts is never gets considered as significant; anything received with ease can never be transformative. This golden rule applies to meditation verbatim. Putting in subtle, substantial and constant efforts behind your meditation practice alone help deepening your practice to desired levels. The point to remember is that 'efforts' are essential to accomplish 'significant' results while 'enormous efforts' alone can be the cause for 'sizable effects'.

Let us also guard against the advocates of law of inertia. Proponents of this law suggest not making efforts so that body and mind feel relaxed. They claim that if you do not make efforts in thinking, your mind will remain relaxed. But is it far from truth. The desired quality of mind for being effective at meditation is to be quiet and not relaxed. A relaxed body or mind, obtained without efforts, is an inactive body (good only for sleep) and lethargic mind (good only for day dreaming). How can we expect a lethargic mind to be fit for becoming completely quiet, devoid and introverted? Letting go of all efforts may calm a mind alright but it will not take it to the deeper states of meditation. As we will later see, meditation requires an agile body and a willing, spirited and vigilant mind.

Let us also not confuse efforts with forced labour or coercive force. That may be suitable for a physical drill but not for meditation. Meditation requires right efforts; one which is gentle, willing, firm, aimed at right subject, all at the same time. This concept of right effort is directly from 'Noble Eight Fold Path' popularised by Buddha where the wise train their mind with right efforts to give total attention to one thing at a time. As we all know well that mind is constantly busy in moving from thought to thought, or in imaginations or generation of new ideas, and all this keeps happening in an automatic manner without us even becoming aware of the process. Diverting such a mind to pointed attention on an object of choice is a long and treacherous journey best facilitated by meditation.

Persistence is yet another critical quality for right efforts required for meditation. Beginning with early days of meditative journey, you start realising that on some day you make good progress and do enjoy pure experience but the very next day the entire sitting may be filled with endless doubts and frustrations. Our very own mind cooperates on one day while next day it starts behaving like a 'bull in bazaar' showing no sign of respecting efforts made to bring it under regulation. Later, such undesired episodes may continue over weeks and weeks in a row. All this is very normal and is perfectly to be expected. Continued persistence alone will be the key for getting over such episodes.

Buddha was once asked "What have you gained from meditation." He replied "Nothing!" "However" Buddha said, "Let me tell you what I lost: Anger, Anxiety, Depression, Insecurity, Fear of Old Age and Death."

Meditation for Practising Silence-filled Efforts

- Please start your session with deep and relaxed breathing. Let duration and sequence of your inhaling, exhaling and the space in between remain natural without you trying anything deliberate. Continue for about 4-5 minutes.
- Over next 8 to 12 minutes, slowly and progressively move the point of focus from nostrils along the entire respiratory track. First you may focus on inner nose, later shift the point of focus to throat mucous membranes, voice box, windpipe and entry into the lungs. You may continue it until the focus point reaches to heart in the chest. The idea is to ensure exclusive engagement of attention on the breathing to the entire exclusion of all other mental activities. With practice you start realising that flight of thoughts is diverted from all directions to the inner space, bit by bit.
- It is interesting to feel the sensations associated with expansion of chest and relaxation of diaphragm during inhaling and exhaling. You have plenty of variations to observe like temperature, smell and feel of the breaths at different points on the respiratory track. All these sensations were not noticed earlier when you were breathing without attention diverted inward.
- It is essential to keep the whole exercises as relaxing, enjoyable and de-stressing without expecting exotic experience. Extra efforts made to seduce faster results in meditation are destined to fail. Patience together with relaxation is the key. Although we are looking for extraordinary results but it is possible only with normal and ordinary efforts over longer period of time. People disrespecting this equation fail, so often, to make progress in meditation. Use of force results in letting the door of inner cave shut even harder.
- Observing breathing with intensity explained before brings in real feel of each palpitation and throb of the heart.

Interestingly, watching this activity itself works as a highly effective therapy as it calms down the entire thought process which brings a unique sense of pure existence that is blissful and meaningful at the same time.

- In a way this is the first step of entering in our own treasured cave of heart. Many people consider this stage itself as end of meditation. No, this is merely a first glance of things to come and settling just for this is surely a poor bargain.
- Ensure that the whole session is voluntary and there are no resolutions made.
- When the breathing reaches right up to the lungs, assume opening of a narrow entrance into a dormant cave sort of space somewhere around the heart. Place your formless self somewhere in that space and feel the thoughts playing on a stage in front. This state ensures your complete disconnect with the external world including your own body. When you are successful in this stage, you do not even know if your breathing is inhaling or exhaling. Similarly, the entire body is reduced to being a statue. The formless self becomes the 'observer' and the thoughts played on the stage of the cave become the 'observed'.
- In one session you may focus on your thought, in next it may be some problem, some unanswered question or some such thing that you decide to be the object of your contemplation for the particular session. Alternatively, you may start imagining your symbols of power and grace. Ultimate objective is to hold your attention within void of your inner core with all connections with the world severed completely.
- With advanced practice and simultaneous growth on other fronts, this imaginative space will turn out to be a virtual space with endless possibilities. It can now accommodate visualisation of every kind of thought, object or emotions and feelings.
- It is here that you come in contact with your immaculate silence. It is the silence that holds answers to every possible question you may have faced ever.

15

Meditation Techniques and Practices

> "Meditation should not be regarded as a learning process. It should be regarded as an experiencing process. You should not try to learn from meditation but try to feel it. Meditation is an act of non-duality. The technique you are using should not be separate from you; it is you, you are the technique. Meditator and meditation are one. There is no relationship involved."
>
> — *Chogyam Trungpa Rinpoche*,
> A Tibetan Buddhist meditation master

A giant mountain always looks different to people looking from different sides and angles. Same mountain may not look that big to a person standing at its base but once you start climbing, the real picture continues getting bigger and bigger. Meditation is that very giant mountain in dimensions and as cumbersome in terms of scaling its peak. To climb such meditation mountain there are too many methods propagated at different times, by different cultures, by different teachers. At times those methods may appear even sitting in diametrically opposite corners.

Some methods strongly argue for silent ways while others propagate chanting and mantras. Some recommend focus on physical objects while others focus only on abstract ideas, thoughts and/or experiences. Some suggest regulation of mental processes while others plead for letting the mind roam freely as it pleases. Few see merit in following time tested ancient methods while others argue newer experimental methods. There are deep divisions on other levels as well. Some believe meditation a uniquely secular practice but others link it to their own religious traditions. Indeed, there are too many conflicting indications about various techniques available in the market. Both techniques and confusions associated with each remain in super abundance giving rise to genuine dilemma for a practitioner.

Under this situation a learned aspirant must essentially take a rather wide view of all that is available before making equitable decision. Going for a detailed theoretical comprehension of all types and techniques available is aimed at that very objective. Different practices also maintain their allegiance with specific traditions which also need to be acknowledged and appreciated to further refine the understanding about their origin. The contours of this chapter are defined with this very objective in mind. Every meditation aspirant must obtain a bird's eye view of entire horizon of plethora of techniques to pick and choose the most optimum selection keeping in line his orientation, background, progress status and expected destination.

Meditation journey passes through unknown territory and the aspirant is more often like a person stranded at unknown location in a dense forest on a rugged and rough terrain. The person trapped is able to see vastness of the unknown saddled with innumerable peaks and valleys having wild variety of vegetations, shrubs and trees. The sounds and droppings also suggest presence of all sorts of wild animals and resultant danger to life. To make matter worse, the person does not have access to specific maps or definite knowledge of known landmarks. All he got is a general idea of the place and stories from people who claim to have passed through similar challenge as a part of their personal journeys in the past. It may not be difficult to visualise the plight of such a stranded soul.

Different techniques are like trails which allow this person to explore the surroundings of entire landscape albeit in a very distraught and jittery manner. Those trails seem to go in different directions while crossing over each other at irregular distances. Some run parallel for some distance before merging with each other. Others go together and later fork out in different directions. Some look difficult to begin with but take smooth direction later on while some look rather comfortable to follow but fail to take the aspirant very far. In this maze of multiple trails, none of the trails seems long enough to take him out from his mess. Still, those trails are all he got to follow.

The only other choice is to make a new personalised trail by his own efforts which, in any case, is bound to consume more time certainly delaying his progress.

Broad Categorisation of Meditational Practices and Techniques

Speaking generally, different types of practices are broadly classified under three distinct categories. To begin with we have techniques that call for focusing attention either on some object or some word or even some concept. The object of concentration can even be a sound, visual form, breath, body part, a subtle idea or even an inner experience. Such attention focusing, or concentration, increases activities associated with beta and gamma EEG waves. Tibetan meditation of focus on love, kindness and compassion for beings are also part of this category. Second broad category include contemplation based meditation types and techniques which basically involve pure observation of thoughts arising in mind. Here meditative awareness gets integrated with ordinary experience. These types are popularly called as *mindfulness or Zen meditation practices* and have gained much more traction in recent decades, especially among the new practitioners in the Western world. Here the practitioner relies on own experience of thoughts without involving any judgement, desire, regulation or manipulation of some sorts. These are in general focused on inward attention. In scientific terms, these practices work on theta waves leading to relaxed state of mind.

The third and last broad category involves *transcending of individual self* culminating into experience that is beyond boundaries or limits. In these practices, processing of sensory information gets reduced while the frontal area of brain responsible for moral reasoning gets super activated. Here Alpha waves are supposed to increase leading to relaxation and calm. Transcendental meditational practices are said to bring coherence which make brain work in a holistic manner. These actually help the mind to occupy the position of CEO and help it function as an authority in charge overruling irrational responses arising out of sub-conscious or unconscious mental systems. Interestingly, it is said that these techniques are comparatively easier to master.

Why Grading Meditational Practices not an Option

Every individual is different; some have visual bent of mind and some kinesthetic; some are attuned to sensations while others to auditory. Many others respond better only to feelings. There is no 'single size fit to all' technique. Each aspirant has to try alternate techniques and come up with his own comfort levels, effectiveness and conclusions. Also, our attitudes and convictions are not concepts that are cast in concrete. Attitudes and convictions change all the times and so do our maturity and world view. Progress on our path of meditation also goes to refine clarity about subtle perceptions. Techniques of meditation practice, therefore, must change accordingly to continue being relevant, interesting and productive. Like for game of golf, techniques are different clubs where each player picks up a club as it suits him for different shots at different holes considering terrain of the fairway, his ability and expertise, the ball position, wind conditions and many other such conditions. However, in the final analysis or scoring of the game, the type of club used has no relevance.

All techniques are worth attempting and may prove successful at different stages of our practice. At times, people practising different techniques end up reporting similar benefits and vice versa. Thus there is no way to hold a particular technique superior or inferior in any way even when different people take to each of these techniques with their own levels of comfort or complexity. Practitioners are better served when they constantly experiment with alternate techniques to realise what works better with them at that stage of their practice. Also, techniques can be combined and alternated at will. Never feel stuck with any technique at any point of time of your practice.

The techniques are just like scaffolding supports required for erecting any big structure. You require a different configuration at different levels of construction. Your selection is also different for interior and exterior, for lower floors and higher floors and different scaffolding for vertical or horizontal pillars and slabs. Surely, you cannot think of erecting a structure without variety of scaffolding during the construction phase. But the same scaffolding is removed and stored in some obscure corner once the building gets completed. Usefulness of multiple techniques is just as important to each practitioner but only until such time that sufficient progress is achieved in the practice.

Let us now look at some important and popular techniques. Their categorisation under different cultures is just to simplify the classification without any overt or covert attempt. Otherwise just a random listing of these would have served the purpose equally well. For better grasp, the individual techniques are explained with little bit of historical perspective.

(A) Buddhist Meditation Techniques

The original words used for meditation in Buddhism are Bhavana, *Janana and Dhyana.* Real meanings of these words mean mental development, mental training and/or illumination of mind. Ultimate objective of meditation in Buddhism is to achieve liberation, awakening and Nirvana, the superior stage of spiritual growth. Buddhist practices are aimed at taking control of the mind so that it becomes peaceful and focused taking practitioner's awareness intensity to higher levels. Buddhist practices endeavours to stop the mind from aimlessly going through the thought streams to a stage of stillness. Core meditation Buddhist techniques have been preserved in ancient Buddhist texts and have proliferated and diversified through teacher-student transmissions for over last two thousand years.

Buddhism principles revolve around peace of mind, compassion for beings, mindfulness, care of environment, etc. which directly resonate with modern day's population. As a result, Buddhist meditation practices are gaining increasing popularity in the West in recent times. These concepts and practices are accepted as more social and secular when compared with other Eastern techniques. Buddhist techniques are seen reshaping character and behaviour of the practitioner without expectations of big mystical experiences. People prefer Buddhist practices for their 'come and see yourself' approach as against complex 'do as being told' approach of some other faiths.

Let us look at most popular techniques having roots in Buddhism, one by one:

Zen Meditation (Zazen)

Literally meaning as 'sitting in absorption', Zazen is a unique method aimed at an attitude of not getting attached with any experience, condition or feeling. This technique credited to Japanese Buddhist

Priest and an acclaimed Zen Master, Dogen Zenji (1200-1253) literally means doing meditation while sitting. Tracking the expansion of Buddhism to Japan via China, Dogen Zenji's school is firmly rooted in Chinese Zen Buddhism tradition which in turn is tracked back to Indian monk Bodhidharma (6th century CE). It calls for sitting in conscious awareness for a desirable length of time. Thoughts generated during the sitting are to be simply observed and released until they gradually become less and less developed. Idea is not to actively suppress/push thoughts to achieve an empty mental state. The practitioner has to focus on what lies behind those thoughts until such time that consciousness becomes entirely free from discursive thinking. Because of the process involved, this practice is called a method without method.

Zazen is also called the study of self. As per Master Dogen "...to study the self is to forget the self...". Normally we see body, breath and mind as separate identities, but in Zazen all three come together as one reality. Under this technique, images, thoughts and emotions are allowed to emerge over the mental surface from the subconscious mind. The practitioner is advised not to pursue them, nor fight or escape in any way. It is rightly believed that any effort to get rid of thoughts and emotions involves only go to increase attention on them. Under this technique, you have to let go thoughts without either judging or getting attached with them. Thoughts are to wither away in due course exactly as the clouds do in the sky.

It is generally practised seated on the floor over a mat and cushion, with crossed legs, taking lotus or half-lotus posture. But other postures with erect back are also practised by many. Mouth is kept closed and eyes are kept lowered, with your gaze resting on the ground about two to three feet in front. The popular way to practise Zazen is to focus attention on the movement of the breath going in and out through the nose. This may be aided by counting the breath in your mind. Each time you inhale you count one number, starting with 10, and then moving backward to 9, 8, 7, etc. When the practitioner arrives at 1, he resumes the counting from 10 again. If you get distracted and lose your count, you have to gently bring back the attention to 10 and resume from there.

Zazen is a very sober meditation practice with plenty of information available on the internet. It is the most common practice used by communities practising meditation in groups. There is a lot of emphasis in keeping the right posture, as an aid for concentration. Under Zazen, there is no meditation object or abstract concept for the sitter to focus on. Basic objective is to still the mind and later to reach a state of pure thought-free wakefulness so that true Buddha nature is realised by the mind. In other variations of Zazen, one also comes across additional elements associated with Buddhist practices, e.g. traces of ritualism, chanting, and group readings of the Buddha teachings.

Vipassana Meditation

"Vipassana", originally a word from Pali language, means "insight", an essence of the teachings of Buddha, who attained that very experience himself by practising meditation. Buddha's own words are records of his personal experiences of meditation. His teachings include detailed instructions for practising same meditation technique for his followers to reach the goal of experiencing truth in a manner similar to the one he reached himself. Within the Buddhism sects, it is attributed to Theravada Buddhist tradition. Vipassana meditation got popularised in different parts of the world under several teachers, writings of many Buddhists from Thailand as well as the Vipassana movement. In recent times, Sri S.N. Goenka figures as a prominent teacher credited for popularising this technique.

Vipassana meditation is a way of transforming self through pure observation and bringing focus on deeper connection of body and mind. Advocates of this technique believe that this observation based self-exploratory journey to the common root of mind and body can dissolve all impurities and achieve a balanced mind full of love and compassion. In that sense, the doctrine of Vipassana is not far from Zazen meditation.

Taking nothing out of its recent spread all over the world, Vipassana meditation technique is indeed revival of the ancient technique conforming to the teachings of Buddha without any shade of religion attached to its practice. There is no dogma and it is a simple technique taught normally in courses of ten days. During the course days, the participants have to remain within the defined course area without having any contact with the rest of the world. During this time, they suspend all their religious practices and reading or writing and only follow instructions given by the course instructors. During the course period, all participants follow basic moral code of celibacy, abstention from all types of intoxications and maintain total silence.

The course requires participants to practise exercises of mental concentration for first three days before getting introduced to Vipassana proper. All other steps are introduced one by one, such that, by end of the course entire technique gets laid out in open. It is reported that during their retreat, at times, participants do go through peculiar experiences. Besides they also realise efforts required to withdraw all thoughts from external world and directing the mental processes inward which indeed prove real hard work. This technique expects practitioners to make full efforts without any tension. This simple rule, however, offers its own challenges, especially in the beginning.

Practitioners also report surprise when they come across their real self. Normally, untrained mind maintains a very selective view about self (which is more of what one wants rather than what he really is). But pure observation during the course brings people in touch with their reality, which at times is full of many dark and grey shades, diametrically opposite to what they may have believed until now. Vipassana leads them to see through their own mental image being different from, for example, an admirable personality with least defects to a discourteous person fraught with vulnerabilities. These surprises are known to excite agitations and irritations rather than inner peace that one goes wishing.

But by the time the course comes to end, provided that all sincere efforts are made as instructed, many participants also get surprised for their new found ability to make effortless efforts to sustain a relaxed alertness along with detached involvement. At this stage, the struggle paves way for the engrossed practice; the mental calmness gets established, the discipline becomes bearable making visions of positivity and peace.

The real practice goes like this—most teachers emphasise starting with mindfulness of breath in the first stage, to stabilise the mind and achieve "access concentration." The first aspect is to practise concentration through awareness focused on breathing. You have to focus all your attention, from moment to moment, on observing the subtle sensations of the movement of the abdomen rising and falling during breathing. This is more like focused attention meditation. Then the practice moves on to developing "clear insight" on the bodily sensations and mental phenomena, observing them moment by moment without clinging to them in any way.

At a later stage of your practice, you can also focus on the sensation of the air passing through the nostrils and upper lips. While noticing the breath, you cannot miss perceptions and sensations appearing continuously including sounds, feelings in the body, emotions, etc. You are required to simply notice these phenomena as they emerge in the field of awareness, and then return to the sensation of breathing. The attention is always kept on the breathing which works as the primary object of attention. Idea is to feel those other thoughts and sensations as if you notice background noise while you are in a public space, that is, you hear the noise but you neither pay any attention nor does it disturb you too much. The practice trains you to focus on secondary object for a moment and return back to primary object without giving much attention to secondary objects. This way you take a general note of the object but not in any detail.

Later, after mastering access concentration, the attention is turned to the objects of practice, which are normally thoughts or bodily sensations. One observes the objects of awareness without attachment, letting thoughts and sensations arise and pass away of their own accord. As a result one develops the clear perception that the observed phenomena are pervaded by the three "marks of existence": impermanence (*annica*), lack of satisfaction (*dukkha*) and emptiness of self (*annata*). As a result, equanimity, peace and inner freedom is developed in relation to these inputs. The entire practice recognises the process of experiencing reality by self experience. It brings back focus on your inside redirecting your attention from habit of looking outside. This works as a proven practice of self-purification resulting in inner darkness getting dispelled leading a person to gain insight into his own nature, the nature of his very existence.

Vipassana technique is said to be easy to learn. One can find plenty of reading material, audio video supports and individual stories to learn from. You can get access to a number of teachers and websites on the click of few buttons and mostly for free. The retreats are always conducted by trained teachers so there are lesser mistakes to be made. There are a number of retreat centres available in different parts of the world offering these retreats on regular basis. Practitioners also find it more suitable for the beginners.

Mindful Meditation

> "Your goal is not to battle with the mind, but to witness the mind."
> — *Swami Muktananda*

Over the years another type of meditation started taking shape out of adaptive mixing of traditional Buddhist meditation, Vipassana, and Vietnamese Zen (identified with Master Thich Nhat Hanh). It is popularly known as Mindfulness and is currently much more in vogue in the Western world. John Kabat-Zinn is considered leading influencers for Mindfulness meditation in the West. His Mindfulness Based Stress Reduction Programme (MBSR) developed in late seventies at The University of Massachusetts Medical School has been used in several hospitals and health clinics in the past decades.

For the general public, this is perhaps the most advisable way to get started with meditation. Being simple to learn and practise, this is the most common practice taught at schools and hospitals. Its initial advantages are felt immediately in terms of good physical health, mental health and general wellbeing. Non-association with eastern concepts and philosophies is yet another convenient thing about this technique. As one can visualise, those concepts are generally aligned with religious shades and are relatively difficult to grasp and practise. Best suited for beginners, one may have to opt for Vipassana, Zazen, or other type of meditation when looking for deeper transformation and spiritual development. Hence, this concept is best taken as initial step before growing into some other purer forms of techniques.

As we already know, in Buddhist teachings, mindfulness is used to develop self-knowledge and wisdom that generally leads to freedom from sufferings and finally help us reaching the state of enlightenment. Mindful Meditation is just modern adaptation of this very context to be readily applied to modern day practitioners. Mindfulness meditation is the practice of intentionally focusing on the present moment, accepting and non-judgmentally paying attention to the sensations, thoughts, and emotions that arise and subside from moment to moment.

One major variation of Mindful Meditation over its traditional technique is to practise mindfulness on subjects other than thoughts. Mindfulness can be practised while doing the most mundane activity of day to day life. It can be done while walking, while taking bath, while watching TV or while doing any and every daily activity. Its refined version is called 'Present Moment Awareness' where the practitioner watches every moment so closely that there is no spare moment even to comment about that.

Ajahn Brahm, a very popular British-Australian Theravada Buddhist monk, who has written many books and articles on the subject, explains this technique in simple terms and talks about experiences entering in the mind one by one through the doors of our senses on a continuous basis. Well, if the practitioner starts talking to any experience in particular, surely the experience entering right behind gets completely missed from being observed. The mind, therefore, should only indulge in observing of each experience/ thought.

As a basic concept underlying this technique, anything done mindfully becomes meditation. Even a mundane ritual like brushing teeth can be carried out in the state of being mindful by moment to moment observing the taste of toothpaste, by sensing the feedback from receptors active in different parts of the mouth, its touch on the tongue, feeling bristles rubbing gums on the inside and outside, sensations felt on different teeth and molars, variations one feels with every motion of hand, etc. Only condition applicable is to remain in present moment and bring back your attention to present activity and observing your thoughts, feelings and emotions without following them and without holding any judgement or comparison about any of them. The moment you go along with sounds, sensations, and thoughts, your mind is destined to get distracted. Whenever that happens gently recognise that you have distracted and bring the attention back to the object of notice you were focused before that distraction. All you need to differentiate is being '*aware*' *of* the thought/sensation and to avoid 'being into it'.

The advance stage of this technique is called 'Silent Present Moment Awareness' focused on a single object. Instead of being silently aware of whatever comes into the mind, here, one chooses silent present moment awareness of just one thing. It can be experience of breathing, idea of loving kindness, a coloured circle visualised in the mind or some such single object of choice. The time span during which generally the practitioner is able to retain his attention on his single object works as a measurement of success achieved in the method.

The basic principle of the practice simply says that we actually live life without distractions when we live in present moment. We also avoid desiring particular outcomes of events. And it is not living a life of status quo. You still find areas requiring betterment but we must understand the subtle difference between identifying points of improvement and desiring outcomes of a particular nature. Being mindful, similarly, adds to our skills and enhances quality of everything we do for self and others. Actually, the approach of being mindful can be easily traced in attitudes displayed by all super performers from every walk of life, for example, sports persons.

Loving-Kindness Meditation (Metta Meditation)

Some meditation practices are designed to emphasise particular strength of its practitioner. *Metta,* a Pali word for kindness, benevolence, and good will, is one such method focused on developing love and compassion. Rooted in Buddhist traditions of Theravada with Tibetan lineage, this practice is popular with English name as 'Loving-kindness'. The teachers of this practice claim many demonstrable benefits like boosting one's ability to empathise with others, development of positive emotions through compassion, evolving loving attitude towards every living being including self, increased self-acceptance, greater feeling of competence about one's life and heightened feeling of purpose in life.

This meditation practice is about inclusive love adorned with wisdom. Under influence of this love, it does not matter if other person is from our inner circle or just an outsider. Also, this love is completely selfless with no expectations in return. One begins this process by loving himself because only a person with overflowing love and acceptance for self can extend it to others. As a second step, it includes persons having special relationships with the practitioner (spouse, lover, child or friend included). This circle of love keeps expanding step by step such that ultimately all living beings get included. This meditation spreads warmth for living beings by focusing on intimate human feelings of care, concern, tenderness, kindness, friendship, and spreading. Continued practice of this technique ultimately leads to softening of mind and heart of its practitioner.

The practice starts with sitting in a comfortable and relaxed meditation position with eyes closed and invoking generation of feelings of kindness and benevolence. The practitioner starts by focusing on solar plexus, the area around heart called *'Manipura'* under the famous system of Chakras of Tantra Yoga. The practice begins with focusing breath on heart chakra by anchoring all attention on the sensations arising in this area to the exclusion of all other body parts.

This practice is especially useful for people who are very hard on themselves, those having faced difficult relationships, those generally categorised as self-centred or those suffering from modern day's ills like insomnia, nightmares or anger/frustration issues.

(B) Sanatan Meditation Techniques

Scriptures belonging to Vedic Traditions are certainly the earliest sources of meditation. Dhyana, the Sanskrit word for meditation finds repetitive mention in Rigveda, Taittiriya Aranyaka and many other later Upanishads where it is generally used in context of contemplative, reflective or meditative practice to further spiritual realisation. 'Prashna Upanishad' takes it even further and describes in details that meditation on a single but most powerful word having unique combination of three distinct syllables, "AUM" is the most effective tool to reach 'Brahman', the Ultimate Reality. As per Raja Yoga of Maharishi Patanjali, *Dhyana,* the deeper concentration of the mind is only a refined meditation practice which is taken up only after mastering the preceding exercises such as Pranayam (breath control) and Dharana (mental focus). Dhyana, in fact, is a central theme of all practices originating on Indian soil and is adopted by all subsequent home grown traditions of Buddhism, Jainism as well as Sikhism.

But single biggest push to the concept of meditation under Sanatan traditions is revealed in the Bhagwad Gita. So much so that its Chapter Six titled as "Yoga of Meditation" most extensively deals with the concept of meditation. The Bhagwad Gita prescribes meditation as one of the four practices to reach the pinnacle of spiritual growth, the other three being Nishkam Seva (selfless service), Jnana (wisdom) and Bhakti (devotion).

It will not be out of place to comprehend as to why Sanatan culture considers meditation as a life changing practice of the highest order. To appreciate this point, one has to go back to the roots of philosophy governing concepts and doctrines of Sanatan era. Here human mind is viewed as a storeroom where thoughts move back and forth from the universal pool of thoughts. Another very important concept also states that human mind has the creative potency of the supreme creator. Every person is considered as a sum total of thoughts and desires which remain active cumulatively over the lives; a person is said to become what he thinks. Sanatan philosophy has always propagated thoughts at par with actions. Speaking philosophically, this equation makes Sanatan doctrine stand at a much higher pedestal when compared with other religious thoughts in vogue.

Speaking logically too, thoughts are known to grow and become part of one's latent impressions. These very impressions start influencing actions in the course of daily life, here and after. Influencing thoughts is comparable to sowing seeds for the crop expected later. Meditation has been long considered the most effective way for exercising desired regulation over one's thought process to impact actions for the actual life. A person withdraws his mind and senses from the distractions of the world and contemplates upon a chosen object or idea with full concentration only through meditation.

Further as Sanatan thoughts are based on an open source concept, and as an extension of its defining peculiarity, multiplicity of individual orientation is accepted with open arms. Here every person is expected and encouraged to make his own individual efforts following his own liking and suitability and see what works most effectively for them and practise the same. As such, under the single umbrella of Sanatan tradition, quite a few distinct practices got evolved and got practised by different people.

The concepts being discussed here are purely pragmatic, non-sectarian and completely secular approach where its reference to any specific tradition denotes only historical moorings and not a religious connect. Actually, religion, as we look at them today, have not even evolved in those times when Sanatan traditions had fully developed systems and methods covering all aspects of individual and social lives of human beings. For example, it is at least one thousand years before the word "Hindu" even arrives in existence. That is why every reader must look at them as techniques evolving and getting used on Indian land without looking at them from the prism of Hindu religion.

Let us now look at some important practices of Sanatan traditions:

Basic Yoga Meditation

Basic principle of Dhyana is to focus mind on a body, part, object or concept with the aim of becoming one with it. As an initial ritual, and for every successive session, one has to first try out some yoga and pranayam routine to bring the body and mind to a calm and relaxed state. This golden rule applies even if you have spent decades for your meditation practice. Practising this routine is to silence the senses and achieve a mind ready and willing to focus attention inward. Later, one takes his place on a cushion, mat or chair as the case may be and starts deep breathing to gradually release tension in muscles, starting from toe and going up to crown. Once all the muscles are felt completely relaxed, the practitioner is required to hold his attention on breath. Primary aim for such breathing is to clear the mind of all other thoughts except breathing. Visualising the lungs filling from bottom to top with every inhale and getting emptied out with every exhale is considered an effective way of achieving the said objective.

While undertaking this synchronised breathing, it is quite possible to expect some thoughts emerging on the mental screen. The practitioner just acknowledges such discursive thoughts and lets them go away by slowly pulling his focus back to breathing. After 15-20 completed cycles of such slow and deep breathing, the practitioner invokes an object or image selected to be meditated upon. It can be a deity, symbol, statue, or such other object considered important and worth connecting with for that very session. This selection is best done in advance to avoid doubts and distractions after achieving good mental state. You continue maintaining deep breathing and simultaneously focusing or staring at chosen object until it remains the only thing holding attention to the exclusion of everything else.

The focus on chosen object must be without any attachment or judgement towards its form, feature or quality, lest your attention start enjoying its qualitative aspects. The objective behind holding such non-attached focus is to lose any separation between the practitioner and his object of focus. One is supposed to have mastered the required focus when even the process of observing the object goes away from the thinking process—when you become one with the object without anything emerging in between all through the length of time of your observation. Duration of 15 to 20 minutes of such concentrated focus is considered sufficient for most practitioners. Restraining the mind is a big part of dhyana practice where duration of the practice determines the quality of restrain achieved.

Mantra Meditation

Sound is known to have vibrations, the same vibrations that exist in all our body cells and everything else in Universe. A mantra can be explained as a sacred utterance, a numinous sound, a syllable, word or phonemes, or group of words in Sanskrit believed by practitioners to have sound based psychological and spiritual powers. Speaking technically, all our feelings and thoughts are also vibrations. Actually, our entire psyche is nothing but a collection of patterns vibrating with their own frequency, speed, rhythm and volume. This reality was well realised by ancient Sanatan Yogis who mastered the art of repeating powerful sounds for achieving desired state of consciousness. Much later, some of those sounds got evolved as specific syllables. That is why contemplative traditions under all cultures use the method of regularly repeating different sounds (words) or combinations thereof for regular practice of their belief systems.

Speed and rhythm of sounds indeed have profound effects on our body, mind and emotions. Mantra Meditation makes use of these effects with ultimate objective of calming, decontaminating and finally transforming mind and heart of the practitioner. A Mantra is said to be much stronger than the syllables or words used to compose it; beyond its literal meaning, mantra draws power from the conviction and strong belief of its pronouncer. As a Sanskrit word, mantra combining verbs of '*man*' and '*trai*' which individually mean 'mind' and 'tool' respectively but collectively come to denote the 'equipment capable of regulating mind', the basic effort of all meditation techniques in general. Mantra by itself is a complex but complete subject of study by itself and frequently used within all religious shades emanating from Indian soil including all their offsprings and variants.

In the Mantra Meditation the practitioner can choose a mantra for himself depending on what he is looking for in life. While choosing a mantra, you should consider your inner motivations for practising meditation. Many people may be more fortunate to have access to their Gurus who are known to gift appropriate mantra to their disciples considering all factors important for right selection. There being no restriction on the length, the mantra can consist of just a single word but generally every mantra is a combination of couple of words. Since the mantra ultimately becomes the anchor for entire meditation practice, it ought to be selected with abundant caution, should be mastered well with its meaning fully imbibed, with all its issues relating to punctuations, speed, volume, impact, pronunciation, etc., fully mastered. The mantra aids in concentration and has to be repeated over and over again in each sitting with the aim to rotate entire consciousness around. Mantra's sound also need be amplified to optimum levels for maximising the effects.

Every word of the mantra has to be pronounced with right emphasis on each syllable and the meaning of each word has to be fully sucked up each time the mantra is recited. Unclear pronunciation, or pronunciation without realising the real meaning with full impact, will degrade the practice to mechanical repetition with loss of benefit on every count. Besides real meaning, the practitioner's firm conviction for the mantra is of paramount importance. Correct intonation of the selected mantra is equally critical to generate right energy. Mantra represents a strong philosophy and each time we repeat it, we must repeat our resolve and conviction in that philosophy. Rightly developed Mantra is like access control 'password', which is biometrically authenticated and hypersensitive to sound, providing all critical admittance to desired state of consciousness. Hence, it needs to be applied correctly else the access stand denied.

Practising mantra meditation requires perfect synchronisation of speed and decibels with breathing, which in turn is linked to state of mind at that given moment. For example, when your mind is clustered or agitated, mantra is better advised to be repeated in faster speed with higher decibels. Later when your mind regains its peace back, voice level can be lowered along with slowing your pace. And it is not difficult to understand why as you will not be able to repeat your mantra for innumerable times unless it matches with your natural rhythm. So, just remember to go with the flow. At a later stage you should be able to repeat the mantra only in your mind without any voice. Over and over repetition helps you to completely disconnect with your thoughts and finally enable you to even peep in the gap arising in between your thoughts. But that is quite an advance stage and will be realised with far greater efforts and combined progress on so many other subjects explained throughout this book.

The most popular mantra is undoubtedly the Gayatri mantra:

> "Om bhur bhuvah swah
> Tat savitur varenyam
> Bhargo devasya dhimahi
> Dhiyo yo nah prachodayat."

Originating from Rig Veda, the Bhagwad Gita also describes it as a Divine mantra. It is a hymn dedicated to Savitur, the Sun God who is credited for flourishing of all beings as well as non-beings. The mantra begins with an offering of gratitude to the all powerful Sun God and ends with seeking blessings to augment intellect, intelligence or reasoning/discriminating faculty as a tool for attaining higher wisdom and enlightenment. It is because of these virtues that this mantra has remained in use all through the Vedic traditions spanning over 5000 years of recorded history. This mantra also happens to be the most often used mantra for Jap as well.

Let us now look at some other favoured mantras in both Hindu and Buddhist traditions. 'AUM' or 'OM' is the obvious pick being an extremely repeated word ever since Upanishadic times. Invariably all prayers start with this powerful word and its use in meditation is no different. To its credit, this unique combination of three distinct syllables creates a profound sound and vibration which is just not repeatable by any other combination of sounds.

The four 'mahavakyas' from the Upanishads namely, 'Prajnanam Brahma', 'Aham Brahma Asmi', 'Tat Tvam Asi' and 'Ayam Atma Brahma' are next in line of selection by meditators since ancient times. In recent times, the most popular mantra used by a majority of Hindus (and in Hindi language) goes as under:

> "Hare Ram Hare Ram, Ram Ram Hare Hare
> Hare Krishn Hare Krishn, Krishn Krishn Hare Hare"

The practitioner is expected to recite his chosen mantra for a certain period of time, or for a set number of "repetitions" like 108 or 1008. As the practice deepens, the practitioner is expected to feel the mantra continuing "by itself" like the humming of the mind. In fact, mantra can be repeated in between doing any other work at any time of the day to fill the empty time as and when few minutes are available. Few times here and few more times there also help practitioner accumulate his power of mantra and such recitations also protect against injurious habits that an empty mind is likely to pick during such free times. Mantra also does wonders to guard you against attacks of negative emotions. All you need to develop is to switch your mind to your mantra as soon as you come across any less likeable scenarios of daily life. Thus, mantra is much more than just a tool for practising meditation.

Mantra meditation is especially useful for beginners who find focusing on breath comparatively difficult. Every mantra is a combination of words and words engage our thought process more effectively and easily as compared to abstract approach of focusing just on breathing. Mantra repetition demands constant attention of the mind and it is less likely to chase after other thoughts while busy with reciting mantra.

Transcendental Meditation (TM)

Essentially an extension of Mantra meditation, TM is a silent mantra meditation technique which is reported to be most widely practised. It is also among the most researched meditation technique. It is credited to Maharishi Mahesh Yogi (1918-2008) who first started teaching this practice in India during mid fifties. Derived from ancient Vedic traditions, this technique got a big boost during world tours by Mahesh Yogi in the decade beginning 1960. The Maharishi continuously worked on his technique and included even technical presentations to especially attract people from business and students community. Around 1970, TM further got a big boost in popularity when many celebrities adopted this with big benefits. Around this very time the Maharishi started training teachers and created specialised organisation to manage spread of TM as an established meditation technique. From its beginning until now TM had been taught to millions of people and continues to remain popular even today,

Supporters of TM claim that this practice results in ordinary thinking process 'transcended' and replaced by a state of pure consciousness. While in that state, the practitioner achieves perfect stillness, rest, stability and order. Hundreds of scientific studies have already been conducted on TM and their conclusions clearly suggest that regular practice of TM leads to verifiable reduction in chronic pain, anxiety, high blood pressure and cholesterol.

TM is taught by certified teachers under a seven step course. The course starts with an hour-long general presentation where the aspirant is presented with normal understanding of meditation in general and TM in particular. This is followed by a personal interview and more specific hour-long instruction about how to undertake the practice. The mantra is always given by the teacher to the practitioner and is to be kept secret. It is said that the teachers consider individual orientation of the person and other relevant factors, such as age, education and gender, before entrusting the mantra. The actual practice is advised twice everyday in sessions of about 15-20 minutes where, the secret mantra is to be repeated in silence. First session is recommended before taking breakfast and second session before taking dinner. The seating, posture and all other hygiene factors are similar to other techniques already discussed.

Kundalini Meditation

Kundalini is supposed to be a bundle of latent energy lying dormant in the shape of a coiled serpent located at the base of spine. The practice of awakening that dormant power is called Tantra, a separate branch of Yoga that is no more as popular. Tantra is based on the assumption that Fabric of human life is made of several layers of Nadis, subtle currents continuously flowing energies through the body. There are three principal Nadis in the body going through the spinal cord and the chakras: the energy centres of the body. Asanas, Pranayam, and chanting are said to be the most common ways to move prana around the body via these Nadis. These currents are weaved and re-weaved in an integrated manner is the conceptual belief in tantric traditions. It suggests that accumulated dormant potential can be awakened by a difficult process involving opening of each of the seven Chakras. Those Chakras are said to be located at specific places within our upper body starting from the spinal base going all the way up to the crown in the skull. Tantra demands that as human beings it is our obligation to access the broadest range of powers and privileges bestowed upon us and use them with great responsibility.

According to Tantra school, the natural life forces that pervade through the universe are assimilated through our Chakras, the psychic centres. Chakra is said to be a point where consciousness intersects with flow of energy. It is estimated that normal human body has over fifty different places of Chakras but awakening of Kundalini involves only significant seven Chakras out of which five are located all across the centre of spine and remaining two in the brain area. The Chakras are generally depicted as little wheels of energy holding our invisible energy fields together.

In addition, as per ancient Indian texts, there are 72000 Nadis interconnecting through ethers within and around our physical bodies. The subtle body around our physical bodies is called the aura. All the Nadis work similar to physical bodies running through our nervous system. There are three most important Nadis named as Shushumna, Ida and Pingala. Shushumna is like body's great river flowing from the base of the spine to the crown of the head. The ida and pingala nadis spiral around the sushumna nadi like the double helix of our DNA, crossing each other at every Chakra. As per Kundalini system, exercising around seven specific psychic centres goes a long way in bringing regulation within our physical bodies.

Kundalini Meditation aims at awakening each of the said seven Chakras, and thereby achieving enlightenment. Awakening of Kundalini is said to be an effective system of cleansing entire body and mind combine for getting rid of all tensions, stresses, garbage accumulated within the subconscious system due to all types of emotional and psychological processes going on and on in normal human life. But, as a general disclaimer, the entire concept of Tantra, Kundalini and Chakras is full of scientifically unproven assumptions and working around these involves great amount of belief, discipline and efforts which is an independent subject matter.

However, Kundalini Yoga is neither about invoking some sort of magic nor following any particular belief system. It is simply a technique driven practice that uses mind, senses and body to establish unique communication within self, body and mind. A kundalini awakening is not so much a physical force, but the movement of the energy of the subtle body. Therefore, one should not attempt the awakening without taking the right steps to open and purify the channels of the subtle body. Even in recent times, one finds many teachers and centres focused entirely on the Tantra branch of Yoga and many people confirm experiencing awakening of their Kundalini.

The practice of Meditation for awakening Kundalini focuses attention on one Chakra at a time starting from the base. The coiled energy at the base is regarded as primal in nature and very powerful in its impact. Awakening of the Kundalini leads to profound conscience and ultimate bliss.

There are several ways suggested for undertaking Kundalini Meditation and all these ways are quite prolonged and slow processes. Each of the practice is required to be attempted very responsibly as well as holistically. Special mention is required to ensure that practitioner's mind, body and emotional status must be matured enough to deal with flow of powers through the body. Due to this reason, all practices around Kundalini and Chakras are required to be undertaken under the close supervision of specially trained and accomplished teachers and that too only after ensuring that the practitioner has gone through certain degree of proficiency in the concepts and rituals associated with Tantra Yoga. If you are not rightly prepared, a kundalini awakening might cause a big commotion that can feel very disturbing and may even cause a breakdown. That is why practising this technique is always recommended with abundant cautions.

According to Dr. David Frawley, "The awakening of kundalini requires that prana or life force entre into the sushumna or central channel. This occurs when the prana is withdrawn from its fixation through the thought process on the external world." In order to open sushumna nadi, one can practice alternate nostril breathing along with a number of yoga and tantra practices of focus, breath, and movement.

Most recommended Kundalini Meditation practice requires attention focus on three major Chakras located at Heart, Third eye and Crown locations. While undertaking meditation sessions, the practitioner must focus and redirect his attention to the selected centre as a means of silencing the thought process with the aim of enlarging gaps, in between alternate thoughts, as long as possible. All this while, carefully selected Mantras may also be chanted regularly as an additional aid for achieving undisturbed attention. Most prominent of all the Chakras is the Third Eye Chakra located in between the eyebrows. With Sanskrit name Ajna, as per yogic metaphysics this Chakra is the centre where one transcends duality, where I-consciousness is absorbed into super-consciousness. In psychological and behavioural characteristics, this Chakra navigates vision, intuition, perception, access to mystical states and connection with wisdom. Third eye chakra works as an instrument to process the more subtle qualities of reality. Its awakening directly opens up to an intuitive sensibility and inner perception and thereby guides entire process of spiritual growth.

Yoga Meditation

Indian tradition of Yoga is the world's oldest tradition and is well documented ever since 1700 B.C. as also the most widely practised across the world in endless variations built upon a single solid basic block. So Yoga meditation works as a broad umbrella covering multiple meditations within its aegis. As we know, Yoga means union and its ultimate goal is spiritual purification to achieve perfect and complete Self-knowledge. Its initial practice involves strictly following rules of moral conduct, mastering physical postures, and regular practice of Pranayam (breath control). These limbs are followed by contemplative practices consisting of pratyahara, dharana, dhyana to ultimately reach for Samadhi. It may be added that Pranayam is an excellent practice to calm the mind and prepare it for meditation besides having multiple physical benefits.

Yoga emphasises that basic preparations over morality, personal conduct, stilling the body with the help of routines of postures etc., lead the mind becoming receptive for self regulation and willing to focus attention on desired sound, word, organ, chakra, thought or such other object of choice. As such, these underlying principles equally apply to all practices explained hereunder. Similarly, all practices under Yoga Meditation never aim to stop the mind or make it go blank. It is because Yoga philosophy believes that effort to stop the mental activity or to forcefully bring it under regulation is a battle lost even before starting. Yoga believes that such efforts result only in endless frustrations.

Let us briefly discuss some such Yoga based techniques practised in brief:

Visual Meditation

Also known as Subjective Visual Meditation, this practice requires your focus on a visual image inside your mind. Most of us directly believe in physical power but have doubts about mental powers. But visual cues are undoubtedly better for learning as compared to auditory or kinesthetic cues. Visuals are best suited for harnessing the energy of our imaginative powers and that is why imagery is considered most fundamental language. Yoga also suggests mental power to be more potent if applied properly. Visual meditation is the technique that uses this great power of human imagination to bring about desired results in physical forms. Basically the formulae used here are the same that some people call as power of positive thinking. Imagination or inner visualisation is sometimes taken as a gift for select few individuals but visual meditation technique reinforces that visualisation is purely a attribute totally open for cultivation and perfection by everybody with determined efforts and patience.

Proven with scientific studies in recent past, imagery and visualisation is found effective for alleviating stress, physical pains, anxieties and such other tensions. That is why visualisation, in addition to meditation, is also considered as a healing therapy. Visual meditation works on the basic fundamental point that human minds comprehend every idea first in the shape of an image and, based on such image alone, directs various body organs to translate that into actual physical form. This can also be corroborated with individual experience that constant presence of a negative image about a person or event often end up damaging our peace of mind and induces our interaction with such person with certain bent of caution and negativity.

Sitting posture and all other cautions desired for other meditation practices apply equally to this practice as well. After reaching a certain degree of calmness in the mind, the practitioner is expected to imagine a broad image of a likeable landscape. Once the basic image takes a good shape, you are required to increase your imagination over finer details of the landscape to make the image more realistic. Experience of other practitioners suggest that calming scenery of a natural setting having running water stream or a sandy beach with gentle waves or setting around a calm lake provide desired results. After achieving clarity of the finer details of the image, you should also imagine about likeable sounds (like running water or chirping of birds) to achieve higher concentration. Later you may also add the feel of smell and touch to complete your imagination for all senses.

All this is done with eyes closed as open eyes take notice of tangible objects in front which will inevitably work as unwanted distraction. Later, once your imagination completes the picture in all aspects, you are required to narrow your focus back on a single specific detail out of the big picture. Let it be a small part of the big image so that your vision is able to grasp its details completely without losing its minor details. It is similar to concentration on a physical object with a magnifying glass. For example, out of your big image, you may select only a stone or a leaf or a flower or even a stem of the tree. The attention on those finest details should be sustained as long as possible to harness imaginative energy that equally applies in all spheres of normal life.

Harnessing of imaginative energy of mind is achieved by evolving positivity and influencing the body to act accordingly. While undertaking this meditation, the practitioner assumes that everything around is positive and conducive, the environment is facilitative, people around are all loving and caring. This constant imaginary, over long periods, results in complete absence of negative tendencies from thoughts and actions of the practitioner. All through this meditation, special attention remains on deep breathing which works both as a relaxation tool and a technique keeping the mind stable and receptive for positivity. For example, seeing yourself as completely healthy person in your own thoughts or visualising the image of a healthy person, helps your mind to send strong signals to body to understand the desire and work towards it.

Kriya Meditation

According to Paramahansa Yogananda, the most vocal proponent of Kriya Yoga, it is a simple psychological method by which human blood is de-carbonated and recharged with oxygen. The atoms of this extra oxygen are transmuted into life current to rejuvenate the brain and spinal centres, The Yogi further added that by stopping the accumulation of venous blood, the practitioner is able to lessen or prevent the decay of tissues. In his autobiography, Yogananda calls Kriya technique as the revival of the same science that Krishna imparted to Arjuna millenniums ago. The Yogi quotes his guru and writes;

> "Kriya Yoga is an instrument through which human evolution can be quickened. The ancient yogis discovered that the

> secret of cosmic consciousness is intimately linked with breath mastery. This is India's unique and deathless contribution to the world's treasury of knowledge. The life force, which is ordinarily absorbed in maintaining heart action, must be freed for higher activities by a method of calming and stilling the ceaseless demands of the breath."

Yogananda also laid out a well defined and well explained process of practising Kriya Yoga stating that the practitioner has to direct life energy to revolve upward and downward, around six spinal centres. One-half minute of revolution of energy around the sensitive spinal cord of a person aids subtle progress in his evolution. He mentions that for people living normal materialistic life, the flow of energy is towards the outward world resulting in the wasting of currents on senses. According to Yogi, the Kriya practice reverses that very flow and guides the life force to the inner cosmos, reuniting the same with subtle spinal energies.

In a major deviation over most recommended meditation efforts of sitting in silence in an attempt to hold normal introspection, Paramahansa Yogananda boldly called such efforts unscientific way of trying to force the mind and senses that are firmly tied together by the life force. He maintained that an untrained normal contemplative mind will constantly get dragged back towards the attractions of senses no matter what quality and quantum of attempts made for directing such a mind towards divinity. According to him, Kriya Yoga, the art of controlling the mind directly with the help of life force, is the easiest and most effective and scientific approach to the infinity.

Kriya Yoga is an advanced level practice which requires a whole lot of ground preparation before making desired progress. The objective of this effort, here in this book, is to generate interest in the minds of readers to revisit this practice once significant progress is achieved in their meditative journey. The authority to bestow Kriya Yoga instructions and initiation on eligible students lies with Yogoda Satsang Society formed by respected Paramahansa Yogananda himself. He also provided for the perpetual dissemination of the Kriya Yoga science through Yogoda Satsang Lessons available from Yogoda Satsang Society of India. Interested seekers are advised to directly get in touch with the said institution for further inquiries.

Sound Meditation

Different types of sounds and their synchronised variations are the basis of everything musical and have been used in entertainment, expressions, celebrations, ceremonies, leisure and communication in general all through the evolution of human civilisation. It is simply because sounds are known to have direct influence over our emotions, psychology, spirituality, devotion, physical condition, social interactions as well as over mental states and such influence can be positive or negative alike. Scientific studies carried out in recent past prove impact of sounds conclusively establishing proven correlation with responses and signals sent to various body parts and systems.

Sounds convert into electrical signals that travel into auditory cortex and thereby alert emotions by releasing hormones and chemicals that affect body and moods. In India, many musical instruments have been used to create special sounds which go to help advance spiritual advancements besides providing immediate relaxation to mind and body combine. Out of traditional Indian music instruments associated with creating specially likable sound for sustaining effective meditation practice, special mention need to be made for Tanpura, Flute, Sitar, Sarangi and Tabla.

Sounds are also used for healing patients of certain backgrounds for effectively helping them recover from illness or reducing their pains. Use of such qualities of sounds aimed at focusing attention inward is called Sound Meditation. The sounds can originate from any musical instrument like drums, gongs, bowls, chimes, whistle or any other physical objects in solo or from multiple arrangements made by using a symphony. Sound can also originate purely from a natural activity like flowing of a river, a water fall, or chirping of birds, etc. The idea is to recede down internal chatter by absorbing in external likable sounds. This objective can be achieved even by adopting concept of DIY for chanting, singing or loudly reciting a mantra, song or poem of choice. In its final analysis, and without losing focus on desired outcomes, the practice is open even for silent recitations.

The technique of sound meditation requires the practitioner to listen each and every note of the sound with full attention. This helps in suspending usual fly away desire of the mind by positively engaging it on the sounds. Sounds motivate the mind to attentively listen and absorb sounds with complete willingness. For this meditation technique, the impact of sound is as critical and significant as the impact of mantra explained earlier.

Sound Meditation necessitates a likable sound in sync with practitioner's breathing to ensure practice to continue for longer duration. Tonality or notes synchronisation, otherwise so important for producing music, are not relevant for sound meditation at all. Objective here is not to create music with better arrangement but to engage the thought process and letting it stay focused on object of choice. So, the practitioner need not worry about pitch, tone or notes of the sound as any focus on such qualitative issues is bound to make the practitioner self-conscious and thereby making ego separation that much more difficult.

Staring Meditation

The Sanskrit name of this meditation is 'Trataka' which means 'to gaze' or 'to look with intent'. This practice is very similar to other practices aimed at one pointed focus. This practice involves staring at a single point of a small object, like tip of a statue, or an incense stick or flame of a candle. The object can even be simply a black dot on a white wall, one's own nose point, the image of some deity or some such symbol within immediate vicinity. People with sustained practice also suggest use of third eye position as a preferred object. The object of focus need not be only external, it can very well be some internal image visualised in the mind. The practitioner may also fix attention on a symbol considered significant, such as the Om symbol, Swastika, Linga, Lotus or Chakra, and stare at it. At the very advance level, in fact, the object can be anywhere in the space. Intentional focus of your stare on a chosen object or image is supposed to bring energy and promote various psychic abilities.

Staring meditation accentuates highly desirable combination of two critical mental states, the power of concentration and stilling of the mind. In due course of practice, the gaze gets stronger and stronger such that everything other than the object of choice gets blacked out. It is in this situation that mind gets completely isolated from things existing or active in the surroundings. Once the practitioner reaches this stage, benefits like enhanced intuition, reduced distractions, and increased energy starts accruing in visible manners.

An eager reader may have a genuine curiosity about sight being chosen for meditation instead of other senses. Well, sight is arguably most powerful sense that we possess. For touching and tasting, you need to hold the object in close proximity and still you cannot continue having ongoing experience. Sound, on the other hand, has much wider range and variations. But variations generate their respective excitations which are worth avoiding for success in meditation. Eyes, especially internal eyes, however, can visualise an object situated at distance of miles apart. Human eye's capability is estimated to be equal to a 576 megapixel camera. Human eyes can easily establish a difference from among thousands of colour shades. The feedback from eyes to mind also is faster than optical fiber cable ever invented by man. No wonder, around eighty per cent of data processed by human mind is obtained through eyes alone.

The basic approach of Visual meditation technique requires focus on a central point where vision gets concentrated to the exclusion of everything around. Even when a candle flame gets chosen, the practitioner fixes his gaze in the centre of the flame such that normal flickering on the outer side continues as usual without hampering his concentration. Every object chosen should be placed at a suitable height and distance so as to facilitate proper gazing. This is to ensure relaxed posture while spine remaining erect at all times.

As an alternate to external object, one may as well decide to use internal imagination to evolve an image of choice and fix gaze on that image with eyes closed. At this point, this practice will get merged with earlier explained Visual meditation. Internal image may actually work out better as it gives the flexibility of choosing an object without restriction on its time horizon, distance restriction, living or dead, and size limitations since imagination can suitably accommodate or resize any object to bring it within gazing. Many people report use of moon, image of a soul, deity of choice, trident, etc. as the object of their internal visual object with positive results. The philosophy behind gaze meditation is again to become one with the object. But internal gazing requires mastery of certain level, hence, is more suited for practitioners in their advance stage of practice. Normally, people begin with external object and later graduate to focus on internal objects.

Just to help the beginners, set your gaze on the object and continue gazing without blinking the eyes as long as possible. Once your eyes get tired and start tears, close your eyes and continue your focus on afterimage of the same object with closed eyes. As and when you start losing clarity during internal gaze, open your eyes and focus on the actual object once again. This entire period shall be counted as one cycle. In the beginning of your practice, you need not worry about the actual time spent per cycle because eventually with practice it will improve for sure. For those interested in specific time, with good progress, people report achieving a timing up to five minutes per cycle. It is just that beginners will require larger number of cycles to achieve the desired duration of their daily practice.

Let us now briefly touch upon some of the precautions required to ensure effective Staring practice. To begin with, one should not hurt the eyes. There is no point in continuing gazing even when the image is already blurred. Secondly, to ensure that your focus quality is not compromised, prepare a darker background for fixing gaze on a lighted candle or lamp. Thirdly, let your gaze be somewhat investigating, as if you are trying to find something that you do not know already. Without this investigative attitude you might lose interest in continuing your gaze for longer durations. Remember that our mind does not like doing something already known.

Self-Inquiry Meditation

The simple sounding question of "Who am I?" remains within us in a latent state and requires tons of work on the journey of spiritual advancement before letting us make a fruitful meaning of our very own divine existence. This power of recognising our very existence remains buried deep down under the mountain full of materialistic and egoistic overburden which needs to be removed layer by layer before we get a peep into it. *Kleshas* and *Vasanas*, or toxic desires and responses, in the form of familiar stories, emotions, self-images, beliefs, and reactive patterns keep us tied with our ego-based personality as a big curtain hiding the actual content. These known tendencies continue to keep covering our essential nature under thick layers of ignorance which need to be peeled off before accessing our shiny sun, the timeless, silent, ever-present place of being. This very existence is called Self by Vedanta and True Nature by Zen Masters.

The practice of Self-inquiry propagated by one of the most acclaimed Indian sages of modern times, Sri Ramana Maharshi (1879-

1950), is recommended only for the matured practitioners. Like in most other meditation practices, the mind flying from one thought to another in an endless manner needs to be brought back and focused on our contemplative being. Under Self-inquiry, however, the mind is required to rest on Self, the feeling of 'I'. In a way, this practice focuses on awareness of the awareness itself such that we are able to cross over the forces of duality. Success of this method is said to have been achieved when the object of meditation (the 'I') ultimately gets revealed as the subject (the Transpersonal Consciousness) itself.

In this simple but powerful method, the practitioner is expected to convert his gaze into a laser beam turned inward for illuminating the path of self-inquiry permeating right through pure consciousness. Many of the meditative practices explained before this practice succeed only in relaxing the body and calming the mind and years go by to master even those practices. But at the advance stage of practice, the practitioner invariably comes face to face with one of the ancient question baffling intellectuals of all times "who am I?", a question that calls for very relaxed receptivity and a deep sense of inquiry requiring even deeper inner penetration before coming across secrets lying hidden deep inside our own self.

Simple meditative techniques aim at multiple objectives but do not really help us in turning our light inward to connect with our real and true nature. If we were, once again, to take our mind as a pool of muddy waters, those techniques do help us to calm the pool of the mind and allow the sediment to settle, but they do not suffice to take us to the bottom where the treasure of truth resides. It was for this very purpose that the great 20th-century Advaita sage propagates an ancient path called "Atma Vichara", self inquiry. Wikipedia page on the subject defines Self-enquiry as ".... is the constant attention to the inner awareness of 'I' or 'I am' recommended by Ramana Maharshi as the most efficient and direct way of discovering the unreality of the 'I'-thought."

Let us also see the reply of Ramana Maharshi himself to the question of 'What is the method of (this) practice':

> "As the Self of a person who tries to attain Self-realization is not different from him and as there is nothing other than or superior to him to be attained by him, Self-realization

> being only the realization of one's own nature, the seeker of Liberation realises, without doubts or misconceptions, his real nature by distinguishing the eternal from the transient, and never swerves from his natural state. This is known as the practice of knowledge. This is the inquiry leading to Self-realization." (page no. 19 of the book titled "The Spiritual Teaching of Ramana Maharshi", Foreword by C.G. Jung.)

For sure, this method is appealing only to spiritually adventurous practitioners with years of practice behind them as underlying fundamental question does not usually bother normal beings. The names of people engulfed by this question in human history are countable few but it does not mean others cannot have the potential to catch a life-altering glimpse of the radiant sun of true nature. In fact, only such glimpses have the potential to free us from suffering once and for all.

As per Stephan Bodian, a psychotherapist, teacher and an internationally known author of many known books on the subject including "Beyond Mindfulness—The Direct Approach to Lasting Peace, Happiness and Love", the twin practices of abiding (or resting) and inquiring work together like the left and right foot in walking. First, we rest in the calmness and clarity of our basic sitting practice, whatever it may be. Then, when the waters are relatively still, we inquire, and the inquiry may reveal a new level of insight into the silence and stillness of our essential nature that allows us to rest even more deeply. And from this deeper resting, we have the capacity to inquire even further."

Explanation of this practice may sound abstract but actually it is very subtle yet simple practice. This can be realised by following the explanation by Stephan Bodian. To begin the practice of self-inquiry, he advises to sit for meditation as usual. If you do not already have a regular practice, just sit quietly and allow the mind to settle naturally. Do not attempt to focus your mind or manipulate your experience, just rest as awareness itself. After 10 or 15 minutes, when the mind is relatively open and present, introduce the question "Who am I?" The point of this question is not to engage the mind, because the mind inevitably gnaws on questions endlessly like a dog on a bone, with little nutritional benefit. Instead, drop the question into the stillness of your being like a pebble into a still pond. Let it send ripples through your meditation, but do not attempt to figure it out. When the pond is tranquil again, drop in another pebble and see what happens. As you continue your self-inquiry, you may notice that the question begins to permeate your consciousness and soon you may find yourself asking it not only during meditation but at unexpected times throughout the day.

Instead of "Who am I?" you may prefer asking, "Who is thinking this thought?" or "Who is seeing through these eyes right now?" Such questions direct your awareness inward, away from the external world and toward the source from which all experiences arise. Indeed, anything you can perceive, no matter how intimate—including the cluster of images, memories, feelings, and beliefs you take to be you, in reality, is merely an object of perception. But who is this entity experiencing everything? Who is the real perceiver? Who is the ultimate subject of all of those objects? These are very real questions at the heart of "Who am I".

For the practice of self-inquiry to work its magic, you must already recognise at some level that the word "I", though superficially referring to the body and mind, actually points to something much deeper. When we say, "I feel," "I see," or "I walk," we are talking about the person experiencing, the doer we imagine to be inside. But what does this "I" look like, and where is it located? Sure, your mind thinks, feels, and perceives, but do you really believe you reside in the brain? If not, then who are you really? Let your inquiry be earnest but effortless, without tension or anxiety. Here is a hint: You definitely won't find the answer to this question in the file folders of spiritual beliefs you've amassed over the years.

(C) Chinese Meditation Techniques

Confucianism, Buddhism and Taoism in general have long history in China and a unique mix of all these philosophies and thoughts has emerged there over time to become integral part of Chinese cultural landscape. Meditational techniques practised in China also got evolved out of this very mix. While Chinese have been practising meditation from ancient times, spread of specific techniques from China to outside started gaining traction only in last century or so. The basic focus of Chinese techniques is on harmonising the body, the mind, and the breathing until the entire being is in deliberation. Besides this harmony, Chinese techniques seek wisdom by guiding the mind towards a specific direction. As a result, some experts recommend them for students engaged in research work. Let us now look at some specific techniques grouped under this category:

Taoist Meditation

Taoism is a Chinese philosophy that dates back to Lao Tzu. It emphasises living in harmony with Nature. Its main text came into existence as back as 6th century B.C. Later, many lineages of Taoism also got influenced by Buddhist meditation practices travelling from India around the 8th century C.E. The chief characteristic of this technique is generation, transformation, and circulation of inner energy. Making body and mind quiet, unifying body and spirit, finding inner peace, and harmonising with nature are its ultimate purposes. Some styles of Taoist Meditation are specifically focused on improving health and gaining longevity.

Most of these meditations are practised seated cross-legged on the floor, with spine erect. The eyes are kept half-closed and fixed on the point of the nose. People that are more connected with the body and nature may especially find Taoist meditation working for them. Willingness to learn the philosophy behind the practice helps its practitioners even more. However, this technique is practised within China alone as Taoist centres and teachers are not so easily available in outside world.

Qigong (Chi kung)

Qigong is a holistic system of coordinated body postures, body movements, breathing and meditation. It is used with the belief that it promotes health, spirituality, and martial arts training. With roots in Chinese medicine, philosophy, and martial arts, qigong is traditionally viewed as a practice to cultivate and balance qi (chi), meaning "life energy cultivation". It typically involves slow body movements, inner focus, and regulated breathing. Traditionally it was practised and taught in secrecy in the Chinese Buddhist, Taoist and Confucians traditions. In the 20th century, Qigong movement has also incorporated and popularised Taoist meditation together with employing concentrative exercises.

Qigong practice typically involves moving meditation, coordinating slow flowing body movements, deep rhythmic breathing and calm meditative state of mind. It is practised the world over for recreation, exercise, relaxation, preventive medicine, alternative medicine, meditation, self-cultivation and training for martial arts. There are thousands of different Qigong exercises involving varied types of breathing. Some are specific to martial arts while others are for nourishing the body functions or for curing specific ailments. Several other exercises are practised mainly for meditation and spiritual advancements. Some of these movements are conducted in static position (seated or standing) while many others are practised through a dynamic set of movements, the dynamic being more popular.

Qigong meditation may be more attractive to people that like to integrate a more active body and energy work into the practice. If seated meditation is unbearable for you, try some of the more dynamic forms of Qigong. Again, there are several styles of Qigong out there, and you may need to try with different teachers or DVDs to find the one that suits you better.

(D) Christian Meditation

There is a perceptible difference in Christian meditation when compared with traditions associated with Eastern Traditions. While Eastern meditations are practised with the purpose of transcending the mind and attaining enlightenment, the goal of Christian tradition is basically focused on moral purification and deeper understanding of the Bible. Christian contemplation is aimed at establishing an intimate relationship with God/Christ. While Eastern traditions focus on disengaging the mind from ongoing thoughts, memories and desires, Christian meditation aims to fill the mind with thoughts related to Biblical passages or Christian devotions.

Here structured efforts are made to become aware and reflect upon the revelations made by God/Christ. In Christian teachings, meditation is usually believed to involve the inherent action of the Holy Spirit to help the meditating Christian understand the deeper meanings of the Words of God and what those words reveal about Him. David found this to be so, and he describes the man who is "blessed" as one whose "delight is in the law of the LORD, and on his law he meditates day and night" (Psalm 1:2). True Christian meditation is an active thought process whereby one gives himself to the study of the Word, praying over it and asking God to give him understanding by the Spirit, who has promised to lead us "into all truth" (John 16:13). Then we put this truth into practice, committing ourselves to the Scriptures as the rule for life and practice as we go about our daily activities. This causes spiritual growth and maturing in the things of God as we are taught by His Holy Spirit.

(E) Islamic Meditation

Islamic meditation is simply captured in following teachings of Prophet Muhammad who emphasised on gaining good character by engaging in constant practice of prayers, contemplation, remembrance of God and other practices that result in changing the heart of the true Muslim and thereby bringing him closer to Allah. Meditation, thus, is one of the most important aspects of a successful Islamic lifestyle. Every Islam follower goes through recognition and cognisance of the Oneness of God by contemplating and accepting Allah being the only one worthy of worship to the entire exclusion of everybody and everything else. The Prophet was well-known for frequently visiting the caves in Mount Hira for meditation, contemplation and prayer. It was during those meditative sessions that he first received Qur'anic revelation opening the door for entire Islamic tradition.

The practices of Salat and Dhikr may not completely fit in traditional definition of Meditation practice but are perfectly used by followers of Islam in a symbolic way to purify their soul. These practices involve both worship and spiritual advancement besides helping getting rid of stresses and tensions created by pressures of living normal daily lives. Salat is a ritual of praying five times a day. Each session can last anything from five minutes to an hour depending on the time the person wish to pray. The practice involves concentrating mind on God as well as afterlife. This ritual starts with standing posture and involves bending, bowing and finally full prostration. During Salat, a Muslim is supposed to concentrate and meditate on God through reciting Qur'an. This meditative contemplation opens and strengthens a connection between God and the human being. That connection helps the person to be guided to Truth and maintain internal peace despite all of life's distractions and challenges. In fact, a sincere and well-practised follower of Islam continues his meditation even while in sleep.

Meditation in Islam combines spiritual benefit with worldly benefit and is taken as a means for healing and finding creative solutions to life problems. One form of meditation is called Tafakkur and refers to reflection upon the universe or pondering the creation of Allah. It is a means of intellectual development that awakens and liberates the mind to help it achieve higher levels of growth. Contemplation is always a form of meditation and many Muslim contemplate by reading few lines of Qur'an or an Islamic book and reflecting on it.

Sensating is yet another method of Islamic meditation. This is a developmental practice to help one find focus and presence of mind and help eliminate distracting thoughts, anxiety, and stress. It is done by sitting erect with eyes closed at the edge of a seat, feet on the ground, and focusing on just being aware of every sensation: the way each part of the body feels, searching out tension in any body part and relaxing it, noting thoughts that come and go while not following any of them, being aware of sounds, feeling of clothes against the skin, feeling of the rise and fall of breath, feeling of the eyes in their sockets, etc. Engaging in sensation meditative practices for a few minutes can help in performing Salat with increased concentration, making its spiritual experience even more rewarding.

Special mention is required for the philosophy of meditation practised by a mystical tradition within Islam, called Sufi. This tradition came into being in the Middle East in the eighth century, though some people authoritatively claim Sufism predating Islam. The chief aim of the Sufi tradition is to release the ideal of duality, embracing and understanding the universe as one unified part, and this is where a strong practice of meditation comes into play. The mystery of Sufism is to shift the center of life from personal to the Divine. It believes that the lost knowledge of the Universe continue to reside within our consciousness and needs to be retrieved expanding our consciousness through meditation, prayer, and glorification of Allah. The goal in Sufi meditation is to reconnect our personal self to the transpersonal dimensions of our being.

Popularly known as Dhikr, the Sufi tradition revolves around remembrance of God and often consists of the repetition of God's name. It can be silent or vocal, private or in group. The practice is sometimes done in conjunction with breathing exercises and at times with uncontrolled movements designed to disrupt normal consciousness.

(F) Guided Meditations

This hectic pace of life due to juggling of career, finances, family and personal priorities, undoubtedly results in volumes of stress and anxieties. Under such situation, finding time and energy for pursuing any meditative practice is a tall order. It is a reality that modern day situation offers many more attractions and distractions in comparison to people from earlier generations. Today one prefers going for ready to use options in most things like eating, reading, entertainment, sports or even social interactions. Meditation is also part of what people are and, hence, expecting them to have entirely different approach for meditation (following traditional techniques alone) is rather impractical, at least to begin with. That is where Guided Meditations are gaining increasing popularity across the globe. Guided meditation is the ready to serve, packed for delivery, and consumed on the go versions for the fast and furious. By some estimate, majority of new aspirants are making use of one or the other guided system for their spiritual requirements.

What is a guided meditation? Well, it is a process by which one or more participants meditate by following guidance provided by a trained teacher or guide. The guidance may be in form of supervision in person, under a classroom setting, via written text, through CD/DVD/MP3 (audio video supports) or a combination of all such options. Guides are also seen using suitable music or environmental sounds or imagery or some such exotic aids to attract larger following. Such guidance is at times available for free in public domain but most of it is by payment and like every other business, the providers (teachers, preachers and guides) come up with some attractive, appealing factors in order to attract their clients with a profit-making perspective. In most cases you listen step by step instruction while the guide leads you to a series of levels starting with relaxation of body parts, getting a still mind, emptying your thought process and finally achieving concentration and focus with clarity.

Guided meditation actually works very well for beginners who can make quick progress in lesser time. Traditional meditation practices need a lot of personal preparation and continued efforts in terms of dealing with moral readiness and sorting out philosophical issues. Whereas guided meditations could be started virtually without any preparation except, maybe, a money transfer. Guided meditation also helps in situations where the person finds it tough to let go of thoughts in spite of making efforts over longer periods. It also helps at times when you are, somehow, low on personal motivation to continue practice of your own and need a push to make a beginning under duress. It may also be effective when you have tried, but got lost on the way or when you hit a dead end. People also go for it when they wish to seek some specific benefit – like improving self-esteem, working through a trauma, or just letting go of some tension in body.

If pursuing meditation of your own is similar to arranging a visit to new country, opting for guided meditation is like joining a conducted tour offered by a travel agency offering their rep to accompany the group to ensure smooth travel, lodging, boarding and sightseeing included. Guided meditation, for sure, will cost more money but it ends up freeing your valuable time. It can be hassle free, especially when you are just starting your meditative journey and are riddled with many unknown questions. Another good example may be to call guided meditation like learning to cook with the help of a recipe from an established chef. In due course, you will, in any case, start cooking yourself and enjoy your food even when your own cooking may have different combination of spices and ingredients.

Does it work better? Well the presence of an experienced guide may make it easy for your subconscious to get ready to receive positive suggestions. People with self experiences may vouch the volume of efforts required to reach this very critical stage. Experience of a trained guide may also save you from experimenting with various techniques in a non-sequential manner and that will certainly avoid some detours. Furthermore, the trained guide leads you to navigate through obstacles like personal empowerment, positive thinking, and work life balancing. In the beginning of guided process itself, the practitioner is also helped to secure emotional healing. So, yes there are some obvious pros out here.

Side by side, guided meditation practices also suffer from many obvious cons. To begin with, continuous guidance kills practitioner's self-initiative. Human mind is lazy and works better when it is self-inspired and not instructed or supervised. Guided meditation goes against this principle through and through. Because of auto pilot nature of guided procedure, the mind is bound to get disinterested. Guided initiatives also go against the ongoing tussle of the wandering nature of the mind. Ongoing guidance expects the mind to follow instructions given. This makes the mind continue its wandering because it is very good in creating defence to protect its ego imagery by evaluating new instructions with what it already knows. Guidance also involves unavoidable repetitions which ultimately lead to stagnation.

One may suggest switching from one guidance source to another but that is bound to open another can of worms with comparisons and evaluations of process, simplicity and effectiveness. Ultimately, the regular meditator has no option but to become an independent practitioner.

Conclusions

For sure, there are plenty of techniques with countless variants with each offering something unique of its own. But in order to get most optimum results, selection of particular technique at specific time of practice must remain an open option for experimenting available alternatives intermittently. One should be open and willing to changeover or mix and match as much as workable and effective. However, irrespective of the stage of practice or personal belief system or psychological orientation of the practitioner, there are always some golden rules to help in selection of the right technique at each stage.

First of all, a practice must be practical to adopt. Best of best technique is completely useless if one is not able to practise it with ease. Secondly, the practice should invoke serious engagement. It should be able to involve practitioner completely; else that inward focus of attention will remain a pipe dream. Thirdly, it should be challenging enough to bring out the best; else the mind loses interest and goes back to wondering, its option of choice. And above all, the practice should be enjoyable. If a practice feels burden, it is impossible to practise it daily. If it is enjoyable, the practitioner looks forward eagerly to get extra time on the mat.

Those familiar with the game of golf can easily relate the technique selection with the selection of club at each stage of the game. Golf is basically about 18 different holes of varying length, terrain and obstacles created at intermittent positions. The golfer carries a bag full of clubs where each stick has its own angle and height. The whole game is to hit the ball from the tee to the hole where the choice of club selection is always with the player. Different players are seen using different clubs as their go to options to deal with peculiar situations. At the end of the game, nobody cares which particular stick got used. The winner is based on the count of total number of shots taken.

Meditation techniques are just like a bag full of golf sticks. There are many to choose from, each little bit different from other. Every player develops his own preference and expertise. Because club selection is only one of the multiple factors, every single stick used under identical situation yields different result for different people or same person using that very stick at different point of time. Each has something unique to offer and selection is critical for moving forward at desired count. But that very selection does not matter at the end.

Reaching your spiritual advancement is like that very final hole where time taken to reach is all that matters. Every golfer is tirelessly busy in improving his handicap and spends a lot of time practising in the driving range, sand bunkers or on the greens besides developing wisdom to take into account factors like wind speed, wind direction, moisture in the ground, dryness in the soil, layout of the course, quality of grass on the ground and what not, before selecting the club to be used and power to be applied in the shot. Goal of every meditation practitioner is no different as he also has to identify his own spots to improve and practise hard on multiple fronts, be it fighting distractions, safeguarding against lethargy, focusing attention, gaining concentration or lengthening duration of mindfulness. Most of the elements impacting final score in a game of golf, most challenges faced on way to making progress in meditation also personal in nature and internal in character.

16

Mindfulness Meditation as most Recommended Practice

"Mindfulness is the aware, balanced acceptance of the present experience. It isn't more complicated than that. It is opening to or receiving the present moment, pleasant or unpleasant, just as it is, without either clinging to it or rejecting it."

— *Sylvia Boorstein*

Multiplicity of alternate practices, with their connections to religious and cultural roots, adds to the complexity of choosing a particular practice. Individually trying most suitable technique for your own style is always a lengthy process and involves many detours and trials. So why not start with something having proven and positive track record for many others. It is with this background that modern version of Mindful Meditation deserves recommendation especially for beginners. It is secular, is not too abstract to grasp and is comparatively simple to practise for an average person of current era. Mindfulness requires more of practical efforts and less of faith or cultural background.

Mindfulness happens to be most preferred technique relied by practitioners the world over. Many direct benefits offered by this practice are experienced by practitioners irrespective of their current position on the long journey of meditation. Some of its assured advantages are listed hereunder in a purely random order. Interestingly, these advantages are equally useful in enriching normal life and not exclusively for meditative journey alone. Hence, Mindfulness is recommended for you even when you have no desire to pursue Meditation as a tool for awakening your spiritual growth.

- Mindfulness broadens your span of choice before responding to any emerging situation.
- It enables you to regain real self rather than living life just like a lifeless puppet, a bundle of accumulated experiences.
- Mindfulness makes perceptions sharper and stronger thereby strengthening intuition.
- Mindfulness sharpens insight, promotes objectivity and helps lessen subjectivity.
- Mindfulness helps in circumventing usual distractions.
- Mindfulness helps in avoiding abstract decisions, overreactions and misinterpretations. This ultimately results in improved emotional balance.
- Practising regular Mindfulness reduces usual melodramas played by normal mind like 'what if' scenarios.
- It helps reduce mental agitations.

Why to Cultivate Mindfulness

Our normal mental attention generally remains gripped by unconscious or subconscious activities linked to sense organs and contents of discriminating mind. That is why attention is momentary and keeps switching to newer subjects emerging in conscious space. Mindfulness, on the other hand, requires sustained attention for longer periods which demands stronger conscious power. Mindfulness is also a demanding practice as it aims at reducing external awareness and diverts focus on inside contents. This skill needs to be honed and cultivated. Mindfulness curbs external awareness and energy thus saved gets applied for conscious working. This increased energy also helps in providing better context and enhanced sensitivity. This immediately results in sharper focus on activity being carried out at that moment. That is how practitioners of mindfulness live richer and more satisfying life on and off the meditation mat.

Our unconscious mind constantly communicates with the conscious mind via the subconscious. Subconscious helps us make a meaning of all our interactions with the world. As such subconscious provide colours to our thoughts and actions. Unfortunately, the subconscious is like a dark, crowded and neglected storehouse somewhere in the lower basement of our mental space. But we have very low control to avoid its involvement in thinking process. Every past conscious experience leaves behind its imprint enabling the subconscious space to expand with time. Later whenever something similar triggers, these old impressions become the very basis for sending the signals to the conscious space.

Mindfulness works like installing new and upgraded software that brings each such buried impression for review, repair and replace with well thought out versions. Mindfulness helps to reevaluate those earlier experiences in light of new realities, knowledge and wisdom making them contextually relevant at present. Now this newer version becomes part of conscious space, an area where we have better control and choice. In terms of computer programming, it is like rewriting the old patch in new language and integrating it within the new systems. To begin with, it moderates the behaviour by replacing self-generated actions in auto mode. That is why even little practice on mindfulness helps improve earlier emotional outbursts. This enables intentions and rationality to play a larger role in the initiation of actions and allows calmness remaining intact even under testing situations. Slowly, you see your behaviour getting filled with increased positivity and intent.

At next level, Mindfulness helps you becoming more logical. You start using your intelligence and discretion before deciding your responses towards emerging situations. Your internal system will still keep throwing reactionary impulses but your conscious mind starts looking at current information available in the light of new knowledge. Slowly but surely, practice of mindfulness helps you to lose grip over old impressions. At further advance level of the practice, you will be able to bring most of your earlier impressions to surface by making them object of meditation one by one. This is absolutely like updating an operating system. Over years, continued practice helps you bring sufficient purity of mind to live in present. Thus, you start new life of living in present, free from accumulated baggage.

Normal mindfulness can be practised while working on most mundane activities of normal life. To that extent, it is similar to Living in Present Moment technique explained in earlier Chapter. But mindfulness as a meditation technique is to be practised in daily sessions. That is why selection of specific subject for a specific session gains significance. As a practice, it is absolutely open where practically any subject can be picked up for practising. It can be an incident, a person, a concept, a relationship, a deity, a thought, a philosophy, an experience, a sound, an action plan or even a physical object of any shape or size. The subject can also be changed as often as desired. Due to this very openness, Mindfulness is considered inclusive and called 'mother of all other meditational practices'.

Process Recommended for Mindfulness Practice

The transition from our ordinary untrained state of scattered and constantly changing attention to mindful attention must always be gradual and slow. As a first step, you may establish open and relaxed attention within immediate vicinity like the room used for the practice session. Once the attention is withdrawn to the room, try bringing attention on body and its sensations. Later, attention can be restricted to upper body alone. Finally, let the attention remain on the tip of the nose or at third eye position. All these steps may take ten to fifteen minutes before every session but it is worth the time invested. Doing it faster runs the risk of failure or reduced quality of focus.

Over longer periods of practice, benefits like gaining greater self-control, increased self-awareness, improving communication and relationships, increased sense of positivity and your ability to accept changes in general are going to be obviously visible. Drastic reductions will also be seen in over-reactions, compulsive behaviours, disorders and phobias alike. The calmness prevailing in the mind hours after each session will become motivating factor for taking the practice to higher and higher levels.

Stage Three

The Regular Meditator

Qualitative issues start dominating meditation practice at this stage much more than physical and quantitative issues. As hygiene factors of finding time, sitting in right posture, sensations of body parts, gaining desired peace etc. are well settled by now. Critical issues relating to past, people (including all types of relationships both at work and personal space) and pertinence still hold sway and disturb practice much like earlier stages. Focus gets fixed on meditational objects but only for few moments. Frequent distractions are most critical matter to handle at this stage. That is precisely the reason for this stage being aptly called 'the stage of gross distractions'. For people continuing in worldly life this is certainly longest time taking stage.

Fewer issues, but with mammoth size stubbornness, bring new challenges in terms of maintaining high level of interest in the practice and keeping the hope for success stronger than ever before. Longer time required in making real progress of this stage offers unique defiance in maintaining passion for practice. During previous stages, you could experience progress made almost on a daily basis with visible improvements. You were getting regular thrills similar to a climber climbing to new heights on the way up. But third stage is like having reached the plateau, fewer chances to go up but plenty of possibilities of sliding down hill. All of a sudden, wham! The results turn into a trickle and no matter what you try you cannot seem to break through to the next level.

Continuing with our comparison with structured educational system, this stage is comparable to the College based graduation level. The learning at college is rather voluntary and expensive. You balance your responsibilities and priorities all by yourself. You are required to face moral and ethical decisions you have never faced before. There is no one to force you to learn or complete assignments. You have to do that at your own sweet will. For support, you may have access to Professors (trained as experts in their respective areas of research) but only on appointed time and schedule. You are expected to research your own pool of texts, illustrations, background information, and reference material. You are also expected to think and synthesise seemingly unrelated topics. As a guiding principle, college means a learning environment in which you take responsibility for thinking through and applying what you have learned.

Interestingly, moving from school to college level education is quite a daunting task as you are forced to leave friends and known surroundings behind which is overwhelming for many but exciting and rewarding for select few. At college level, you decide your time of learning, you take a call to spend time in class, internet, library, laboratory or canteen. In general, a college student manages his own competing priorities like studies, sports, jobs for side earning, social circle or pursuing social-politico-religious ambitions. At this stage, subjects are fewer but depth of dealing is much deeper. You also do not have the option of being selective in topics as you must master all topics. All these statements apply verbatim to meditation aspirant of Third Stage. Due to higher costs and commitments required, demands of this stage of meditation journey force many people to abruptly drop out of their practice exactly as many students drop out of college.

Plateaus are realities of life. Passing through a plateau one wishes to take long strides but steps seem too stuck in the sludge. Every effort made seems to be nullified by internal obstructions. Efforts to remain motivated result only in procrastination. These intractable barriers to further growth can indeed be incredibly frustrating. Many people report following questions occupying their thought processes around this stage. Readers can compare their notes with these statements to identify their own dilemma, if any:

- Nagging internal concerns for slow progress and repetitive question if the time has come to call off meditation practice.
- Bossing around by thoughts dictating that nothing much has changed with meditation, that it is too overrated, and there is nothing more to achieve.

- Internal voices showing craving for other options available to achieve better and faster advancement on assured spiritual realisation.
- Self-doubts wondering if your method or approach of practising meditation is effective at all, fuelling frustration that nothing much is likely to happen anytime soon.
- Mind justifying failures in meditation and constantly suggesting that meditation, after all, is not for everyone.
- Sudden impulses of feeling that everything possible to gain is already gained and life is much more than sitting in meditation.
- Mind coming up with comparison of successes achieved by those others who did not indulge in meditation but enjoying success in life.

If you identify yourself with one or more of the above statements, it is time to rejoice rather than feeling delinquent. All practitioners face these challenges at this stage in varying proportions. Hence, these are good indicators of your progress on desired path. It is unfortunate that, in the absence of proper guidance, many aspirants lose steam at this crucial juncture and fold their mats. Yes, qualifying this stage is tougher than all of IAS, CAT, IIT, CLAT, CA, etc. put together where only *crème de la crème* qualify for moving forward.

Most critical subject at this stage of practice is to achieve sustained inward focus with conscious concentration. This in turn demands mastery over the issues involving self-awareness, overcoming emotional structures and evolving right understanding of your real self. There is no escaping anymore. Also required is living consciously in the present moment where you neither entertain past memories nor face fear for future.

Subjects to be mastered at this stage are fewer in number but rigorous in scope and complex to comprehend. There is plenty of supporting material available from multiple sources but you alone are expected to pull out, put together, screen, investigate and inquire into the same and prepare yourself to be ready to face all conceptual, philosophical and practical issues arising out of these subjects.

17

Controlling Mental Distractions

"Don't hate the arising of thoughts or stop the thoughts that do arise. Simply realize that our original mind, right from the start, is beyond thought, so that no matter what, you never get involved with thoughts. Illuminate original mind, and no other understanding is necessary."

– *Zen Master Bankei Yotaku*

Who is not well aware about conflicting thoughts erupting in an endless manner? One voice suggests we eat food, another suggests better finish the work in hand first. Soon we get reminded to return that important call promised earlier while yet another thought goes to check current score of the ongoing cricket match. These conflicting demands arising at the same time suggest that there are multiple parts within our own mind where each part is pushing for its own agenda. All these agendas are invariably at variance from each other. But ultimately, mind alone decides on what to take first and what to ignore or postpone, be it willingly or reluctantly. All those voices which create these mental intrusions, interferences, confusions, obstructions or diversions are collectively called distractions. All these distractions have to be dealt with squarely before we achieve a conducive state of mind for effective meditation.

As already learnt, open arm willingness of the mind is a prerequisite for making headway in meditation. To be free from all types of distractions is quintessential aspect of such willing mind. Attempting meditation with a fragmented and divided mind is destined for disappointments and failures. To counter distractions and disturbances and for ensuring enjoyment of meditation, working of the mind and its sub-systems need be understood in much greater details, something which was not so significant to attend to many other activities carried out in life so far.

Human mind is not a single entity operating of its own. Mind comprises of different mental processes having their own specific purposes and processes. To begin with, we can compartmentalise the Mind into two distinct categories, the conscious and subconscious. Conscious space works like a central processor or a CEO. It receives signals and inputs from all around, processes them and decides course of action. Its most important job is to prioritise the signals to be processed and selecting next thing to be picked up after concluding the last. At a given point of time, conscious awareness contains many subjects/thoughts seeking its attention. As soon as a new subject/thought is picked up for contemplation, other competing thoughts make way to the periphery, a space shared with many other attention-seeking subjects which could not get central attention from conscious awareness. All these subjects are potential sources of distractions.

Than we have the subconscious space, which incidentally holds much more information, patterns and experiences than the conscious space. This subconscious space is like a thick folder having several individual software programmes and Apps operating independently but linked with the main processor of conscious space. Most of these software systems over years become beyond edit. Sustained mindful meditation is said to be the only tool that allows re-logging into them either for deletion, rewriting, overwriting or delinking them from the central processor. Within the total space, multiple parts and subparts of both conscious and subconscious systems are connected with each other in a manner like a super speed e-way.

Within the subconscious space we have the sensory sub-minds linked with each sense organ. They constantly take inputs from the sense organs and leave it in the conscious space, as already explained earlier, hoping for seeking attention of the central processor. It is their obligation to interpret the raw sensory data being collected and feeding it as it gets received together with the intensity and density of the sensations involved. These sub-minds work as relay switches and keep feeding inputs irrespective of active involvement of the conscious sub-mind. This is how new inputs from surroundings and outside world at large get thrown at the door step of conscious mind at all times.

In addition to sub-minds linked with sense organs, we have internal sub-minds within the subconscious space itself dealing with thoughts, emotions and past memories. They normally work on highly autonomous and simultaneous basis to keep looking at the information received from sensory organs, assimilating the same with established patterns based on past data and transforming their inputs to conscious space as complex mental representations to help it decide desired course of action. Combined together, all these sub-minds (those connected with sense organs and those dealing with internal subsystems) can be called parts of discriminating mind systems. These very sub-systems of the discriminating mind are also responsible for producing conceptual images including thoughts and ideas for consideration of the boss, the conscious space within the mind. The feedback of emotional response to any input received from the remaining unconscious space converts these very perceptions as likable or such other overtones of joy, fear, anger, happiness and likewise.

In short, within a mind we got innumerable other sub-minds constantly engaged in feeding emerging inputs to the conscious mind to receive the feedback, select it for consideration, process other associated inputs about it, initiate action desired and instruct concerned parts to take that action. This helpless boss has the power to choose an input by deciding priority but got no power to stop receiving inputs being fed by all other sub parts. Let us also remember that the subconscious sub-parts also have the power to trigger many actions even without involvement of the conscious space, for example, our limbs can react to a sensory input relating to fear or safety. These are called automatic reactions where, for want of speed, action gets generated bypassing directions from so-called boss, the conscious space.

Let us also briefly look into process of the conscious space to choose one input for action from among many options available at any moment. After all, it is the one who decides what input is to be entertained first and for how long and with how much concentration. Once we understand that process, we should be able to live stream what we desire and stop streaming of what we do not wish. The objective behind explaining working of subparts of the overall mind systems at this length is to highlight why poor mind is unable to easily surrender its wandering and why it is so complex to achieve its willing focus on object of meditation. In a nutshell, the mind is always surrounded by multiple demands from its subparts and it is really hard for it to pick the one out of many for considering at a given point in time. Conscious mind is genetically trained to prefer more interesting, exciting, intense or important subjects to focus attention on. Depending on its initial evaluation of the level of interest and excitement, it moves to another subject seeking attention and this process continues.

Kuladasa, the co-author of *The Mind Illuminated*, in this very book calls information projected into conscious mind as intentions. Multiple intentions interact with each other for problem solving, decision making and creating new responses to situations. Ultimately, strong intentions get acted in preference over weaker intentions. Each intention gets supported or opposed by different sub-parts before a final action gets initiated. Complete consensus among all attention-seeking competing subparts is the ultimate situation where we say that our mind, body and soul are in sync. Just imagine how difficult it is to arrive at this consensus among all subparts of our entire conscious and subconscious spaces. Unless all these mental processes are not in complete harmony, the mind is unable to achieve its unification which means it remains involved in internal conflicts. Bulk of entire meditation practice goes in achieving this unification.

Are You in Control of Your Mind?

Having understood the working of mental processes, it is clear that even the thought that one is in control of his mind is too tall a claim. The learned even warn against one's association with the mind control intentions. Unfortunately, your own self has very little role to play in this whole process. As a result, you should not even feel responsible for failure to control the mind. If you have no role in controlling what is thought by your mind, what good it will do to blame yourself with your failure on this count. So avoid becoming annoyed or self-critical about mind wandering.

But all is not lost. Owing to the fact that each thought remains in the conscious space for a short time only, there exists a silver line.

Soon some other thought will be taken up by the conscious sub part. If you work on strengthening of intentions, you may ensure that the next intention to be picked up is as per your desire. In Cricket parlance, you maintain your chance to hit a big hit on the next ball if you are already not out. In short, while you cannot control wandering of the mind but by strengthening of desired intentions, you may bring the attention of mind on your subject before the wandering inflicts real damages.

In the whole process, interestingly, scolding or such other strong arm tactics are destined to fall flat. Any deliberate attempt to force your attention to remain stable on a subject matter is similar to pulling a plant to make it grows faster. All such efforts are considered negative and not liked or accepted by all other sub-parts. They immediately turn rebellion and start reacting against suppressions. Consistent and reinforced behaviour is more likely to be effective over any punishing or applying coercion. Many chapters explained earlier are intended to make one of these Conscious or Subconscious Subparts agreeable such that it stops sending newer intentions to the conscious space. This is also the precise reason Yoga gets so much focused for success in meditation. Yoga and pranayam ultimately help is drying up physical sense organs sending stimulations to subparts attached with each of them. Lesser stimulations directly means fewer intentions thrown at conscious mind and hence, fewer distractions.

It is only over longer periods that each sub-part starts seeing the advantages of agreeing for consensus with other sub-parts rather than continuing cravings of 'me first' approach. One also has to learn to make all these sub parts still, as long as it takes because only a still mind can enjoy the happiness and only a happy mind can be a focused mind.

Gaining control over own mind is akin to the working of a seasoned gardener. The end result of his efforts is, of course, beautiful flowers on the plants and healthy fruits over the trees. But much before that gardener has to go through a difficult process of preparing the soil, sowing using well selected seeds, weaning away the weeds, adding desired manures, proper watering, protection against all types of climatic extremes, timely arranging supports, etc. The underlying activities call for tons of patience and hard work. Gaining desired success in ensuring willingness of our mind to extend desired focus on meditation is equally tough and long drawn process.

The process of achieving right mental attention, in a way, calls for complete reprogramming of our default software. This process is slow, boring and unsophisticated but best possible cure for purifying the mind of all its afflictions accumulated during ignorant living. How to achieve attention is no more a big secret. Progress achieved on topics already discussed like acceptance for world as it exists, practising Santosha, becoming fully Self-aware, improving Moral Standards and Ethical behaviour, living in Present Moment and strengthening of will power, are all steps that add up in bringing sharper focus of attention on desired subjects bit by bit. Success achieved in practising the technique of Mindfulness also goes in calming all mental sub systems to operate in sync with each other. Getting rid of normal distractions becomes the springboard for carrying out all initiatives of personal growth finally leading to spiritual awakening as well.

> "One morning, you'll hit mental inbox zero, and that is a pretty amazing feeling. It's a state somewhere between joy, bliss, and peace. Once you have that, you won't want to give that up. If you can get a free hour of bliss every morning, just by closing your eyes...that's worth its weight in gold. That will change your life." — *Naval Ravikant*

18

Other General Practices for Improving Meditation

Nothing ever happens of its own. Best of seed needs fertile soil, desired humidity and initial care to germinate and grow to become full tree. At each stage of the growth, you continue watering the plant in good proportion, take care of its nutritional requirements, maintain your vigil against apparent dangers, keep taking out harmful weeds, occasionally spray pest control when required and take every other care to ensure that the plant grows well and get ready for flowering in due course. Flowers of such cared plants have to eventually bloom and spread their smell in the entire vicinity. Of course, you have to have patience, show vigil, work hard, stand firm against sudden changes in external climate. You are also destined to come across situations where growth stops for no reason.

Purifying ethical and morals standards, as discussed earlier, is just like ensuring that very fertile soil to facilitate germination and growth of the initial Meditation practice. General practices explained under the current Chapter, on the other hand, are similar to nourishment and protection required for that very tree to stand tall against all odds. Standing firm against known obstructions is like taking out weeds as and when found. Control over anger, aversions and materialism work as spray of pest control. Acceptance, self-awareness, contentment are similarly protection against external climate. Ethical and moral advancements ensure unhindered growth of roots of the said tree while practices decoded below contribute towards matching growth of trunk, branches and leaves of this tree all through its growing period. These practices provide desired tending and watering to let the tree sustain and grow at the same time.

At this advance stage of our meditation journey, the practice gets expanded far beyond the scheduled sessions as it is to be practised both 'off' the mat as much as 'on' it. While sitting in regular sessions of his practice, the practitioner at this stage gets used to frequent vision of sense of bliss and serenity. Majority of issues in terms of obstacles and conceptual roadblocks stand duly dealt with. Strong influence of earlier issues like ego, materialism, temptations, loss of focus, etc. is not dominant as before. As a natural progression, the seeker aspires for living the familiar transcendent state of being over remaining hours of his day as well.

In the journey so far, the seeker must have already made significant changes in living life but this stage asks for much radical changes in living normal life. Biggest of all changes is suspending all money making endeavours. This single change releases a whole lot of additional time available with the practitioner. Practices suggested below suddenly become feasible due to extra time on hand. Interestingly, following these practices also elevate seeker's happiness quotient and help him achieve most effective equilibrium among forces pulling normal lives in different directions. The random sequencing of practices touched upon does not speak of their relative importance or effectiveness as they all combine together to bring the required transformation.

A. Continue Working on Improving Emotional Balance

Emotions influence our feelings, thinking, actions and responses on moment to moment basis. Actually, emotions are part of our system of sensing and responding to the entire world and differentiate human beings from robots. Significant overarching impact of emotions on our life demands deeper understanding, appreciating their interplay and finally ability to exercise regulation so that merit of our actions and responses is not lost. Improved emotional balance is equally essential for living and moving on meditational path. Also, emotions are very pragmatic and audacious; they keep reappearing in our system even after years of working on them. Regulating them is always tricky and a lifelong challenge. Few emotions pose problems to advance practitioners due to their capability of striking at lightning speed. That is why dealing with emotions remains critical even at this stage.

Familiar instances like outburst, yelling, getting angry, feelings of jealousy are all too instinctive stress responses suggesting poor emotional balance. Feeling bad or angry at times or getting burdened with overwhelming situations are just natural occurrences but how one deals with them depends on emotional balance. An advance meditation practitioner learns the art of managing emotions without involving other people. Emotions are always at play with human beings but a seeker has to advance self-regulation such that desired balance is not disturbed even in testing situations. Mastery in this art also pushes up all critical sense of self-worth. Also it is very important to appreciate that suppression, denying, intensifying, weakening, curtailing, masking or replacing powers of emotions are options that may sound good but are completely impractical and are bound to fail every time.

Actually, our emotional mind is just like an elephant symbolising its size where good volumes of intelligence, aggression, anger, empathy and power, are all rolled into one. Rational mind, on the other hand, is the mahout of that very elephant, characterising sense of discrimination, patience, perseverance and responsibility. Sitting on top of the elephant and holding the reins firmly, the mahout is expected to be in command. But the precarious mahout is too small and fragile in comparison to the elephant. The moment the elephant does not agree with the mahout, the command gets lost resulting in all round chaos. Interestingly, this elephant (our emotional side) is always hungry for instant gratification and does not think beyond the moment. The mahout has capability of thinking long term and analyse repercussions but is forced to use the power of elephant to do anything good. So long as they lack agreement, they go nowhere.

Ability to acquire emotional balance involves matured refinement of moral and ethical preparations, evolved self-awareness together with identifying real purpose of human life. This also calls for perfecting acceptance for every person, objects and situations around as given. One must be able to filter and let go everything outside individual control. All these initiatives, however, give results in bit-by-bit manner, in the continuous circle of learning, practising and perfecting in baby steps. Regulating emotions in nothing short of discarding the original skills one has lived with for ages. All these are big ticket changes and results for people in making such changes is not very encouraging. Loads of dedication and perseverance are required to fight this endless battle but fight we must.

Every instance of lost balance of emotions needs to be contemplated in greater details. Now that you have more time and lesser social interactions, please go back to the depth of each violation and look for real reasons. Maintain a full journal of all episodes and continue refining your practice. Sooner than later, the numbers of episodes are destined to reduce.

B. Practising Pranayam Regularly

Entire meditation practice revolves around sitting and breathing. Meditation necessitates reaching the state of still breathe which in turn necessitates still mind. Aimless wandering of mind is also best managed by regulating breathing. The link between breathing and thinking is both direct and deep. As per Ayurveda, process of contemplation consists of two distinct parts called physical and psychological where breathing is physical part while thinking is its psychological sibling. Obviously, the second is conditional to the existence of the first. Actually, conscious awareness and regulation of breathing are two distinct pursuits that differentiate meditation from normal human mental activity.

Pranayam takes care of both breathing and thinking. It invokes a number of benefits on physical, mental, and psychic levels. During pranayam routines, breath is skillfully inhaled, exhaled and retained like a symphony at work. For smooth meditation, our breath has to be shaped well to ensure that it is deep, smooth, even, without sound, without pause and has very tender transition between inhaling and exhaling. Pranayam involves systematic working on change in depth of breathing, changes in rate of breathing and most importantly at varying patterns of breathing. It leads to perfect relief from physical and mental tensions arising due to breathing.

Desired shaping of breathing patterns requires long practice, perseverance and determination. Only a practitioner with years behind knows challenges faced in establishing proper rhythm in respirations such that the breathing during meditation is able to avoid all known adjectives like being laboured, unlaboured, gasping, too fast, too slow, too deep or wheezing. Practising regular Pranayam routines achieves that very purpose. It also brings balance among *doshas* of *Vata, Pitta* and *Kapha* resulting in significant health benefits. It brings tremendous balancing, strengthening and cleansing of internal organs by offering unmatched exercise. The obvious physical benefits from Pranayam are—

- Clearing and cleansing of nasal passages, lungs as well as respiratory system
- Drawing out of carbon dioxide from entire body
- Renewing body tissues
- Imparting massage to stomach, liver, spleen, heart and pancreas.

As part of mental benefits, Pranayam makes mind steady and calm. As a very first step, it augments supply of oxygen to the mind to reduce stress levels. Regular practitioners of Pranayam report increasing mental alertness and higher feeling of exhilaration. Pranayam is also very useful in reducing blood pressure and cholesterol numbers, alleviating nervousness and toning up nervous system. It is an excellent exercise in keeping mind cheerful for long periods and maintaining higher levels of enthusiasm and energy for all of its practitioners.

On the psychic level, Pranayam allows introversion of mind paving way for subsequent activities relating to self-awareness, self-observation, self-acceptance and finally self-realisation.

Taking sufficient time in between changeover of Pranayam routines is strongly recommended to properly recuperate. This is not like session in the gym that higher the flow of sweat better it is. Doing it mechanically brings only physical advantages while the objective at this stage is spiritual advancement. The loop of *'study to practise to perfection—to study to practise and further perfection'* remains true for years and years. The more you practise, the more you know about faults in your previous sessions. So you practise, make mistakes, see the results and finally practise some more. Over periods, we begin to make fewer or smaller mistakes. In a way, practising of Yoga exercises and Pranayam cycles are similar to a singing maestro who keeps improving his skills by undertaking daily practice all his life and still keep realising how much more is there to learn.

Pranayam is advisable on empty stomach only. Sitting for Pranayam within one hour of eating, sexual activity or bath is prohibited for obvious reasons. Similar to Yoga, having these exercises with regularity is the surest way of seeking all possible advantages. As a practical suggestion, on a day when one is short on time or energy for both Yoga and Pranayam, skipping Yoga may be suggested but not Pranayam.

C. Care for Health

Life is said to be a journey of mix bags. It inevitably entails breathtaking views on the sides and some potholes too. Your health is the vehicle used for taking you towards your destination. A passenger feels comfortable in taking long journey only in a well kept vehicle else it runs the fear and risk of frequent breakdowns. Even if there are no real breakdowns, the driver of a not well kept vehicle always remains apprehensive and full of anxiety for possible breakdowns. A top level vehicle for ensuing long journey necessitates top level working of all its parts and processes operating in sync. Material wealth, in this example, is equated with gas and lubricant. Yes, you need it at every step but only so much. To reach the destination safe and sound, quality of vehicle is certainly more critical than having tons of extra fuel.

In reality, however, people take health for granted. We fallaciously presume that our body will remain subservient irrespective of the count of atrocities we commit. No, human body keeps perfect score of everything good and bad is done with it. Right eating, right sleeping, regular exercises, remaining tension-free, spotting unwanted variations by periodical check-ups, abstaining from use of substances (including alcohol and tobacco) are all matters of personal choices that are made many times on each day. All these measures reflect on state of health on cumulative basis.

Besides physical fitness, several aspects of mental well-being impact our overall health quotient. Depression, anxiety, diabetes, stress are obvious despised symptoms of imperfect mental health. These afflictions are breaking known boundaries of age, gender, financial status, cultural background etc., and are labeled as modern-day curses. Every responsible person should take cognisance of these signs and work around to get rid from them by doing whatever works for them.

Uninterrupted practice of meditation presupposes a perfect health and demands strict regime of do's and don'ts. An unhealthy person is destined to overwhelm in meditation as well. Both fitness targets and meditation success need disciplined life, dedication, self-motivation and practice. Again, only reading about it cannot help achieve targets. Working for improving mental health requires being watchful of thoughts, words, actions, emotions, logics, habits and attitudes. No wonder, health-conscious practitioners are seen making faster progress in meditation as well.

D. Spend Time in Solitude

> "Touch your inner space, which is nothingness, as silent and empty as the sky; it is your inner sky. Once you settle down in your inner sky, you have come home, and a great maturity arises in your actions, in your behaviour. Then whatever you do has grace in it. Then whatever you do is poetry in itself. You live poetry; your walking becomes dancing, your silence becomes music." — Osho

Every demand on our time is a drag on mental concentration. Quality of interaction does not even play any role out here. But what we have is a funny world around where daily schedules are packed, multi tasking is fashionable, having free time on hand is considered fearful and not having something urgent to attend entails unknown fear of missing something substantial. Empty mind is branded as 'devil's advocate'. People sprint from morning till night, switching from work to leisure and back to work as if there is no tomorrow. Monkey mind certainly loves such a scenario as it enjoys hopping from one thing to another without even a desire of master exerting any control whatsoever. In this background, the significance of spending quality time in solitude away from the noise and pressures of modern life becomes important more than ever in the past.

Spending time in solitude is critical for freedom from distractions. Solitude helps in concentrating focus on a subject of choice. Most importantly, solitude enables our brain to think outside the box and come up with unique, extraordinary solutions to problems. Time spent in solitude runs counter to the norms of being social beings but spending some time away from the hustle and bustle of society ultimately proves beneficial for a meditation practitioner. And it has not become important only recently. As per Christian tales, God created the world in six days and he took rest on Sunday, the seventh day. To this day Christians are expected to take Sunday as a day of rest and reflections.

In modern times, we may do better to create solitude corners within our private space and spend time there in regular intervals as often as possible. But solitude, as being discussed here, mean much more than being physically alone. Solitude is being in a state where one is able to park worldly baggage in a separate space and allow the body to perfectly catch up with mind. Our world is full of over stimulations and poor mind also needs free time to suspend its over-activism. Let us look at solitude as anti-adrenaline system that kicks on when there is no danger of fight-or-flight response. Solitude helps us feel deep connect with the entire creation in a timeless and spaceless realm where soul feels at home and heart enjoys its quivering.

Success in meditation practice calls for proficiency to swim against the tides. A mind can develop that ability only when it remains free from all types of compulsions and pressures. For this purpose, you are advised to get yourself bored rather than loaded with activities. Please find regular time intervals when you have nothing to keep you occupied. Cellular phones, TV, newspapers, social media, internet, books, thoughts, sports, entertainments, to do list etc. are all essential, but not at all times. Persistent switching from one engagement to another is neither good for happiness nor for spiritual growth. Activity less boredom is the recharging time that does wonders to creativity; it germinates seeds of self discovery. Solitude is must for contemplating big questions in our life.

Solitude helps our body to catch up with mind thus balancing the 'Doshas' as prescribed under Ayurveda. Solitude does wonders towards enhancing creativity by keeping distractions at bay. It is a must-have tonic for curing toxins of normal living. By keeping you out of touch with others, it brings you in touch with yourself in a profound manner. Human life is a journey with billion others travelling alongside. Solitude facilitates you looking around and enjoying the scenery on either side of journey rather than blindfolding driving towards an unknown destination that can arrive any time.

Time available without any immediate pending 'to do' list allows observing internal tendencies in new light. This process brings us face to face with our realities, something that we never knew before. How much time of the day is good for solitude? Well not the entire time of the day but certainly few hours of quality time daily. Solitude is more a matter of rescheduling than shunning human interactions. So do not worry, your other demands on your time will still be met now that you have luxury of time at your disposal. Away from immediate worries, the free 'me time' on hand prepares our mind for undertaking contemplation, a must have habit on the way of meditation.

Solitude demands periods of personal time away from mails, internet, messages, mobile phones and every other social media platform. Let us not forget that all these time-consuming activities cropped up only in last couple of decades. Humanity has survived millions of years of its history without these devices and Apps. What is the use of connecting with the world on moment to moment basis but not connecting with self for months and years? It is indeed a poor bargain. More importantly, you need not leave the world for a hill top or for a boat on the sea or for a cave in the mountain; you can enjoy blessed solitude well within four walls of your own crowded house. Loosening of attachment with the members of the family and letting them live their own life is good enough to practise solitude. All you need is a sacred place for a defined length of time all to yourself.

Meditation practitioner who has practised thus far must have realised that the central point of all contemplation is nothing else but self inquiry which necessitates silence and seclusion. This inquiry cannot be carried out with the help of instruments or physical matter similar to conducting experiments inside a scientific laboratory. Here we are dealing with subtle sensations which are to be accessed in the silence of our own inner core.

> "The mind that is alone is not only innocent but young—not in time or age, but young, innocent, alive at whatever age—and only such a mind can see that which is truth and that which is not measurable by words." —*Jiddu Krishnamurti*

E. Replace Old Learning with New

Learning depends on the intensity of the passion with which it is pursued. Learning is not limited by age or any other constraint. A learning mind remains a fresh mind and makes every experience exciting. Conversely, a mind that is unwilling to learn is a dumb mind and it remains engrossed on past impressions. Such a mind at best is a lazy mind that works only for justifying what it knows already. It considers old knowledge alone as accurate, appropriate and sufficient. Unfortunately, making fool of ourselves is mind's primal quality. It also loves to take over master's role very quietly converting the master as its obedient servant. Keen observation based constant openness for new learning reduces the status of mind as a good servant. This facilitation of change of roles is the biggest contribution of meditation as a tool and technique. Once the mind becomes a good servant, it regains its ability to do wonder to help his master grow on all dimensions.

What to learn? Well that is never a problem. The moment you start learning the smallest of a thing, you are bound to realise how little you knew about it. Digging in the most obvious subjects opens unending expansion of the unknown. The more you learn new, the more you realise your earlier false impressions. What to learn is the least of the problems to be tackled as one thing always leads to another.

F. Reading for Learning

Reading was always considered a good habit for every knowledge seeker. Reading is a skill worth acquiring and the easiest of the trait to learn more with fewer efforts. Throwing your towel by saying that 'I am not into reading' is a sign of your mind fooling around. Mind needs to be told in no unclear words that it is obliged to read and retain the content of every good material it gets exposed to. Reading connects us with the wisdom of others in the fastest possible way. But in general we get used to casual and cursory reading which is simply flipping through pages with the intention of reaching to the end. It is too casual an approach and may be ok only when reading is for fun or thrill. Reading for gaining new knowledge is an entirely different ball game. Meaningful reading demands profound look at why to read and what to absorb, much before the book gets picked up. Knowledge is gained only when the reader begins with the attitude of gratitude. Reading for spiritual quest for superior objectives of human life is even more pious an activity. Here one has to swim deep into words and absorb their true subtle nuances rather than understanding literary perception alone.

Serious reading aimed at wisdom via serious knowledge is entirely different than fictional reading. There are many who pick a novel and continue reading until the last page in one sitting. It is just like going over a long story where even the names of the principal characters were in the conscious mind only until the last page. Reading for subtle realities of life and subjects like meditation is much more objective in nature and is in absolute contrast of casual reading.

Think for a moment as to why people write in the first place. The magic trick inspiring people to write entertaining fictions is called PIE which refers to persuasion, information and entertainment. But the foremost inspiration of every author, writing on subjects of our interest at this stage, is sharing his wisdom with deserving others. Authors dealing with significant subjects basically carve out their life's learning in the form of their books or blogs. In that sense every such book is sort of a biography. Selection of your reading material is your exclusive prerogative and you have every right not to pick up a book. You are also within your rights to fold the book in between if you find it digressing from your expectations. But so long as you are reading you ought to remain hospitable for its content as well as its intent.

Do not let the message of its writer get lost for want of your attention. True reading requires a sharp focus to grasp the knowledge contained in the writing. You have to read the lines as well as in between the lines. If you read without focus, your efforts of reading will fail to fire your imaginations. Objective reading requires very open and slow approach to facilitate grasping. The focus should be to chew the words and sentences until every drop of delicious juices contained therein are extracted in full. Let the knowledge conveyed by words sink in your conscious mental space without any ambiguity. Let us remember that words have to travel the distance from mind to heart before they really become ours. Physically that may appear a very short distance but it is full of long lasting detours and sinkholes which, at times, prove too long to travel.

You decided to learn about meditation, and the fact you have come to read this book so far means you are serious to make considerable improvements in your life and thinking process. Train your hands not to pick up a book unless it has potential to enhance your knowledge and wisdom. Apply your judgement to be very selective in what to read but once you decide, please do justice with it. Also, do not limit your horizon to a particular language, time period, religion, faith, nationality, zone or any such other limitation. With any such condition operating, you are depriving yourself of the treasures well within your reach. Wisdom contained in words originating from all corners of the world and from all times is equally precious.

G. Do not Judge Everything Around

Passing judgement over the smallest thing is a pretty big deal. Before pronouncing the judgement, a judge goes through lots of records, testimonies, arguments, counters, and a whole lot of evidence evaluation. Facts are studied, both sides get opportunity to cross examine each other, evidences are corroborated and verified, then alone the judgement is passed. Pronouncing a ruling casually invariably leads to defective judgements. But if we take a pause for a moment and assimilate situations in our real life, we find that quite inadvertently we do pass judgements at the drop of hat.

So and so said this and that it was not right. That guy interpreted my words wrongly. I should have been consulted by so and so before finalising this and that. I deserved that promotion before my colleague. That TV debate should have been conducted with this and in that manner. That actor in the film was not up to the mark in acting and dialogue delivery. One can go on and on endlessly to spot normal life situations which are clear instances of our actions as if we are self-appointed judge. We want everybody else to do things in the way that we approve. Our mind may argue as to why we feel the way we feel and why we are right in coming to our conclusions but in reality such pronouncements are inadvertently passed judgements and nothing else.

Our jumbo sized ego is very intelligent to hold upper hand in its dealing with the poor mind and coerce it to manipulate its judgement to justify what ego likes disregarding all other versions around. Please see through this scenario, are we being manipulated? Are we being belittled to poke our nose in matters where we have no business to poke? Every other person is a small world by itself. And each world is a big place and has systems and rules in place to run and take care of disturbances. Also, we are too miniscule to deserve a say in working of the outside world. Let us be cognisant that we do not know well about others and their situation to conclude their actions and words. Also that one person's right may be other person's wrong. Eyes can see wrong, ears can listen wrong, testimony of others may be wrong. How many times in past our impressions about others were found wrong? How many times we regretted our reactions being hasty or being out of place?

We are responsible only for ourselves alone. Let us accept words and actions of others as given. It is not so hard to consider them as their best and echo them with our best. This simple harmless principle has power to significantly reduce most of day to day problems arising from interactions with all others. Letting the world move as it does is a big sign of maturity. Let us focus only on our own direction and try reaching our destination. Even while evaluating improvements, our focus must remain on self and nothing else. This approach is simple, practical and assures positive results. The moment we firmly refuse to stand as judge for matter of others, a whole lot of ugliness, pettiness, shallowness and selfishness disappear from life.

So, every time you get an impulse to take sides, control yourself, handover the matter to your logical mind and let it ponder what needs to be done, that is, if at all there is a thing to be done by you. Tell your ego to rest and let the judgements be delivered by actual judges. Please make your delay devices stronger than before so as to avoid enumerable extempore assertions. This is very significant for making the mind still. In a way, this is an extension of the concept of Acceptance we discussed in Stage One. Desire to detest from passing judgements contributes to mind's willingness to surrender for focusing inward.

H. Realise Your Modesty

Just imagine that as late as 1920, Milky Way was supposed to contain all the stars of the Universe. Over next 100 years, however, developed Astronomy has already established existence of hundreds of bigger galaxies. Advancements in telescope further enable space observatories to identify more and more distant galaxies. Each galaxy comprises of innumerable systems. Milky Way of its own consists of up to 400 billion stars and over 100 billion planets. Our entire solar system is just a miniscule part of Milky Way. Just the Sun, the centre of our solar system, is large enough to hold approximately 1,300,000 Earths into itself. Just imagine the relative size of Mother Earth in reference to known dimensions of our Universe.

Mother Earth itself has population of about 7.8 billion human beings at present (projected to touch 8 billion by 2022). Billions and billions have lived and left this place in the past. We are just one of the billions living in this world in some small corner. Are we not just a tiny small dot with iota of relevance for this Universe? Are we really so important for smooth running of our nuclear families, let alone our societies or nations? Can we accept our inconsequentiality and forget about desiring how things should be and start accepting things as these are. It is hard to imagine any worthwhile point in feeling burdened with the encumbrances of this world. So many other people have already faced everything possible to imagine. Our burden of living this minuscule life can never be so unbearable.

Please continue practising your modesty and keep reminding yourself that you have only so little role to play on this stage called human life. Under this scenario what is the point in controlling destinies of others including your children or spouse. Allow others to take lead and move on with what they deem fit. As soon as you accept your modesty genuinely, a whole lot of mental agony just disappears within moments and of its own. This realisation always leads to impressive progress in our meditation progress. Time and energy so saved is best used to polish uncut diamonds (unused skills) lying deep down in our internal pockets. Letting those diamonds remain wasted or convert them into gems by cutting and polishing are the options awaiting our decisions. So, we must make well considered choice to deal accordingly.

I. Say Bye-bye to Hurry

Famous American cardiologists Meyer Friedman and Ray Rosenman coined the term "hurry sickness" after noticing that many of their patients were diagnosed suffering from similar symptoms. They defined hurry sickness as an ongoing struggle and continuous attempt to accomplish or achieve more and more things or participate in more and more events in less and less time. People with hurry sickness think fast, talk fast, and act fast. Most unfortunately, they consider it a virtue and genuinely work hard to excel in this race and do not mind committing more than they have time for. Soon enough, an unfounded fear of missing out makes them reluctant to slowdown. They multi-task and rush against the clock, and enjoy feeling pressured to get things done. Over longer periods they lose ability to stop and lose objective thinking. Thus, they become less effective and poor performers across all aspects of their life. They tend to stop seeing the big picture. Any person suffering from these common symptoms is indeed a real patient and needs medical intervention.

Current society standards appreciate, recommend and reward fast paced life on all fronts. Evolving technologies and gadgets are fuelling this fire further. There is no realisation that fast paced life is playing havoc and actually crushing sensitivities and vulnerabilities. Fast pace instantly makes us dull and blunted turning reality into deception and non-acceptance. Hurry is also contagious and forces others as well to respond back in same currency. Work done under hurry inevitably generates pressure killing all the joy which could have been celebrated while going over the very process doing things. Being in hurry may save a few minutes here and there but it steals feelings-filled moments that had potential to turn out precious experiences worth treasuring for decades.

Let us remember that people approaching life without hurry enjoy their present and also preserve vigour to live a grand life in future. Let us not forget that the years of working life are normally lesser than years of post retirement lifespan. So we ought to ensure that quality of life in later years is well prepared and protected. Else one will have a life but no meaning. One can see around in the inner circle of relatives and friends to realise that most senior citizens glowing with strength, satisfaction and happiness have one common thread of living life, and that is calm attitude and slow pace. Hurry leads to shortcut solutions which always open doors but only for sloppy progress on the way. Also, initiatives implemented in hurry are always uninspiring and unfulfilling. Why should there be any taker for such a thing?

Living a hurried life is similar to driving your vehicle in overspeed. Consequences of frequent overspeeding may vary from engine to engine but risks of collision remain eminent. Overspeeding also reduces engine life and at times leads to engine's catastrophic failure. Sense of hurry is that very overspeeding in our life. Unfortunately, hurry comes in a very attractive packaging (offering promise of thrills) and with a price payable in future installments (long-term negative health hazards). People infected with incessant struggle to achieve more in less time, end up becoming aggressive, inflexible, insensitive and unemotional. These traits, very unfortunately, mirror exactly the very traits found among all drug addicts. Moving away from all this is possible for those who work on their behaviour and attitude. And behaviour is the gun firing bullets of addiction. Bullets are bad but they do no harm unless fired using a gun.

Let us revisit our sincere and original inclination of living a blissful life free from habits, behaviours and attitudes once again. Let us aspire to have loving and respecting individuals around, enjoying natural health and vitality. We should surely wish to grow on many fronts simultaneously but let us resolve to make these attempts with our calmness and happiness intact. Well, all this is possible once we learn and practice to slow down and take our foot away from the accelerator pedal of our life. Than alone we might have chance to enjoy the beautiful surroundings on either side while we still remain in journey called life. How does it impact meditation journey? Hurry keeps the mind occupied and kills possibilities for its willful surrender to withdraw from external world to inside. Hurry leaves no room for frequent reflections inward which are essence of meditation.

J. Let Simplicity be Philosophy of Life

> "Meditation could be said to be the Art of Simplicity: simply sitting, simply breathing and simply being."
>
> — *Dilgo Khyentse Rinpoche*,
> Head of the Nyingma School of Tibetan Buddhism

We make countless choices every single day. Each choice ignites new options for many more choices, and the process continues. It is a must to have own philosophy in place to deal with multiple options because future is built on those choices. Being that very philosophy, simplicity has guided millions over centuries to live life without pressures and impediments. Simplicity differs with Eastern traditions focused on overcoming desires and attachments. It is also not to be confused with minimalism, outdated and impractical in today's time. Simplicity believes in gaining control over optional choices inclined on self-sufficiency. Simplicity is practical, uncomplicated and pragmatic and must be obvious way of life for everyone. But it stands on the opposite side of uniqueness, a quality deeply adored by our ego. Ego always projects us as special, and not being part of the crowd.

Simplicity has hostile relations with consumerism much more than minimalism. Consumerism has simply turned present day majority as its slaves. It involves acquiring a thing, owning it, using it and keeping it on display for others to appreciate. Be it entertainment, social media interactions, experiences, news feeds, holidays and even relationships, for people suffering from consumerism, material enjoyment is at the centre. This very paradigm of possessing and consuming is unfortunately proliferating many wrong things in our life including stress, unhappiness, unfulfilment and discontentment. All this is orchestrating lot undesired complications in people's life.

The moment a person reboots his default preference, replacing consumerism with simplicity, he immediately finds spare time and energy, most limited and perishable resources a man can have. Surplus time opens new dimensions for attending to important, transformative, life changing activities. Now you get time to fine tune, for example, your inner microscope to see, know and realise the real truth of own purpose of human life. Simplicity is indeed a powerful tool capable of pushing many complexities out of life.

Life is known to throw up overwhelming issues and it is normal to expect complications here and there. But even when there are genuine complications, people following simplicity swim back to normalcy faster than those chained down by complexities. For example, simple approach to start believing things like 'I don't know' is a strong beginning. No one needs to know all the things, after all. Similarly, saying a clear and straightforward 'no' guards against many possible complexities. 'No' is much stronger a word than most other two letter words. Its use offers many solutions having great potential. It is a proven antidote against unreasonable demands/ expectations from undeserving people. It got power to save you from overwhelming situations such as forced to set unachievable targets, accepting challenges to try things outside your set plans, getting involved in matters where you do not have interest, etc. Many such situations tax mental peace, ingenuity and dynamism. Saying 'No' where it matters offers opportunity to smell the roses of our garden.

Simplicity fundamentally is a state of mind rather than a standard of living. It is also a very dynamic concept and keeps evolving by the day. For example, in today's time simplicity is not having a smart phone but to use it judiciously. Money or possessions do not corrupt simplicity so long as there is no 'love' for money or 'addiction' for 'possessions'. It requires, however, a strong awareness of the subtle tipping point for drawing a line between necessities, usefulness and beauty on one side and superfluous, wasteful and vulgar on the other side,

Simple, disciplined and regulated life offers strength to face occasional heavy burdens with ease. Excesses of all types sow seeds of complications. Avoiding excess in eating, sleeping, talking, working, exercising, entertaining or even in thinking, creates simple eco-system banning entry to many problems. Simplicity fosters harmonious relations among everyone around. It promotes sense of fairness and equity. Simplicity paves way for living life in balance; be it between work and life, between money and health, between urgent and important, between temporary and everlasting, between momentary and significant. Simplicity allows us to appreciate beauty and blessings on offer by Mother Nature. Meditation by itself simplifies mental processes which soon lead the practitioner to embrace simplicity in other spheres of life.

People indulging in justifying their complex actions must remember that every form of intellectualism is a sure sign of complex personality. Simplicity runs away from all sorts of manipulation, justification and fabrications. Besides loosening the grip of materialism, practising subtle art of simplicity enhances unconditional acceptance for everything around, helps you appreciate contentment, makes you self-aware, helps in living in present moment and most certainly helps in crossing over the attachments to materialism. Simplicity is the real key to brilliance.

K. Mastering the Art of Giving

In the modern material world "charity begins at home" has turned out an often used cliché to justify self-serving approach by those who believe in doing nothing for others. They suggest that forget about others as this life is too small to solve own problems. But an old African proverb saying that "when the right hand washes the left the right hand gets cleansed too" is the eternal truth equally relevant even in today's interconnected world of mutual interdependence. The Bhagwad Gita goes one step further when it says that "one who enjoys abundance without sharing with others is indeed a thief." Let us agree that even the most selfish person is better served by helping others in so far as charity is a proven antidepressant and takes care of the longing to overcome feelings of isolation and antagonism.

Virtue of charity has been admired and practised across time, culture and race. Charity celebrates interrelatedness of all creations (people, things, animals, plants, mother earth, environment included). It is a reminder to feel responsible for nurturing, supporting and showing solidarity with others around us. Undertaking charities has always been a powerful freedom from greed, one of the most negatively active emotions among living beings. Charity is being generous in sharing our presence, time and money; an art of giving without expecting anything in return. Charity encompasses a whole range of acts that connects external surrounding with our personal sphere. Most importantly, it is measured by the quality of attitude and not with the size of donation. Also, giving is not limited to money or material assistance alone. Giving means sharing what you got; it can be your professional abilities, your time, your material possessions, your skills, your knowledge, your thoughts or your experiences alike.

Many of us extend regular financial help to others in need. But every giving does not qualify as charity. Right giving must be without any relation or attachment to either the recipient or people around him. There are other conditions also to qualify as right giving. First of all, it better be something substantial, something which represents a part of what we have in totality. A millionaire giving away few dollars cannot mean a thing? But some Fortune five hundred businessman pledging half of his fortune for philanthropy shall certainly get counted. Sizable parting involves an element of sacrifice on the part of giver. Giving away what you do not require or something lying surplus with you, as such, fails to qualify as proper giving.

Secondly, charity must be for a just cause and to someone genuinely needy, someone whose life undergoes a change with your giving. Feeding an expensive meal to a person who has regular access to normal food two times a day cannot obviously qualify for charity. Your giving must also ensure that its purpose is legitimate, the process is verified with proper due diligence and there exists a monitoring system in place to ensure that money is used as intended. One can identify a just social cause to associate with like education, health, sanitation, self-help, housing, social awareness, gender equality, skill development, etc. and work alone or associate with other reputed agencies already working in that field.

Giving with modesty is third and equally compelling prerequisite for a genuine charity. Undertaking charity with the intent of displaying one's richness or with indecent and impropriate behaviour will certainly fail to bring the real benefits of giving. That is why in

Ancient Indian context, we come across big charitable activities where the identity of the giver remains anonymous. Real giving is always without expecting a reward and regard. Else it fails to shred selfishness, bringing peace of mind and purifying the heart. Perfect motivation for giving is freedom from greed and nothing else. Giving with right qualities is really transformative. Right giving accrues karma credits like a fixed deposit.

L. Get Rid of old Systems and Harness Imagination

Crossing over attachments, pleasures, aversions and fears is mandatory at the advance stage of meditation practice because mind has to gain access to its essential qualities of original purity, freshness and receptivity. This stage lies far beyond the starting point where preconceived notions rule mind and heart; where soul remains influenced by traditional systems, preaching, religious dictates, racial restrictions, and gender generalities etc. Personal habits of all sorts are also nothing but chains of such systems as a habit is defined "more or less fixed way of thinking, willing, or feeling acquired through previous repetition of a mental experience". Stereotypes rule thinking and actions of people so possessed. They get stuck in the status quo with no desire to come out of these iron shackles.

Scholars of behavioural psychology identify this roadblock as 'negative memory' because of its constant interference with new learning. Old systematic knowledge is worth condemning due to its blocking of new learning. In normal life, forgetting old memories and knowledge is considered a curse but in spiritual quest it is considered a blessing, a boon, a distinctive virtue, a great accomplishment. You are indeed fortunate if you are able to sink your old moorings every so often. This sinking is similar to rebooting one's operating system to go back to original/default settings escaping negative impacts of all types of system corruptions/virus infections that creep in while operating the software over longer durations. Meditation practitioners with certain degree of expertise are able to experience this freedom during their sessions whereas advanced practitioners continue in this state for much longer periods.

Going back to default setting allows our mind to regain its innocence making the mind completely receptive for fresh knowledge in sight. Layers and layers of acquired experiences and impressions colour perceptions with darker shades of subjectivities. Multiplicities and urgencies of normal life compel us to discharge most of our daily activities with that subjectivity in place. Since the ego keeps fooling us to take pride in those subjectivities, normally, we neither detest them nor feel compelled to change them.

In the absence of rebooting, our mind continues suffering from the features identified with robots. Robots are good too but only for performing repetitive jobs. Robots do work fast without fatigue and tiredness but you do not expect them to use imaginations or use activated consciousness. Human mind alone is bestowed with active discretion, the freedom to choose what is best in the given situation. But applying discretion requires a blooming mind, a mind without any bias or subjectivity. Bias generates conflict and subjectivity promotes dichotomy. Both these are big roadblocks for conflict-free pure learning.

Ordinary life invokes too many influences from practised religions and cultural traditions. Unfortunately, both religions and traditions believe in blindfold following and appreciate conformity. New imaginations and experimenting new ideas are sternly admonished. Old traditions survive on moron followers doing as they are told. Questions, other than those already answered in so-called holy books, are not welcome at all. There is no place for fascinating creative powers. They strongly oppose free flow of new ideas because there is a risk of flow moving in unseen/unknown directions. It is like forcing the water to flow through pipelines with pumped in pressure rather than letting it flow freely like a vibrant river. Pipelines have elbows, reducers or enlargers on the way. How can a water transported from pipeline and river have similar sentience and righteousness. To that extent every organised faith deserves criticism as long as it fails to encourage its practitioner applying their free thinking and newer intellect.

> "I maintain that Truth is a pathless land, and you cannot approach it by any path whatsoever, by any religion, by any sect... The moment you follow someone you cease to follow Truth."
>
> — *Jiddu Krishnamurti*

The emphasis on following the prescribed systems closes thinking valve rather tightly ending possibilities of free flow of genuine new ideas. On the other hand, inventions and innovations become feasible only when logic and imaginations are put into use from new angles. And for that to happen, it is essential to have a routine free, system free, method free, tradition free and belief free mind. The fact remains that some cultures/faiths make more scientific advancements (leading to overall contribution to humanity at large) than others. Tight systems and following traditions only promote status quo and thinking logically. Such systems should never be allowed to operate as they fail to help their followers keep pace with positive evolutions of the modern world.

Let us not forget that inquisitiveness is a supple and significant quality of human beings which separates them from other living beings. Sticking to belief systems, however good they may sound (or were proven so at their times), by definition is like imprisoning the mind preventing it from using its unique potency of logic, reasoning and discretion. Critique, evaluation, flexibility and adaptation to changing realities must be central values to every living tradition if they wish to avoid turning irrelevant. History is full of examples where popular and widely followed traditions got extinct from the face of earth because they forced imaginations to remain slept. Moving away from systems of all kinds inject a sense of freedom to experiment, to try options available and evaluate what works better. The same freedom and flexibility proves handy while attempting alternate meditation practices over years.

Besides religious beliefs, getting accustomed to a particular way of living, strong brand consciousness, or depending on any single person, product, routine and habit are all undesired examples. How can one take pride in declaring that I am prisoner to such and such thing? Such tendencies stop people to live normal life. To take a sense of pride in such tendencies is even worse. These are liabilities weighing heavily on consciousness and one has to get rid of these. Systems and habits applicable for most mundane activities are undesirable.

After being free from old systems alone one can work on developing his imagination muscle. Free from old systems, this muscle will remain at work 24/7 and will be a catalyst to help you achieve all your dreams and wishes.

> "Successful entrepreneurs are optimists—what they imagine, they believe will happen. Then, they make it

happen. Walt Disney had such a creative mind that he employed Imagineers in the making of DisneyWorld in Florida. The current Disney jobs site says that "Imagineering" combines imagination with engineering. Building upon the legacy of Walt Disney, Imagineers bring art and science together to turn fantasy into reality and dreams into magic."

M. Ending Duality of 'Observer' and 'Observed'

Memorable experiences like an evening by the lake or a night at music concert of favourite performer turn into cherished moments which eventually convert into our implicit memory staying in our subconscious space for longer time periods. It is natural to gather more and more such unique experiences in our kitty. These experiences have power to engulf attention completely making us forget everything else around. Now imagine you revisiting the same or similar spot once again. Invariably, you fail to repeat the original experience simply because your second visit lacks that original element of surprise.

Repeat experiences always tend to get compared with the earlier experiences without even making efforts for doing so. To quote Scott Fitzgerald, the famous American fiction writer, "there are all kinds of love in this world but never the same love twice." The origin of pleasure is from our thought process and not so much from the external stimulus. Enjoying demands total attention of our body and mind entity. But every repeat experience inevitably involves experience with comparisons and critique. In short, repeat experience dilutes the beauty of pure observation that was there the first time. Unfortunately, on our subconscious level, this very repetition and comparison keep happening days in and days out for many real life situations. This makes our life monotonous and dull making us operate like machines.

Avoiding this situation is difficult but not impossible. All you need to do is increase your sensitivity for the happenings in life. Sensitivity increase will make your mind equally receptive to new observation/learning at all times. Mind needs to be trained to look at everything as if looking at it the very first time; as if you are ready to get surprised by the turn of events. In the process earlier memory gets erased or forgotten. Once your link to past gets severed, the current experience itself feels like the first experience protecting genuine joy and pleasure at every repetition as well. So we have to look at all our fears, pleasures, attachments, as if looking at them the very first time with a clean slate. This involves prompting the mind to use its passion for learning, to intensify its sensitivities for happenings, to maintain its open and pure approach for right observation. Let there be no opinion, no conclusions or formula, because all these spoil our ability to enjoy and deprive us from cherishing experiences in more ways than one.

The entire concept of memory (its creation, retention or recall included) is entangled with an 'observer' and another aspect called 'observed'; the duality of an 'object' and a 'subject'. This duality spoils our propensity to take notice of so many beautiful things around in life. Lack of focus and concentration stops us from seeing the hidden beauty of things around. Hence, every intelligent person must cross over the walls created by this duality as soon as possible.

This duality also create a big ditch full of conflicts because the observer does not look at the reality 'as it is' but more like what 'it should be'. The qualities it perceives are based on its own analyst or expert. Its analysis is based on accumulated incidents, accidents, memories and experiences. Under influence of these accumulations it forms an unreal image of the object. Soon that unreal image gets cast in concrete and we start dealing with situations with such pre-cast false images. Just recall your interaction with a person in your immediate circle (can very well be your spouse) and sum up how many times you assume their words, actions, reactions based on a preexisting image. Surely, we should not deal with false images but real beings.

Yes, ending duality demands tremendous discipline for merging both 'observer' and 'observed' into one. Once you are able to do that, you are going to get direct access to your consciousness. Continuous practice helps in looking at things happening in life afresh by freeing the mind from past impressions and stored experiences. Please acquire the skill of being a pure observer by shunning away all comparisons, expectations and judgements. By focusing attention on pure observation, everything seen and felt will get experienced as a blissful experience. Please attempt it with full knowledge and credence that it is entirely possible to develop such an attitude with practice. This single capability, once acquired, is capable of transforming this very world into haven (as we believe it to exist and if it really exists).

N. Taking Things to Logical Conclusion

Thoughts stay in our mental space similar to uninvited guests who refuse to pack their bags and leave. This especially happens when we come across some big issues with no solution in sight. It is quite a common problem for most except that contours of problems differ from person to person. We are also aware that half hearted efforts result in only half baked solutions. Most recommended suggestion, therefore, is to take up one issue at a time and continue working on it until that issue is taken to its most logical conclusion. This process indeed involves a long chain of subparts like seizing the, collecting its full details, identify connected parts of the main problem, study each part for its own solution, look through all options available, review impacts of each pros and cons, look for longer perspective, ensure that there is no violation of value system codes and finally execute the action or actions, as the case may be. This is precise reason that most people lose steam in taking big things to conclusion. Multiplicity of issues and possible actions inject doubts and fear of failures.

Most of the issues with practitioners at this stage revolve around specific obstacles not caving in spite of best of efforts. Until now, one was able to keep them aside and move on for additional issues but that is no more an option at this stage. Now you have to find the perceptions, physical, mental or philosophical real reason, study about its theoretical perspective, look for experiences shared by others, make required changes in approach, try out alternate techniques, consult teachers and generally do everything else until the issue gets resolved. The luxury of ignoring or postponing an issue no more exits at this stage of practice. Yes, it may require tons of patience and understanding. Leaving a problem unsolved leaves scars making our vision blurred.

Continued meditation practice does its wonders by churning out unique mix of clarity and imaginative solutions and encouraging practitioners to act with courage and conviction. That part comes partly from Acceptance, partly from Detachment, partly from Concentration or Silence or Mind Training, etc. Second important step to take fewer issues to their logical conclusions is to clearly separate out the core issues from peripheral issues, the process referred as 'helicopter view'. At later stages, success achieved in meditation aids discovering appropriate solutions found with own-expertise befitting to an external consultant of repute. Thus, you are able to weigh in long term view, minimise resource involved, draw help from others, and evaluate alternate solutions. Beyond doubt, this approach helps arriving at better and effective course of action to all pressing issues. In any case, meditation prepares you well to accept the outcome without any preference or attachment with the result.

One might conclude that most of above-mentioned practices have no direct relation with practising meditation. Indeed these practices sound way too general in nature and sound like sermons for leading a new way of life. But a close scrutiny will suggest that these practices indeed address common issues that impact living life off the mat. Bit by bit work on these suggestions prove crucial in transforming the way of living life and that too in a practical manner. Most of these suggestions relate to subtle improvements which are difficult to be appreciated by a person struggling in living normal ignorant life. That is why these have been placed at this stage of the book.

19

Embracing Mauna, the Voice of Silence

Perfect silence alone has the power to reflect reality with exact clarity just like a flawless mirror reflecting clear image of an object placed before it. Silence bridges the wide gulf denying access to our inner self; it alone facilitates communication with soul. Silence relaxes the brain and creates prospects for genuine imagination and original thinking. One can hear God only in the quietness of life. Phenomenal physical and emotional health benefits are just other incidental benefits of practising silence. Silence also helps to dispel prevailing uncertainties as most important decisions of life necessitate access to one's pure silence. Perfect silence just cannot be achieved so long as one fails to sever links with past and future. Real happiness and feeling of bliss will also continue evading us unless we learn to experience this pure silence.

> "True silence is the rest of the mind, and is to the spirit what sleep is to the body, nourishment and refreshment."
>
> — *William Penn*

Speaking generally, discussion about silence remains restricted to loud or disturbing sounds falling in ears from speech or noise from other sources. No, that is just a tiny and obvious aspect of silence. Silence being discussed here involves much different horizons as we will soon see. Besides sounds of higher decibels, we are equally perturbed by resonance and reverberations of logic, internal arguments, internal debates, never ending evaluations, comparisons, mental chattering that keep us engaged ever so regularly. Speaking broadly, living in silence need guarding against multiple noise sources listed hereunder:

- Noise from Speech
- Sounds of Emotions and Feelings
- Uproars of Desires and Passions
- Voices of Faiths and Beliefs
- Rattling of Attitudes and Prejudices
- Clamouring of Fears and Anxieties
- Yelling of Ego
- Murmuring of Opinions and Judgements
- Detonation of Habits and Obsessions
- Hissing sounds of Thoughts

This list clearly expands the scope and significance of silence to its real comprehension relevant to our discussions here. Suddenly it is obvious that the most common form of higher decibels emanating from our environment and personal interaction is just a tiny part of the problem we face; that there are many other sources that are more forceful, difficult to control and irritating for our mental peace. Clamours from these dimensions keep our mind agitated even when we are all alone, inside our cozy homes, sleeping in night on well secured beds. These forces do not allow us to even dream peacefully.

Our very existence is indeed noisy and it is deteriorating too badly and too fast. No arguments are needed to realise this reality. That is why importance of silence is much higher today than ever in the past. We are indeed living in an uproarious and rattling world. Cities and towns were never louder in human history. Adulterated noise keeps pouring out loud at all times from neighbourhood, traffic, industries, commercial establishments, public places, religious and cultural centres. To make matter worse, we keep switching from one noise source to another hoping it to provide more agreeable noise. Overtime, people lose sensitivity to prevailing noise and start believing that they got used to it. Noise is disturbing under all situations and no one ever gets used to it; noise does never stop impacting human adversely. Every time one is exposed to noise, and all types of noise for that matter, the brain gets alerted irrespective the nature of noise; likable or unlikable.

Internal Noise Sources

One may brush aside the environmental noise by branding it beyond control but how are we dealing with the controllable noise sources?

How much of our silence is getting harmed by noise from podcasts, blog posts, TED Talks, books, Music Apps, Social media, TV and entire entertainment and news segments. These sources of noise overwhelm us and always end up clouding our ability to listen inside voice. Next in line is the internal noise generated by ongoing monologues, running stories of triumphs and defeats, desires and temptations, inspiration and imagination, past failures and future fears, current pressures and anxieties. These are by far most disturbing noise and can safely be called our biggest enemy. It is critical to discuss above classification of noise sources simply because, the moment we talk about silence, our intelligent mind jumps to blame uncontrollable environmental sources leaving aside more lethal and comparatively controllable internal issues that involve no one other than we ourselves.

Unfortunately, with every passing day we are constantly adding to our noise sources. We have started making even those activities noisy which were always carried out in silence. What else explains constant feeds from earphones, podcasts, sermons, preaching, etc.? Exploding numbers of blue screens have multiplied additional sources of noise like never before. Most recent technological advancements are adding to noise in worst possible proportions. Situation is turning so bad that people are seen opting for checking themselves into silence retreats to just reconnect with sense of quietness away from society.

Agreed that silence is too feeble and every human effort to pursue, protect and promote interest of every kind ends up breaking silence. Actually, life itself is a form of noise and it is almost impossible to avoid it. On the other hand, every quest for salvation necessitates access to complete silence. Silence is capable of being used as an effective tool for human to human communication. It is a unique power to show agreements or disagreements and it can be strongly used to make or break communication. Practising silence is a personal and optional choice. Expertise to use silence effectively is a sure sign of wisdom of the beholder. Here again, most critical is to fight the internal noise which is the hardest of all and is similar to swimming against the current.

Connection with our inner silence allows us to see through our real hurts and wounds. That clarity later enables us to attend to the curses and get cured by acknowledging them, because when you know better you deal better. Silence also provides best possible environment for real communication with other beings. Verbal communication is too overrated. As per research, 93 per cent of real communication is nonverbal (Dr. Albert Mehrabian). Silence is also available for use as a great negotiation tool. Spoken words are always well-packaged lies and are open for loss of message in translation. Silence is stable and substantial; there are no misunderstandings in silent communication. But the real trick is how to access that veritable silence in our normal life. Do we even know that real silence, at all?

Understanding Nature of Silence

Pure silence being discussed here is intimately shy by nature. The moments she listen you talking, even about her, she disappears; to talk about silence is to miss silence. Our mind deals with words and images and we can say that silence is what tells about the noise; otherwise silence is just the remainder. Good thing is that this silence is completely attainable. All it requires is velvet gloves used with great care. It is approachable by any one at any time and any place provided one is well trained to do so. Silence is not felt with mind but requires the connection with the depth of heart. All it presupposes is your ability to turn off all sorts of chatters mentioned before. All it demands is perfect tuning with your innermost voice and shunning of all notions, tangible or notional, irrespective of quality of those notions. Once approached, this silence provides strongest possible results. So much so that all powerful and tricky human mind also cannot ignore its message.

Access to this very silence is pivotal to aspire for faster progress in meditation. You must communicate with your silence regularly. You must make peace with it. Any effort to bring mind under regulation cannot succeed unless access to pure silence is gained. Silence heightens sensitivity to a level where subtle sound of soul becomes audible. This is very stillness and tranquility advocated by people of wisdom. This silence also helps indicate success in shunning away past and future and living in our present moment. Under influence of this silence, our actions may be slow but they are definitely more deliberate and our thoughts may be few but well ordered. In this situation, we may be refraining from reading, writing or all other direct contacts with everything external, but we feel tuned with the very source of everything.

Silence is a quintessential mental state to get connected with our inner self. Initiation of dialogue with our feeble conscience necessitates perfect silence. It is an uncompromised condition and not a matter of degree or options. "In Hindu philosophy, Mauna (Silence), which has a voice of its own, refers to peace of mind, inner quietude, Samadhi and the Absolute Reality. The Hindu texts insist upon proper understanding of silence (called Mauna in Hindi and Sanskrit) by experiencing it through control of speech and practice."—Wikipedia page on Mauna. Sanskrit texts actually define Mauna as state of "non existence". Going a step further Ramana Maharishi equates Mauna to state of Egolessness, where mind is firmly established in heart and primal thought of "I" disappears for the thought of ever-existing real self. This very silence is the real silence for meditation.

Practising Silence

Silence is essential prerequisite for all life changing learnings of substance. When it comes to transforming life, no change can be effected without being grounded in silence. Like other skills, silence also can be acquired and mastered with proper efforts. More than learning, it calls for unlearning of many things already learnt the wrong way. Silence works like a laboratory having space and instruments to make your experiments (similar to all scientific inventions). Silence allows you to know what did exist but was not known. Silence allows germination of seeds of insight perceptions which in turn facilitate the experiments of far reaching consequences.

In normal life we like to achieve more in less time. Most of us wish to achieve maximum possible quantitative targets. These result in tons of sensory inputs communicated to the mind. This basic approach of expecting more, trying for more, getting more, and then some more, needs a total reversal for practising silence. Practice for silence requires erecting strong barriers to filter minutest content before allowing it to entre into mental space. This 360 degree reversal becomes feasible only at Stage Three of your meditation journey.

Simply imagine a minister offering to meet and listen to every visitor offering complaints or compliments. How much time will he be left to attend to make long term policies, conduct review meetings, and monitor progress on initiatives under implementation or making/ revising statues for legalising the plans and policies? Our mind is no less important than a crucial minister of a high level Government. The minister is required to have sufficient time to identify, review, discuss, supervise and finally implement long-lasting solutions to ensure real governance for its population. Else, list of complaints from the very population will just get longer and longer.

Ongoing chattering weakens our concentration and depletes energy to think long term. Silence replenishes that very energy. Nothing else restores brain's receptor centres like silence. That restoration ignites imaginations, problem solving and high order thinking. All these qualities progressively suffer under the overload already talked. Reconnecting to our pure silence is a sure way of recharging those attention centres back to effective levels. In a way, silence allows us to tap into default mode of our mental network. All it asks is to minimise external stimuli and internal chirping. Regaining default mode of our sensory network lets us access inner thoughts, memories and ideas which enable us to think deeply, objectively, rationally and creatively. This very regaining is called opening of 'Gyan Chakshu', the eyes of wisdom.

> "Fools disagree due to ignorance. Intelligent disagree due to excess knowledge. Wise neither agree nor disagree but remain silent. That is why he is called Mauni, the silent one."

Silence and Meditation

'Silence is a true mental workshop'. 'Meditation is dominant and powerful form of work'. It will not be difficult to agree with efficacy of both these statements. The moment these two statements are combined, there remains no ambiguity about role of silence in meditation. No one can carry out this powerful work without access to this critical mental workshop. Silence plays critical role in letting the mind be graced with clarity and stillness, two most important preconditions of meditation. Still and clear mind alone is ready to feel detached and to let go the influence of ego. Clarity and stillness of mind alone sharpens the visual perception to see true reality with eyes closed. Achieving this state of mind coupled with well developed conscious awareness provides the best possible podium for most effective contemplation. Just remaining in this state, it offers feel of bliss and energy to do wonders on every aspect of human existence. Experiencing such a state by itself is the most immediate reason people get magnetised towards meditation.

Off course, our ever spinning mind just despises silence. When we wish to introduce silence to the mind, it starts exposing its efficiency by bringing to surface even those issues that were buried deep down. It is here that meditation helps silence as it systematically prepares that very mind to be receptive in steps before completely submitting to the radiance of silence. Thus, there is a perfect case of both silence and meditation helping each other to progressively grow in stature and intensity. One ought to remember that noise can never be stronger enough to disturb silence, that silence is essential and productive to create wisdom and clarity as against mechanical thinking. The moment one gets this mantra, silence becomes more attractive and important.

20

Concentration—Disciplining the Mind for Undivided Attention

> "There is no limit to the power of the human mind. The more concentrated it is, the more power is brought to bear on one point."—Swami Vivekananda

Concentration is best defined as stable and absolute attention and energy continuously established on an object of conscious choice. Such attention should be sustained irrespective of focus being wide or narrow or object being big or small. Thus, concentration is much more than attention, as attention is generally spontaneous and switching in nature. Only the stable variety of attention is made use of in concentration. Actually, one of the most profound benefits of meditation is its contribution towards replacing spontaneous or switching attention into stable form. Beyond doubt, our attention is a precious faculty and like every other faculty its usefulness depends on how it is put to use. This happens only after mind gets totally diverted from all other ideas it keeps entertaining in its untrained state of being. Best quality of concentration is achieved when one is so attentive to the happenings that all perceptions of world around stand completely dissolved.

Let us understand it with the example of light. Normal light spills over in multiple directions and can illuminate a place only in the immediate vicinity. Its intensity gets lost over small distance of few metres at best. Beyond which it fails to illuminate anything with clarity. But once the projection of same source of light is made directional and converted into a beam, it is able to illuminate the object placed in far away distance. After all, a beam is stream of same light concentrated in a single direction through use of many reflectors. Normal untrained human mind is no different than the spilled light as it keeps leaking its attention from one thing to another, entertaining one thought after another in an endless manner. Diluted attention, without doubt, is an open invitation to restlessness, anxiety and dullness.

Let us quickly look at obvious reasons for lack of concentration. Lack of engagement in a meaningful activity is its first obvious cause. During growing years mind of a child is active as he keep learning newer things. But soon after crossing middle age many things start settling down on personal, career as well as family fronts. At this stage, many of us fall for the routine where there are hardly many new things to learn. Learnings during adulthood actually explain extensive difference in wisdom of people when they are in their seventies, for example. Those who are able to keep themselves engaged all through their adult life in purposeful pursuits are seen standing much apart from their friends going with the normal routine of daily life. Single word for difference in a routine hardened mind and engaging mind is surely 'concentration of attention'. Forgetfulness, something associated with aging actually is first indication that the mind in question is not being properly exploited and used and hence, is prevalent among younger people as well.

Having focused, selective or undivided concentration is not accidental. And there is no reason for one to settle for anything less than sustained concentration. Yes, there can be physical factors like dementia, organic disorders, brain injury or some neurological illness that may result in memory lapses but if one is not suffering from some such condition and still has poor concentration, it is just a case of inactive or less active brain. The obvious reasons for poor concentration are lack of dedication for the work in hand, lack of interest in the task being performed, poor emotional state, physical fatigue or non-conducive environment. These are all manageable issues.

Let us realise that memory and concentration are not fixed qualities but skills that can be acquired, grown and refined like all other critical skills and at any stage of life. Tips for improving brain activity include continuously learning new things, regularly using all senses, repeating and re-repeating things that one wishes to remember for long and attending one thing at a time with full mental and physical attention. So next time when you come across a person remembering thousands of names, events or anecdotes, should work as a reminder to you about the commitment and practice that person would have put in to reach where he is today. Just exclaiming that some other person has fantastic memory and you do not is a clear case of sour grapes.

> "Attention is a limited resource, so pay attention to where you pay attention."
>
> — *Howard Rheingold,*
> An American critic, writer, and teacher

Second critical step to aim for sustained concentration is regular breaks. It is impossible for any human to sustain high quality concentration for longer durations. To lose focus is part of the internal human survival system. Frequent breaks help in overcoming this genetic programming. Do not know why, most people do not consider place of work suitable for any form of physical exercises. No one should shy away in taking small breaks at work, say once every 30-40 minutes and go for some stretching, standing work outs or even chair based exercises. It is wrong to believe that such breaks negatively impact productivity. To the contrary, people having regular breaks at work, in research or even studying for exams, show far superior outcomes. Blocking outside stimuli, proper organising and setting clear prioritisation of activities are some other options to remove physical distractions to sustained concentration.

Buddha's Approach to Concentration

Gautam Buddha is credited with very convincing theory on right concentration for pursuing superior objectives of human life. Actually, right concentration is the eighth and final part of the famous Eight Fold Path preached by Buddha. Buddhist traditions provide that the first seven parts (namely, right view, right resolution, right speech, right action, right livelihood, right efforts and right mindfulness) are all dedicated for achieving the eighth path of right concentration. Practitioners report of refinement in their concentration with step-by-step progress in attending to recommended first seven parts of the path. Buddhist literature also holds shiny distractions of sense organs as biggest challengers in the way of achieving skillful qualities arising in the mind so that it rests in concentration. Sensual preoccupations, desire for aromas, desire for tastes, and desire for tactile sensations are considered big roadblocks preventing a mind from getting concentrated on higher objectives. One has to let go all these ill wills completely before expecting the readiness of the mind to surrender for desired level of concentration.

Making Mind Willing for Concentration

> "Be at least as interested in what goes on inside you as what happens outside. If you get the inside right, the outside will fall into place."
>
> — *Eckhart Tolle*,
>
> Canadian spiritual teacher and best-selling author.

But concentration by itself is not sufficient. One should be able to invoke it on the object and time of choice. Some people choose strictness to bring control over mind but it does not work for concentration and, hence, meditation. Our mind is very manipulative and stubborn. When pushed into a corner, it does not shy away from providing wrong impressions to its master and it is expert in coming up justifications of its own working or lame excuses for its inability to work. That is why it is said that 'mind has a mind of its own'.

We ought to induce active willingness of the mind only through friendly approach. Considering the mind as a subordinate has its own repercussions. You may have heard that mind is a great slave but bad master. But the path of enslaving has to pass through many hurdles requiring very careful navigation. Among all relationships, friendship is the only approach assured of fast and sure way to obtain its willingness. Great amount of compassion is required to make it agreeable as a friend. You have to be forgiving and strict at the same time. Please avoid imposing restrictions too early. Treat it as your friend and give your dear mind as much space as required.

How to Improve Concentration?

Bringing a bit of ancient wisdom in the play, Maharishi Patanjali prescribes only two alternative tools for steadying the mind and making it willingly surrender to work like a slave. These tools are 'Abhyasa' and 'Vairagya'. The first tool refers to the practice of regular efforts to stay with object of choice and second tool is the art of detachment. The most recommended practice for pursuing 'Abhyasa', the efforts, is through breath control. Regular Pranayam secures higher oxygen at the disposal of brain to let it work with vitality and vigour. Use of mantra also is regarded as best possible practice of regular efforts. Repetition of Mantra in a synchronised manner allows feeling the vibrations emanating from concentration. One selects his/her own mantra and use it until it is able to keep mental systems agreeable.

'Vairagya', on the other hand, has already been fully explained in the chapter on Detachment. But for the limited purpose of comprehending its impact on concentration, detachment enables release of tension of the body and mind so that both mind and body work as counter balance. Detachment here is similar to putting the vehicle in neutral gear for disengaging it completely from the forces (of thoughts). Once the car is in neutral gear any pressure on racing pedal does not have any impact on movement of the vehicle.

Let us also look at some proven tips for improving concentration. Having a good physical health by good diet, sufficient sleep and regular exercise tops this list. Physical health is very critical for optimum working of mind. Much more than heart and lungs, mind needs high dosage of oxygen and exercise. Like every other key organs, mind also tends to get lazy if not exercised regularly. Brain as an organ is only two per cent in volume of the body but consumes about twenty per cent of total body energy. Receiving energy is comparatively difficult for brain due to its location at the wrong end of gravity. Oxygen is carried to the brain with blood pumped against gravity. To keep it well oxygenated, blood pumping quality must remain of high order through regular physical exercises.

After ensuring mental energy and stabilising all important moral stability, mind needs to be motivated so that it gains its willingness to seek concentration. Depleted mental energy makes the mind low on patience while low moral stability makes it indeterminate. For making success we need both patience and determination in equal proportions. One must work on both these factors simultaneously because virtue of patience without determination is laziness while determination without patience is just recklessness. Presence of both determination and patience facilitates active willingness of the mind.

Leading a disciplined routine also helps in improving attentive concentration. Avoiding distraction comes next in importance. Keeping notifications on, cluttered environment, having too many activities in hand, picking thoughts on impulse, finding fast solutions are some such examples piling distractions for our monkey mind. It loves to work as a spider always awaiting some or the other things to happen. How can such mind concentrate? Well developed intellect is required to encourage mind to remain in present. Keep things simple and cultivate the habit of taking slow and logical decisions. Spending time in social activities and frequently helping people indirectly keep us happy and it also works like a boost for better concentration. Some people suggest maintain a 'to do' list only for distractions so that they find time to meet you but only as per your appointment. Regularly switching between high attention and low attention activities is also very important since higher concentration is impossible to be maintained for long at one stretch.

Concentration and Meditation

Meditation is acknowledged as the surest possible way to enhance concentration, and that too, while remaining consciously aware. But we must appreciate the very basic nature of concentration and meditation as there is a genuine confusion for what comes first? We also come across articles proclaiming that right concentration is right meditation; as if both these concepts are interchangeable. Thus, there is sufficient room for a far deeper dilemma. Should we focus on meditation to improve concentration or improve concentration for achieving progress in Meditation?

Concentration, by its very nature, requires some immutable efforts. As a result mind, in its concentrated state, tends to develop fatigue in due course. A tired mind is lethargic and dull. This sluggishness is entirely different than the sense of comfort or ease so much required for practising meditation; a state where the practitioner can remain internally focused for longer periods of time. Concentration is by far a very conscious effort while meditation gets ruined by making conscious efforts. So, concentration certainly starts its journey much before meditation.

In reality, however, meditation and concentration become inseparably intertwined except for the initial stage where both these concepts have separate identity. At later stages, concentration and meditation travel together for long distance on the same path. If meditation is a full grown strong tree, concentration is certainly the compost required to help the plant grow faster during its infancy stage.

Once we are able to train our mind and acquire concentration in our efforts, focusing mind on right issues and turning it inside becomes comparatively feasible. Soon a brilliant light begins illuminating all issues placed under its focus. Qualitative illumination so achieved brings clarity and makes comprehension feasible. This very clarity and understanding is called the perfect vision of real truth. Entire purpose of meditation is to gain this very vision. In its very advance stage, when that vision get focused on the Supreme Being, one is said to have reached the Super conscious state, Samadhi, the very ultimate pinnacle of Spiritual quest.

21

Crossing Over Materialism

Continued indulgence in materialism is certainly one of the biggest roadblocks for spiritual awakening. And it has been so all through recorded human history. People from modern world are gripped by materialism like never before. A large majority today justify materialism as a must-have for a happy life. Material resources were always required by humanity but sheer magnitude of resources required today is squarely blamed on Industrial Revolution. Suddenly, the way for societies to live, eat, dress, communicate, cure, transport, educate, worship, celebrate, fight, compete and excel, has all undergone a big change in recent centuries. The basic direction of things required in all these spheres has swiftly moved from 'less to more', from 'minimum to elaborate', from 'survival to luxurious living'. Chase for materialism can safely be branded as the single largest homogenising factor of entire humanity in 21st century.

Corporations, a new form of faceless identities, have started ruling the world and its order is pushing human beings and their rules, ethics, emotions, and compassions out of the game. These corporations function with the sole purpose of maximising profits for their owners. For them everything except profit is secondary in significance and incidental in character. Corporations have converted scientific innovations and technological advancements to flood markets with products and services that never existed earlier. They spend billions on advertising products with the loud claim of satisfying needs that did not even exist earlier. Many of the product features presented are just fictitious and concocted. Riding on artificially created false propaganda, acquiring and flashing these items is already new normal. Society looks down on people not having access to such new products and brands. Having more things is considered inspirational and worth trying for. Under this reality, crossing over materialism is certainly harder than any time in the past.

Even at the cost of being branded as old-fashioned, let us take a pause and look at subtle difference between necessities, comforts and luxuries. Necessities are basic requirements for sustaining life. Items covered here meet primary needs like food, clothing and shelter. Comforts include stuff that goes to make life easy and comfortable resulting in improvement in efficiency and productivity. Comforts available, but only in appropriate measures, with one's own hard earned resources, accumulated morally, can also be justified on some counts. Both necessities and comforts help build, maintain, secure and sustain our physical body, the most essential equipment of soul to enjoy human experience. But expensive things catering to only pleasures and prestige squarely fall under luxuries. These are rather used for displaying wealth and power of their owner. Luxuries have always been looked down in all traditions from the East simply because these are obstructions in making progress on spiritual journey. As such, seeking spiritual advancement demands a clear line of segregation so that proper filters are applied to identify and segregate luxuries from comforts, and finally disassociating oneself with everything falling on the luxury side.

This all important differentiation requires developing strong perceptions about materialism and how stringent barrier it is in the way of our progress in meditation. Unfortunately, materialism plays very soft to begin with but the crossing over from necessity/comforts to materialism happens so ever seamlessly that most of us fail to feel its tipping point. This works exactly like 'The Boiling Frog' fable where poor frog gets cooked to death without perceiving the danger increasing with slow warming of the water from tepid to boiling. Interestingly, the biggest reason for this failure is our own DNA which has evolved sharp sensors to feel pain of only unfavourable changes while incremental changes towards the favourable conditions are gleefully accepted as welcome relief. Unfortunately, 'basic materialism necessary for survival' and 'desire for unending acquisitions' are two sides of the same coin connected in a unique blind fluid where normal human being invariably fails to gauge the switch over. Realisation and practising the blessings of contentment alone helps normal soul in guarding against prevailing dragon fire like lust for materialism.

Does Materialism Operate in Isolation?

Problem with materialism is more complex than what appears on the surface. It does not live alone and encircles us with all its large family members living under its command. Materialism is known to have immediate younger siblings named Fear and Frustration. Materialism is also rumoured to be biological father of Jealousy and Insecurity. Thus, materialism rarely operates in isolation. Materialism hunts in pack where all its siblings and bastards get joined by their common friends named Greed, Egoism and Attachment. Insatiability happens to be the single common thread among all pack members. So letting them indulge with a free pass is not even an option. These evil forces capture their innocent prey where initial attraction gets evolved to a level where necessity loses its differentiation with constant hunger of acquisition. This hunger is different than the cravings by sense organs (which by itself is considered too tempting to resist).

Interestingly, all of our five physical sense organs ultimately get satiated with continuous indulgence. After all, one can eat only so much, lecture for so long, listen best of music or other sounds only for so long. The eyes also can see the best of scenery for a limited length of time only and so is the case for sexual gratification. But our sixth sense, the human mind, which incidentally provides shelter to materialism in its early stages, has no gratification limits. Such strong is the bad influence of its company that poor mind soon gets trapped in its sinister designs. To make matter worse, hunger intensity of materialism keeps increasing every time a previous demand gets met as its normal motto of 'more the merrier' gets kicked in.

Materialism, an unending appetite for wealth and material goods, is initially driven by thrills of acquiring objects. Later the same gets followed by ego-inflating stimulation of owning those very objects. This stimulation continues growing from one object to another, from smaller to bigger, and from fewer to many. Incidentally, Western economic system is based on this very concept which considers human being as a rational actor always seeking to maximise material self-interest based on 'multiplicity of wants'. Of course, one should value the riches for what it can do but should never get ruled by it. Being rich can be logically justified only so long as the owner understands the added responsibility of putting it to good use for helping those in need. It is here that Eastern system fundamentally differs with Western system. Only Eastern concept endorses excess of wealth as a trust to be used for welfare of others now and in coming generations.

Harms from Indulging in Materialism

The lust for materialism is fuelled by prevailing culture of consumption which encourages people to succumb to temptation and acquire things without considering the consequences of the acquisition. People are seen buying things just to improve their psychological well being spoiled by prevailing anxiety and unhappiness. Vitiated forms of materialism have been named as Compulsive Buying Disorders and Compulsive Hoarding Disorders where people experience irresistible urge leading to excessive, expensive and time consuming acquisition spree. These disorders cause severe social, personal and financial pressures prompting mood swings, substance abuse and eating disorders, to name a few.

Insulation from stranglehold of materialism requires constant vigilance against desire to acquire objects which indeed is its ignition point. Ensure that desire to pick up any object, small or big, is always driven by our hardships or necessities and not by inner discontent. Market offers too many attractive products but should we buy those things just because they are available and we can afford? Buying stuff without the filter of necessity runs the risk of falling under materialism. And for the sake of clarity, even on philosophical basis materialism belongs to the opposite camp of both idealism and spiritualism.

Proponents of materialism believe that every human is a born materialist and only unhappy people drift away towards religion, spirituality or some such practice including meditation. They also justify it as an evolutionary mechanism that enhances state of alertness and motivates people to work harder and achieve more. But such views are over-simplification of a correctible phenomenon. Motivation is not the sole legacy of materialists alone. Motivation to do better is a positive stimulation of many other desires; it comes from curiosity to know something unknown, hope for suitable rewards, maintaining a positive self-image, and many such other intrinsic factors. Motivation to do better is a cycle where thoughts influence initiatives. In reality, studies establish that materialists lack sanity to decide how much is enough and generally falter on their priorities.

Philosophical and Spiritual Materialism

In addition to physical materialism discussed above, one has to guard against its even more powerful manifestation called the philosophical materialism. This is less visible but more detrimental in nature. Under this form, the being is captured by strong opinions, iron-clad likes and dislikes, staunch judgements and fictitious pretexts. Such people hold stiff attitudes and are in perpetual confrontation with those having divergent views. And it is not that they are only named as militants, zealots, extremists or chauvinists. People displaying strong brand consciousness are equally covered under this form of philosophical materialism.

Interestingly, endorsements of brands is not limited to usual merchandise as we understand in normal parlance but include religious belief, political leanings, cult followings, racial supremacy, social diktats, gender bias, or advocacy of a race, culture, language, or such usual divisive factors. Youngsters promoting specific product brands, supporters cheering for particular sports team, political followers cheering their parties or leaders, religious followers chanting for their cult leaders are all obvious examples of obsessions with philosophical materialism. And, in every important ways, philosophical materialism is as bad as materialism of objects and possessions.

Spiritual materialism is yet another manifestation of the same problem. Examples of this form are temporarily experienced during meditative state, worship routines, during visits to religious places, while undertaking philanthropy based activities like conducting camps for donations, arranging free meals for needy and such other getaways intended for uplifting ego by developing a superficial self image. In reality, any such activity, unless carried out of genuine compassion, is just a pleasure-seeking trip and provides experiences similar to relief from anxieties post couple of alcohol shots. More than the act, the intentions behind such activities dictate the final outcome. Every activity for helping others must be carried out without any traces of sycophancy or flattery to your own ego. Else it runs the risk of immediately getting degraded as a repugnant form of spiritual materialism. Let each seeker develop good understanding of materialism in its complete scope and see through these adventures. Agreed, it is a difficult path to follow but there is no choice. A meditator must overcome all traces of materialism and detest from these as much as possible.

How to Guard against Materialism

Bonding of materialism with negative forces of life makes it a smoking gun for several mental disorders prevailing in society at present, and we know that well. That is why every stream of wisdom, from every corner of the earth and every time in history, warns against temptations to own and indulge in flashy flamboyance. Situation today is certainly at its worst but it is not that nothing can be done to seek freedom from the clutches of materialism. Gradual progress in practising meditation by itself is a sure way to begin in right direction. Several other conscious efforts can also be made to insulate ourselves against heat of materialism. Following suggestions have proven useful to passionate seekers in their endeavours.

Direct and Redirect focus on Internal Goals

At any moment we have two simple choices to direct our focus. Either we let it wander in external direction or we cajole it to turn inward. So long you continue looking outside all you see are objects and exteriors of living beings. This always is a partial view resulting in wrong impressions and conclusions. Pointing your focus to your internal core helps you truly realise significant human needs like objectivity, competence and relatedness being more important than accumulation of embracing materialism in its different manifestations. Inward focus redirects your view from the obvious to intrinsic; from temporary to permanent and from uniqueness to universalities. Spend time in solitude and come out of influence from external pressures. When you focus inside, you suffer less from distractions and false impressions. And most importantly, inward focus does not involve usual resistance, opposition or after effects.

See Through Subjectivity and Develop Objectivity

External goals like minting money, trashy titles, prestigious positions, artificial awards, clapping from crowd, etc. are completely subjective and clear indications of poor mental health, anxiety and narcissism. A subjective perspective is always influenced by individual emotions, opinions, biases and feelings. On the other hand, objectivity based perspective depends on facts, logic and reasoning. We should focus on promoting objectivity to boost our self esteem, happiness and psychological well being. Objectivity also helps you bring proper balance within divergent goals. It helps to decide about your necessities and help you measure how much is enough.

Evaluate and Conclude that Materialism is Imperfect

Study the concepts around materialism, gain desired knowledge from as many sources as possible (ancient and modern, Eastern and Western), compare all alternates, check history, check people from past or present and generally speaking do everything you wish to do. Take your time and contemplate as much as required but arrive at final conclusion of your own, once for all, about focus on materialism being good or bad for the long term happiness in life.

People of wisdom in past have spoken about it and their conclusions are clear and simple. That acquisitions and possessions of all types and forms are sheer means and can never be justifiable ends by themselves, is the universal culmination of all intelligent thoughts. You may not remain in disagreement from this reality for long that 'ends' are more important than 'means'. Pursuing means is faulty approach as means are always open for misuse. Allow this realisation to completely sink in your internal system. When one starts focusing on 'ends', materialism cannot ever remain main focus of human life, period.

Cultivate and Practise Gratitude

Acknowledging and appreciating all things present in your life is the simplest way of being practical. This by itself is being in gratitude. It is not that you stop chasing what you need but please do that while remaining in appreciation for what you already got. The real joy comes from appreciation and not from possession. The sense of gratitude lessens your hunger for more. It helps you realise that enough is enough.

Look into Your Attitude

You may be engaged in right actions (by avoiding all prohibited, immoral or illegal actions) but that alone is not enough. Your actions must also meet the condition of being an actor with selfless attitude. Generally there are three very important questions like (a) who is performing actions, (b) for whom are the actions being performed and (c) what is the purpose behind those actions. If the answer to any of these three questions involves I, me or mine, there is certainly a big problem because such an action is apparently selfish. It is a clear declaration that you are acting materialist.

Ideally, the answer for the first question should involve omniscient and omnipotent Supreme where you should conduct an action as His instrument or his servant. This teaching comes straight from the Bhagwad Gita in the forms of word of Lord Krishna. The second question should involve society at large rather than you, your family or friends/relatives alone. Similarly, the answer to last question should always be public service. The moment majority of your actions start meeting these pious conditions, grip of materialism gets loosened even when money making happens to be your occupation.

Apply Filters to Information Being Consumed

Flow of information today has just exploded like never before. So it is very essential to apply filters on information consumption. Filters are a must on conscious as well as unconscious levels. Explosion of information from multiple sources makes it like attending a feast with a lavish buffet comprising of signature dishes from all continents for multiple courses. Since you only have so much appetite, and assuming that you are indeed health conscious, you have to be cautious of what you put on your plate. Lack of filters carries the eventual risk of drowning you in non-essential information. For example, choose only one newspaper, browse only limited websites, watch TV only for a fixed period, be member of only limited WA Groups, and so on. Post only so many updates. Follow only so many people, and so on.

Increase Your Investments in Right Social Connections

Behavioural studies conducted establish direct link between materialism and social isolation. Materialism sucks your precious time. That in turn reduces your social interactions. That isolation forces to search recourse in material objects. This is even bigger challenge for people living in metro cities. Be it in sports, hobby clubs, discussions groups, walking pals, meditation retreats or whatever; please ensure that your roots to social interactions are founded firm. But social interaction does not mean parties and late nights but coming together for common cause with likeminded people contributing their individual bit for greater good of society. Idea is to promote human to human interface for common cause.

Emergence of social media is among the leading causes of materialistic mindsets among youth of today. Besides regular channels of advertisement, youth equate their self worth to quantitative data like counting re-tweets on Twitter, Facebook likes and Instagram comments. Social media has given us an outlet where we can hide behind a computer and project our edited version to others. It comes out of social insecurity. Please remain away from these new Apps and rely on establishing proper social connections and relationships, that if you wish to remain sane in the long run. How can one forget that money does not ever reciprocate our love or attention but living people do it all the times. Material objects keep slipping from one to another but affection of real people remains intact irrespective of changed circumstances.

Appreciate that Experiences are Superior to Objects

A good part of adult life goes in attending to occupational and family obligations. Past that stage, however, comes the realisation about stories of life lived (good experiences) alone fuelling the fire for passionate living. At that stage presence or absence of objects is just a hygiene factor. Young people, therefore, are advised to accumulate experiences (to be read as hard earned personal achievements) capable of long lasting imprints. The common thread for these experiences, however, must be your individual endeavours, your personal triumphs coming out of exceptional and stretched efforts.

Once you start realising that these experiences are going to be more important for second half of your life, how can you continue chasing cheap and momentary thrills associated with materialism?

Spending time alone is another important measure to puncture the pull of materialism. Outside world exerts lower influence on a person living in solitude. Solitude directly unburdens you from the clutches of comparisons led jealousy. Silence and peace in seclusion allows intrinsic goals to float ashore inner conscience. Such a person better appreciates presence of more important and substantive activities than senselessly pursuing materialism. Maintaining utmost simplicity in all our actions, thoughts and opinions is yet another effective instrument used to loosen grip of materialism.

Putting a big line next to an existing line goes to make the existing line small. Recalibration of your bigger aspirations and objectives of human life is similar to drawing that bigger line. This subtle increased preference for matters of significance coupled with rising contentment immediately goes to make hearts pure. This very process, howsoever slow it may be, is real progress on the journey of Spirituality.

Materialism and Meditation

Their mutually exclusive relationship is similar to day and night, a perfect either or situation. One represents focus on objects, attachments and possessions while the other focus on finer feelings like learning, knowing, introspection, peace, relationship and respect for fellow beings. These two are irreconcilable extremes standing in opposite poles and historically have been in longest running battle. Both of these concepts are involved in a tug of war where, ultimately, only one comes out as winner, a perfect either or situation. Desire for materialism survives and flourishes but only until spirituality remains in deep sleep. But such extreme positions do not apply at starting or later continuing meditation. It is not that one must abandon things material to even try out meditation. Living a materialistic life does not, in any way, disqualify you from pursuing meditation. Later, only much later, the forces associated with spiritual practices are expected to gain sufficient force in a slow manner where pulls of materialistic attractions lose steam. Ultimately, with you making desired progress on your meditational journey, your craving for materialism is destined to fade away.

Meditation brings back your focus on immanent goals of human life and helps you determine your position in this world. Realisation about impermanence of most things in life, reduction in greed and increase in contentment, letting go of desires and learning importance of minimalism, ultimately pulls you out of gravitational force of materialism. Later, with more progress in practice, you realise clarity of your own intellectual and philosophical aspects. Point to remember is that one can have money, position, power, influence, opinions or views as much as possible and still not be a materialist. You are asked to strive being lotus flower blooming in a muddy pond.

Without negating the role of objects in sustaining normal life, one has to differentiate essentials from possessions feeding to luxury. Let us not lose sight of the fact that excess over essentials will either remain unused or will get misused by others. Once this simple realisation sets in, every person has stronger chances to clearly spot the tipping point. Identifying the tipping point allows the seeker to prepare for freeing from all fears of losing life's comforts, possessions, luxuries, social security, human relations and all types of attachment with '*me*' and '*mine*'. There are no exceptions to this rule neither there are shortcuts available. It is actually so plain and simple.

As it is, there is no need to worry about popular stereotypes making rounds about meditation and materialism. Ultimately, taking the 'middle path' helps you navigate your increasing reliance on your own ideas about materialism. Let there be no place for fantasies, dreams or hallucinations about either extremes. So, keep moving forward and enjoy your comforts and, side by side, continue your meditation practice. With the practice of meditation bearing fruits, your mind is destined to lose its grip over attachments with objects, ideas, approaches, and opinions.

Stage Four

The Skilled Meditator

This last and final stage corresponds to obtaining the degree of Doctorate, the Ph.D, which is most advanced degree possible in an academic discipline. Holders of this degree are regarded as authorities in their specialised field of knowledge. Being the highest credible professional recognition, meditation progress at this stage requires non-uniform lengthy endeavours similar to time required for Ph.D degree. Its final project requires a notoriously difficult to compile original Dissertation which also must be vetted and approved by panel of Professors. The cumbersome process forces many aspirants to cave in under the process and leave the programme mid way. Meditation at this advance stage also commands mastering over self discovery of new knowledge called Self-realisation exactly in a similar way.

This stage necessitates mastering over key subjects, overcoming all obstacles experienced, especially mastering the control over subtle distractions. This stage requires perfecting of real nuances of concepts involved, a stage much ahead of formal knowledge or working understanding. Meditator must have already achieved near perfection in moral and ethical issues and finds himself in new avatar of his previous self where worldly attractions, personal relations, emotions, bonds, religious/cultural moorings are all crossed over. The meditator at this stage graduates to settle confusions arising out of grey shades around the periphery of meditational objects. Constant introspection and contemplation is the only tool used at this stage.

This stage calls for majority of available time of the practitioner invested on spirituality supporting activities alone. Even while remaining part of the dark and murky swamp called modern living, such a person envisions life's beauty and bounties keeping his deeper connection with the Self intact. Like a lotus flower flourishing in a muddy pool, this person lives as an awakened and enlightened human life focused purely on universal spirituality. Two most critical faculties used for mastering this stage are 'attention' and 'awareness'. Attention here is pure in nature, grounded with concentration, and washed of all desires or inhibitions. This pure attention manifests in an integrated and aggregated mind completely free from distractions. Such a mind rests in unmitigated clarity, certainty and assurance and remains beyond influence of responses arising from overstimulation. Similarly, awareness of this stage is conscious awareness grounded in reality that is profound in expanse and is devoid of any form, shape, sound, boundary or sensation. This awareness is luminous of continual knowing and nothing else.

22

Regulating/Training the Mind

> "To understand the immeasurable, the mind must be extraordinarily quiet, still." —*Jiddu Krishnamurti*

Contribution of far exceeds than body for achieving success in life on multiple fronts. This fact is not even contested. Amplification of our happiness and achievements also is generally shaped by mental strength than physical powers. That is why the central theme of practising meditation is focused on mental patterns and habits. Mastery over working of mind alone turns focus inside and allows access to the purity of consciousness. But normal mind itself is known to be the biggest obstacle standing between our deeper awareness and ourselves. Working around this dichotomy is easier said than done. Length of time and efforts required to achieve a clear, relaxed, still, alert and willing mind, the very foundation of this entire endeavour, determines the plot of our entire meditation story.

That is why working on mind and thoughts account for bulk of advices available for transforming human life. The difficulties involved in following these advices, however, are quite insurmountable at times and appear more like mysteries and for very genuine and understandable reasons. Traversing over these mysteries involve realising assumptions that are delicate, complex and intricate at the same time. But the fruits waiting on the other side of the fence are also delicious, abundant, long lasting and worth all the efforts involved. Within this overall trade off, climbing over the mountain of efforts for exerting influence over mind's working is worth conquering. The true seeker has to tame his mind by winning against all its sinister designs.

Thoughts shape our ideas, actions, speech, emotions, etc. and precede all our responses, initiatives, actions and reactions. Therefore, all efforts towards nipping the bud have to begin with management/ regulation/purifying of thoughts. Buddha revealed this understanding long ago saying "What we are today is the result of our thoughts of yesterday." Our thoughts of today shape our tomorrow. Since mind manages generation and processing of all thoughts and happens to be the only instrument available to achieve desired corrections over thoughts, hence, our entire life is creation of our mind. Importance of our mind in terms of its usefulness for our entire existence is a settled issue and good command over its working is essential before mind gets used as a tool to reshape the future on desired lines.

Understanding the Mind

Ancient Indian texts deal with complexities related to human mind in great details. Indian Philosophies define consciousness/mind as 'free will' that is independent of all causes. It is to be understood as ability to decide consciously and independently of all stored experiences or impressions from past and present. In tune with its complexity levels, those texts further segregate this faculty into several distinct levels as Ahamkara, Chitta, Manas, Buddhi and finally Jnana. Upanishads also talk about different states of mind and provide for Sushupti (unconscious), Nidra (sleep with dreams), Jagruti (Wakefulness), Tureeyam (Trance), Tureeya Ateeta (Para-trance) and finally Ananda (Superconsciousness), the state also described as Sat-Chit-Ananda; the timeless and spaceless transcendental state which may feel like relaxed alertness, higher awareness, abundant peace, sublime elation, tranquility, serenity, ecstasy and bliss, depending on the level of underlying experience. Each of these levels and states need their own detailed comprehension far beyond the scope of this endeavour. Suffice to understand that complexities around human mind are indeed real and have been baffling scholars all through the documented history of mankind. For all purposes under this chapter, even at the cost of repetition, any and every reference to 'mind' shall mean this very complex entity called consciousness with all its levels and states duly included.

Much beyond, the physical matter component, mind for our reference is entirely different than brain. For our discussion here, Mind may be understood as Consciousness which is completely independent of both brain and body. This very meaning need be applied every time the word 'mind' gets used in this chapter. Faculty of consciousness holds complete influence over imaginations, recognitions, judgements, and memories experienced all through mortal life. More importantly, it is responsible for processing all our feelings and emotions before actions get initiated in our mind and body combine.

More and more researchers are now scientifically convinced that human mind is indeed the most powerful force that influences body, life and entire behaviour. If our physical body, consisting of five material elements, is hardware of our mainframe computer, brain may be compared to CPU while mind is the actual software that operates the body all its life. Mind's operating system collects stores, processes, manages all types of information and initiates all thoughts, actions or feelings by using the physical processing capability of brain. In short, brain is the disc with processors while mind is the OS. Mind is subtle and invisible but its real magic unfolds only when it works with the body.

Before going further, let us see how this mind practically works and why does it need so much discussions and explanations. In a way, understanding its working is rather simple and straightforward as it happily does things it likes, when it likes, and how it likes. In doing so it ignores getting tired or bored. But it does not like owning responsibilities or consequences of its actions. So long as you do not hold it responsible of anything it does, it feels elated. It hates interference, regulation or suggestions to work in a particular manner. Like a spoiled innocent child, it wishes to enjoy freedom of all types but without accountability of any type.

Considering unique similarities of most of human minds, one can also deduce that in reality an average human mind is generally lazy, ignores long term implications, yearns for quick conclusions and prefers taking the easiest of options. Simplicity attracts it instantly and it always prefers to avoid or postpone everything complex. Invariably the mind also hates to focus its attention on any single object longer than a few moments. Some parts of the mind are responsible for processing sensory stimuli and controlling particular types of information flow, while other parts integrate and act upon information processed elsewhere to generate executive decisions. Constant flow of new sensations reaching it through smells, sounds, visuals, tastes besides its own interplay of feelings and emotions, keep it pretty busy and spoiled by providing opportunities to move from one to another even faster than it likes. Mind enjoys the job of a CEO which provides the luxury of being pretty selective to lay its attention on anyone of the multiple inputs so conveyed. In its normal state, mind's attention keeps switching to the smallest of stimulus. This reality is difficult to digest for people carrying false notion that their mind works under their guidance and command.

Going beyond obvious optics, one finds many layers of processes and systems involved in the working of a normal human mind. Our mind is actually a sum and substance of many mental processes. On one hand, these processes involve familiar sensory feedbacks while, on the other hand, they may pertain to thinking, planning, narrating or processing emotional responses. Other processes dealing with pains and pleasures, physical demands or entertaining memories only add to this existing matrix with more complexities.

Each of these processes is distinct but they operate in a complex interconnected manner. Each of above processes has its own independent agenda which is seldom in harmony with agendas of other processes. Only on rare occasions, these processes operate with consensus. Seeking mind's attention, on priority ahead of all others, happens to be the only common agenda among all these competing rival processes. These processes keep throwing their agenda even after the mind is unable to provide its attention for the required duration. This very abundance of stimuli spoils the mind to operate at its own sweet will. At times a particular process takes dominance over others but only momentarily. This is why we regularly face dilemmas, conflicts and contradictions in our daily life. Establishing harmony and collaboration within this complex and multipart systems, consistently and cohesively, requires crossing over a long, high and scary bridge. Any real efforts aimed at training or regulating of mind exist only across the said bridge.

Multiple Segregations of Mind

Very first step towards understanding this bridge crossing involves understanding of its classifications and its interconnectivity with other body parts/systems. It indeed requires an entirely fresh approach. Let us begin all over again. Human mind is known as a dynamic entity managing rich stream of fresh information and integrating same with pre-existing information with respect to both time and space. This complexity prompts people to look at mind under several segregations, for example, conscious or subconscious, left or right, new or old, controlled or automatic, emotional or rational, etc. The segregation under Conscious, Sub-conscious and Unconscious, merits deeper look for unraveling mystery of mind's working for our purpose. If we assume these three segments in terms of a good visual, shape of a triangle emerges immediately as shown below:

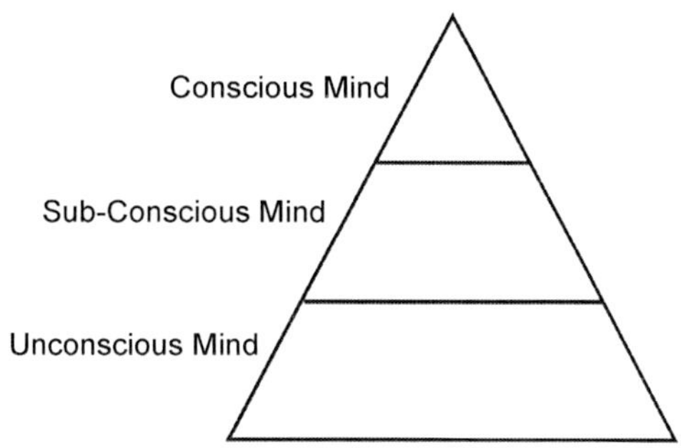

(A) Conscious Mind

It is said to receive all inputs from other subparts and sense organs, process those inputs selectively, identifies patterns, makes decisions and controls short term memory. As a captain in command, Conscious Mind is responsible for communication with outside world as well systems within the body. All thoughts, ideas, perspectives, opinions and beliefs for self as well as the world around are perceived by mind's conscious part only. These thoughts are shaped by a mix of our genetics, actual life experiences and stored memories. Thoughts need be looked as spontaneous and sporadic outputs of conscious mind. Interestingly, these very seemingly harmless, feeble and timid looking thoughts, when repeated over time, get converted into rock solid attitudes. While generation of thoughts is impossible to control, conscious mind has the option to assign priority and duration of attention to those thoughts; it might pick it on top priority, entertain for a while or just ignore and let them subside. Entire regulation of conscious mind revolves around this subtle art of prioritising and entertaining only desired thoughts and letting all undesirable thoughts go away.

In case of normal ignorant living, useless thoughts occupy attention of conscious mind in endless circles. In such situation person is not in command of thoughts, rather such mind is said to work subservient to those thoughts. Poor imagination, dull responses, tired memory, inability to arrive at just conclusions quickly, lack of clarity in thinking are all strong signals of this very syndrome. The quotation "thoughts are thinking us rather than we thinking thoughts" seems to have been coined exactly for this very situation.

The practices of Acceptance, developing Positive Attitude, practising Silence and Solitude, and most importantly developing iron clad morality together with controlling Mental Distractions are the recommended practices aimed at strengthening the working of conscious mind. Higher level of success in practising these tools helps in widening the pause between generation of a feeling and initiation of action. This nano-seconds delay enables the conscious mind to remain firmly in command of the final action it seeks from other subparts. Command over practices mentioned above strengthens the conscious mind to work out its own agenda and action plans. Once conscious mind regains its proper authority, role of other sub-parts is relegated to just take action following command of conscious mind to expedite implementation of its decisions.

(B) Subconscious Mind

Main functions of sub-conscious mind, which generally operates in autonomous mode, is to store and recall all past information; it is like a memory bank that holds endless data from cumulative past impressions and experiences. Working as a powerful layer underneath the conscious mind, it is always active. Over long periods, it develops master programmes by laying out patterns for all normal activities. As and when the conscious mind asks it, it is there to carry out the job without applying any objectivity, reasoning, analysis or criticism. It is that loyal and old time "Ramu Kaka" (domestic servant) who works day and night to make our behaviour fit in a pattern that is consistent with our experiences, hopes and desires. It is indeed that fertile soil which germinates a seed put into it without looking at whether the seed is of a flower, tree, wild bush or a useless weed.

Subconscious mind is also held responsible for imaginations and creativity of all types. All of the intuition or psychic powers also arise from subconscious mind itself. Another critical role assigned to it is managing everything relating to our habits. Occupying roughly half of total space of our mind, it is like real working platform where everything is executed as directed by conscious mind. Subconscious mind takes instructions from above and remains in touch with unconscious for retrieving long term information. It is the most active part of the mind and it remains at work even when its boss, the conscious mind is at rest.

Moment to moment awareness through deep breathing, a practice that has been so strongly recommended in many earlier chapters, results in delaying the gratification impact of senses and weakens impact of emotions on responses suggested by subconscious. Similarly, the practices of Santosha, Detachment, importance of making strong Efforts and developing art of Concentration, augment its faculties such that its dependence on unconscious reduces drastically. Once that link is made weaker, bringing desired changes suddenly become practical and effective to implement.

(C) Unconscious Mind

Unconscious mind is primarily operating all our vital body functions for breathing, digestion, sleeping, blood circulation, nervous system, etc. For all these functions the subconscious part of mind operates fairly independently without any intervention, direction or supervision by the conscious or subconscious minds. Storing millions and millions of our life long experiences, perceptions, feelings, and sensations is another important part of its responsibility. Many of these are not easy to recall as the person might have forgotten all about those. But it will be a mistake to write those long term stuff completely off because directly or indirectly those old and forgotten impressions do impact our behaviour and responses of present time as well. All those repressed and forgotten personal material of past get stored in this store house situated somewhere at the dark and deep store house in the basement section of our mind.

Equally important contents of this store house are collectively inherited experiences of entire humanity passed through to us through genes. These can also be called survival instincts which ignite automated responses of fight or flight syndromes. Ignition of survival instincts flood you with stimuli at a fast speed and actions get initiated even before conscious mind becomes aware of the same. Unconscious mind also guides and advises our conscious mind as well as subconscious mind through its strong underlying over arching influence on our behaviour, experience and response systems explained previously. As a strong corollary of this working, efforts for bringing changes at Conscious level or Subconscious level are dependent on bringing changes at the Unconscious level. This is the reason that making significant improvements in our decision-making, self-regulation, emotional management and holding attention over longer spans prove so much more difficult if not nearly impossible.

It may not be difficult to realise that systems of unconscious mind get formed ever so slowly. Over periods those become as stiff as forged steel. Therefore, making changes at unconscious level to undo all that must be possible only after applying tons of perseverance and endurance. Formed over of a long term and based on accumulation of both personal and genetic inheritance, making changes work at unconscious mind certainly sound Herculean task. It is indeed as true today as it has been all over human history. Ever since antiquity, the idea of unconscious mind has been explored across all cultures but Vedas from Ancient India are the earliest recorded texts that establish this concept ahead of all others. The abstract, silent but completely unified field of "pure consciousness" (which is completely different than the philological concept of 'consciousness' referred in Ayurveda) is attributed by Vedas and Upanishads as the earliest manifestation of unconscious mind.

To bring home a better understanding of this point, let us recall one real life example. Each one of us would have read, seen or heard some sort of new learning that you would have been impressed with. Under logic shared by the presenter you may have instantly resolved to make required changes in your life to benefit from those at the earliest. But why strong impact of those learnings quietly escapes our mind within few days/weeks leaving the life continuing as usual? Why most New Year resolutions, made in all earnest and seriousness, generally die premature death within days and weeks?

Arriving at answers to failure of resolutions is actually rather simple. First of all, all that logical appreciation and resolutions are bought by our Captain, the conscious part of our mind. As per the procedure, Conscious mind immediately passes on the line of action to the subconscious for implementation. But subconscious mind, like all normal clerical staff in the secretariat of the boss, generally remains flooded with too many things to handle at the same time and always works as per priority of the boss. It is well aware that Boss will always give reminder(s) for the jobs to be attended on priority. So, Subconscious mind remains busy on a project only until the Boss, the Conscious Mind continues sending reminders. In the absence of persistence about actionable reminders from the conscious mind, and because subconscious mind deals only with shorter term memory, the information of actionable points and resolutions get quietly pushed out of its 'to do' list, similar to the secretary pushing the non-urgent file by dispatching it into the store for safekeeping.

Bringing changes in the working of Unconscious mind requires you to revisit the chapter of Controlling Mental Distractions all over again. In addition, practices of Uplifting Moral Standards and Crossing over Materialism in particular and other practices in general contribute a great deal in enabling the Unconscious to reprogram itself by deleting many old memories and experiences out of the system. Significant progress on these practices and success in meditation achieved so far greatly helps towards loosening the grip of earlier held experiences, perceptions, feelings, and sensations. Slowly but surely, long practice impact even deeply held values as well as social conscience and prove capable of bringing in desired changes.

Behaviour and personality that we derive from the constant and unique interaction of conflicting psychological forces operating at these three different subparts of our mind makes us a unique persona with singularity. Each of these parts plays an important role in influencing behaviour and hence any reverse engineering required for bringing changes will also be possible within their set interactions. We know that conscious mind forms its impressions very quickly but its span is very short term. Most of its impressions are just handed over to the subconscious for implementation. So we need to strengthen the conscious mind to search opportunities even under challenges, maintain open view, remain flexible, recognise the transient feelings and work with efforts to refine and fine tune support sought from subconscious.

Understanding Old and New Mind

For appreciating difficulties in making changes in our thinking and behaviour, we must also look at another classification of mind as old and new. Old part is dated millions years in age and deals with auto performing functions in the human body. The brain to body proportion of this part is estimated to be similar to other mammals. This part is also called Automatic part of the brain. Being so old, it has been debugged over very long time period. Most of its functions rarely go wrong but simultaneously are much more difficult to change. Lust for basic things like tasty food and carnal desires belonged to functions under its gambit, as a reason, are labeled as most difficult to get over.

On the other hand, 'New' part of our brain, also called Limbic system, has evolved much later. This part deals with reasoning, motivation, learning, conscious planning, controls over behaviour, and stimulations. Similar to newer apps, its debugging continues to take place even today. No wonder, these systems are susceptible to fail more frequently under overload conditions or severe variations in the SOP. Stress and Hypertension are its most obvious recent examples to prove the point. Speaking technically, all our habits and behaviours handled by Limbic are amenable for adopting changes and comparatively with fewer efforts. This understanding can be critical to many of us who can now start their improvement drive with bigger confidence to succeed.

> "A mind that is fast is sick.
> A mind that is slow is sound
> A mind that is still is divine."
>
> — *Meher Baba*

Working of Mind as Emotional and Rational

Practitioners working for regulation of mind often complain that they end up doing certain things as a reflex and find it difficult to control their outbursts ignited by particular situations. This subject impacts most seekers and deserves proper investigation. Understanding these phenomena requires looking at yet another segregation of human mind under emotional and rational divisions. Emotional mind is said to be more intuitive, thoughtful and subjective while Rational Mind is categorised as logical, analytical and objective. The emotional mind jumps into reaction to any signal far more quickly while the other mind likes to take a moment or two to check what should be done. Long time back, when survival carried much more urgency for human, emotional mind indeed helped human survive many scary circumstances. But of late, survival is not that much critical as now we live in secured and safe environment, exceptions apart.

Interestingly, there are two very important studies that have contributed a lot towards insights in the working of Emotional and Rational divisions of the human mind. Their results are very convincing to help us know the working of mind and provide useful tips in looking at how these findings help us make progress on our meditation journey. The studies called as 'Cognitive-Experiential Self-Theory', credited to Paul Ekman, and Seymour Epstein focus on how people use two separate systems dominated by 'analytical and rationality' on one side and 'intuition and experimental' on the other extreme. Our emotional mind is faster in responding to emerging circumstances both inside and outside. People using this part of brain, come up with quick reactions. But their reactions are also based on strong sense of uncertainty. It is because an emotional mind reacts to overall situation in a jiffy. It does not waste time to wait for complete and detailed view of the situation. It looks at the situation in a rather simplified way. Its speed is so fast that the subject does not even entre the conscious mind discussed earlier. Its quick and dirty variety of emotions laced reaction does not even wish to ponder as what has actually happened. What matters here is speed and not accuracy or reasoning. First impression here is taken as representative of situation. The emotional mind takes snap shot of emerging situation and shoots out the first option at its disposal. Many times these responses are ill advised, ill founded and ill timed. Some of these responses are even regretted later on.

On the other hand, the rational mind takes a few moments to grasp and analyse the emerging situation before coming up with a measured response. Actually, in first category, the response is from spontaneous instinct while in the second category it is guided by logically carried out rational thinking. Articulated thought activates the response in a rational dominance scenario in place of feelings and emotions. Rationality allows opportunity for evaluating a new argument or new evidence as beliefs are not cast in concrete. These people are ready to evaluate the same rationally and are open to change their belief without much problem.

So how does this division of mind under Emotional and Rational categories help us in our drive to improve our meditation progress? This is where we get a twist. This twist is the ability of emotional mind to exercise control over rational mind. To understand this, we have to go back to thousands of years ago when it was still period of early stage of human evolution. The emotional mind got evolved fully much (old part) before rational part was to arrive on stage (new part). It is like birth of two brothers in the same family with a long age gap in between. Due to the age difference, surely, the emotional mind is the big brother. As a big brother, it has unique capability to befool the younger one, rational mind, by engaging it in search of justifications and arguments so that quick reactions by emotional mind can be justified as well reasoned, if the situation so desire. As a much younger brother, poor rational mind has to toe the line taken by big brother in front of every outsider.

That a well thought out action coming out of rational mind has, in most situations, merit in replacing instant response from the emotional mind is not a very difficult conclusion to arrive. Needless to mention that such an observation involves careful view that requires few extra moments. This step is likely to function exactly as a time delay device. This simple process of delaying the instant reaction by just a fraction of second itself brings out a wonderful change. The moment there is a slight delay, by virtue of genetic coding, the matter is taken over by rational mind. We may relate it with live instances where, at times, a few moments of delay stop us from uttering some unwanted words or opinions especially under highly charged situations. Just imagine if all our actions taken or words spoken arise from rational mind only. For sure, we will be in a much better situation in terms of morality, empathy, mental peace, relationships and even financial planning issues.

Exercising Control Over Mind

Training our mind is a daring challenge because mind holds a bag full of its own contrivances. It is quite a defiant friend that does not like to be controlled. As soon as we try reining it, mind is master at diverting attention to endless distractions at its disposal. It resorts to pricking you again and again to ignite anger leading to frustrations. It is a master in breaking your concentration by amplifying a tiny sensation into a blown out emotion. Generating reminders for urgent works, calls to be made, reminders to be sent, deadlines to be dealt, etc. are its usual tantrums expected right when you wish it to be quiet and focused. Every meditator comes across its endless tricks all through the practice periods. Challenge in bringing focus back to meditation remains even after decades into practice. But once it knows that the owner is persistent and his desire to keep it quiet is not leaving conscious space, the same mind comes around and ultimately caves in. Once it is tamed down, it converts into a domesticated obedient servant, ready to serve you as you desire.

But to see that day, mind needs to be handled with velvet gloves. Strong arm tactics just do not give positive result in case of bringing mind under control. Tuning the mind for learning new knowledge in a willing manner is the very first step of this long process. Without this active willingness, mind argues that either it is not required or that it knows it already. Ability to develop keen and pure observation without the reflexes of past memories and without the attachment with any particular outcome is the KEY for turning mind to learn willingly.

Exercising control over mind is possible only with the help of an entirely new muscle, called "Focus". Growing this muscle may be as difficult as doubling biceps or reducing midriff to ideal BMI, but it has to be done. Once it grows well, mind achieves its stillness opening the access to its subtle state. This alone opens the door to heart and illuminates the path for practitioner to walk in steadily deeper and deeper. The struggle goes over years. Seeker has to be ready with tons of patience. Thoughts will fly out million times but one have to bring it back as many times. Objects to focus can keep changing on daily basis as already discussed.

The final measure of degree of regulation of mind is a state when both unconscious and subconscious parts are completely receptive to the desires of the conscious part. In this state, other two subparts have no desire to push their own agenda into the conscious space. It is only in this state that there are no misconceptions, illusions or fallacies in any subpart of the mind. This is the mind that is free from attachments, emotions, feelings, attitudes, or other restrictions in term of time and space. Such a mind is in equilibrium without any traces of concoctions, exaggerations or falsifications under any hidden corners of unconscious or subconscious. All types of distractions get eliminated. All obstacles on the way disappear and ego gets transcended into a higher being. The only new information arriving at conscious space is based on pure observation; mental processing is based on logical reasoning grounded on real truth alone. This is the mind that enables righteous contemplation and paves the road for an unknown unity and bonding with the universe. This is here that purest form of meditation becomes feasible.

This state may be rightly called 'unified state of mind', a state where all subparts behave like trained horses pulling the chariot with rhythm and speed in desired direction. Much of the energy of individual subparts of an un-unified mind gets wasted in fighting inner conflicts exactly as different horses pulling the chariot in different directions, where the strongest of horses is able to pull the carriage on its side but both speed and direction get compromised.

Unified mind becomes source of joy and happiness as subparts begin ignoring/overlooking elements capable of disturbing prevailing peace and tranquility. Here alone we expect to have deeper, longer and balanced sense of happiness becoming default state of our mind; it is here that mental behaviour improves to assimilate acceptance, attention, awareness, pure observation, positivity, integrity and realisations. Unified mind is called regulated mind or trained mind and it is here that simple or neutral looking activity like breathing starts arousing feelings of pleasure and satisfaction.

23

Transcending the Ego Beyond all Subjectivities

> "A human being is part of the whole, called by us 'Universe'; a part limited in time and space. He experiences himself, his thoughts and feelings as something separated from the rest—a kind of optical delusion of his consciousness. This delusion is a kind of prison for us, restricting us to our personal desires and affection for a few persons nearest us. Our task must be to free ourselves from this prison by widening our circle of compassion to embrace all living creatures and the whole of nature in its beauty. Nobody is able to achieve this completely but striving for such achievement is, in itself, a part of the liberation and a foundation for inner security."
>
> Albert Einsteen (1879-1955) Physicist and Nobel Laureate

Ego thrives in uniqueness and prompts us to do things differently to leave lasting impressions on others, near and far. It touches every aspect of our worldly existence and helps beings in accumulating and enjoying experiences, perceptions, memories, knowledge and relationships. Surely, human life without ego would become quite dull and lackluster. Our ego is indeed our best friend at all times and defends us with all its might against one and all, always. But for it, humanity may not have progressed as much as it did.

Besides, it defends us and guards our interests by standing for us in front of the whole universe. Lawyers are known to fight for their clients rather than truth and one can never have a better lawyer than his own ego to create best possible defense. Ego justifies our stand even when we are brazenly wrong. Who does not need such a loyal friend? Ego also has a great bonding with our mind so much so that it constantly manipulates poor mind to come up with intelligent answers for finding logic and morale behind our most stupid actions. Such false arguments, unfortunately, are, at times, taken by us as valid arguments.

There are precisely two separate perspectives for ego. The first is scientific or materialistic perspective where it is simply a person's sense of self-esteem or self-identification or sense of self-significance, the very part of mind that mediates between the conscious and unconscious and is responsible for letting us test reality and feel the sense of separate identity. Originating from Latin with literal meaning being I, ego is the name card we use while relating our self with the rest of the world, both in terms of our identity and individuality. But it is not a fixed state and keeps evolving every moment. Also defined as a fiction created in the mind by the mind, it is basically an illusionary image founded on narrow views and interests.

Our entire life gets spent in establishing this ego, exalting it, defending it, championing it and conserving it. Since our ego defines and perpetuates our self-concept, self-construct, self-identity as well as self-perspective, there is hardly any occasion to develop any aversion against it. Ego alone provides us super inflating feeling of pride. In addition, ego interplays such comparisons with strong likes and dislikes. Ego also classifies our actions, thought process and entire mental content as good, bearable, agreeable or otherwise. In this form, it captures poor untrained mind by misleading to take wrong judgements under the colours of our own existence. In depth understanding of this aspect of ego helps one realise why we behave the way we do under different worldly situations.

Major pitfalls of this ego revolve around it being too judgemental, its over emphasis on self-esteem and its ability to wrongly influence mind's working. Ego works similar to an elephant walking through the market and sniffing everything coming across its way. Ego looks at everything and suggests 'like it', 'do not like it', 'pick it', 'chose it', 'appreciate it', 'ignore it' or even 'hate it'. This judgemental nature gives rise to a lot of anger and conflict with their own share of challenges. This single aspect of ego expands working of all human emotions and feelings. Since ego puts too much emphasis on self, it ends up alienating others and keeps them at distance.

This Ego also keeps us trapped in its tricks, i.e. desires, cravings, attention, arrogance, attachments, pride and envy. It generates, then collects and later thrives on vast repository of well layered memories by applying such contents at will. Ego creates that blinding effect where its owner refuses to see things in purer forms and look at them only with coloured lenses. Its craving for uniqueness creates false projections that divide and pitch people against each other and, ultimately, too much focus on advancing self-esteem of self-turns into one of the biggest evil prevailing in humanity. Thus, ego sense results into false moral idealism that is unrealistic, self-obsessed and self-admiring. Eventually, ego is found guilty of being a root cause of unjustified violence as a means to just and moral ends.

Ego's inter play of being irrationally selective, similarly, results in a lot of social divisions. Ego tells us to take a stand on everything either 'for' or 'against'. This struggle is said to be mind's worst disease because it impedes search of real truth. After all, our discrimination of being for or against gives rise to strong likes and dislikes and that initial small difference soon snowballs into extremes like differentiating hell from heaven. The wise people say that perfect way is impossible for those who 'pick and choose' and that everything starts appearing clear the moment influence of ego is ignored.

> "Ego is just like dust in the eyes. Without clearing the dust you can't see anything clearly. So clear the ego and see the world." (www.wisdomquotesandstories.com)

How to Spot that Ego is at Work?

Many practitioners wish to know a quick way for assessing if their ego is still at work or measure progress made by their practice towards loosening ego's grip on them. Let us look for simple signs to work as dipsticks for quick testing of ego's presence as well as its degree of influence. Affirmative replies to some or more of following questions is enough to identify ego's remaining at work. Similarly, vertical variations in the degree of these very points help in establishing the extent of progress, if any, made over practice period. The examples are deliberately picked up from normal life situations to ensure a direct connection:

1. Do you desire appreciation from others for your deeds or thoughts or habits or behaviours and get flattered by their praise?
2. If another person gets credit for your initiatives, do you feel the urge of letting others know about your individual contributions?
3. Do you find yourself more experienced on life matters and desire to be consulted by near and dears for issues in their life?
4. Does criticism of your actions or views disturbs your mental peace and if so to what extent?
5. Do you feel the need of justifying your position and putting things in right perspective every time others find fault in your views? To what extent are you willing to go to prove your point to others?
6. Do you seek attention of people of your inner circle on your opinions, skills, and actions? How much legacy you wish to leave behind?
7. Do you seek approval of others for your life style? Do you secretly desire to be taken as a role model?
8. Do you get the urge to jump in with your inputs when others are in the process of expressing their views? And if yes, what is your level of excitation to do so?
9. Do you indulge in mental comparisons with the speech or actions of others? If yes, how often?
10. Do you get urge to comment on actions of others around?

Let us assume each of these questions is like a single step connecting the egoless universal self at the top with egoistic individual self-sitting on the lower floor or holding base of this ten step ladder. Also assume yourself starting from the top of this ten step ladder with every affirmative answer pushing you down to a lower step on the ladder. Your position after considering all ten answers determines your current location on this ladder. You are welcome to take this test as often as you deem fit and get a feel of your position on this ladder.

Getting rid from ego is one of the longest running challenges that humanity has been facing all over its evolution. Ego does not give up easily neither its grip gets loosened without strong efforts. Ego knows well that giving up means death, and like every other living being, ego is also too afraid of its own end/death. The moment it feels under attack, it panics and comes out attacking ever so strongly. Under attack, it falsely agrees to rearrange all the thoughts and memories but in reality it starts using every dirty trick at its command including deceptively using our mind. One comes across many situations where ego feels purged or purified but it gets tossed back to its original nature in rather quick times.

Getting rid from ego's force demands a complete spiritual surrender. This surrendering demands you to bend knees with hands folded where you voluntarily accept, with all humility, that you are just an ignorant being and do not know a thing. This stage comes after you finally realise that Truth is much away from you, that you are just like everybody else a tiny insignificant part of the giant Universe. This requires drowning all your thoughts, images, beliefs, opinions, impressions and finally arriving at conclusion that there are no ways you can figure out about your role for anything and everything. That leveled sense of emptiness or nothingness is the real indicator of evaporation of ego in totality.

Being egoless simply means putting others ahead of self in every respect, a realisation that being at the outer periphery of this universe is our real place. Most certainly, this involves the less travelled and very tedious process called total transformation of self, one that is greatly aided by spiritual evolution being discussed throughout this book. Egoless also means not identifying with thoughts or being attached to any thought. One has to learn to exist simply as a witness to things happening around. People practising meditation with success are known to reach their state of egoless leading to peace of mind and blissful living.

The second perspective of ego is of spiritual nature where ego is identification of true self with human body. Spiritual ego is created by the false self as a product of conditioned mind. This ego needs to be crumbled before expecting soul to reveal itself. This ego stands in between one's focus on here and now being on one side and state of pure attention without thoughts, commentaries and evaluations on the other side. This ego is limiting in nature and prevents us from expanding to infinite. This very subtle ego needs transcendence to achieve altered state of consciousness; one that is not bothered for any concern for self and thus is able to perceive reality with greater objectivity.

Not knowing ego in full details runs the risk of giant size speed breakers and pot-holes capable enough to derail all further efforts for continuing meditation. So ego must be comprehended in entirety and practitioners must equip themselves to overcome its challenges. Meditation involves the internal evolution of consciousness or self-awareness until we realise our divine state of being. This process gets completed only after sense of ego broadens enough and emerges as transcendence of self. Interestingly, this process requires you to first realise a strong and healthy ego with accentuated subjectivities before you make efforts to cross over that very subjectivity because you have to become somebody before becoming nobody. In other words, you should become human before you become spiritual being. Just as a side reference, Western philosophy encourages the first part of this very sense of strong ego while Eastern philosophy advocates the second part, ego transcendence.

Famous saint of recent times, Ramana Maharishi is credited with the views where he says "the experience of self is possible only for the mind that has become subtle and still as a result of prolonged meditation." Considering this, we may immediately realise that all stages of meditation journey explained until now were largely preparatory in nature as real meditation begins only after first three stages are fully completed and subjectivities of all types are well settled. Also, transcending this ego is not about waging a war against it, but by moving to higher context of self. It does not mean getting rid of a functional self but a self who no longer exclusively identifies itself with individual self alone.

On the other hand, this strong feeling of separateness is despised by all great teachers from different strands. Be it Rumi, Advaita Vedanta, Dzogchen from Tibet or German mystic Meister Eckhart, they all say that there is only one reality and no one is any different from that reality. The very feeling of separateness gives rise to all fears, cravings, feeling of abandoned, selfishness, aggression, or carelessness towards others. In a way, this sense of being separate is also the root of all human dilemmas. Unfortunately, this sense of uniqueness is very tenacious and deeply ingrained which makes overcoming it a very difficult journey. But before expecting any further progress, one must overcome all its challenges.

Ego and Meditation

Ego loves to expand its area of influence to make the owner bigger, better, smarter, stronger, etc. But continuous meditation practice encourages the view sitting exactly in opposite corner of this position. With roots of meditation firmly grounded and meditation promoting universality, the promotion of uniqueness by ego starts getting confronted. At this stage, the ego starts feeling threatened and its confrontation with meditation begins straight and square.

Developed Self-awareness and pure observation skills let practitioners see through ego's dirty tricks in play. But scares of fear and hatred for self created by ego repeatedly prevent him from taking concrete actions against it. Ego is known to cast its ideas in stone and force us to work against new learnings by pushing logical but contrarian knowledge in background. It is the same principle under which some people develop hostility against perceived enemies even when no real reasons exist.

Over longer periods, spiritual practices in general and meditation in particular enable seekers to see through this working of mind. Further success in meditation helps us cross over selfishness or uniqueness and makes us ready to see more similarities with others in the world. This promotes harmony between us and others and eventually makes this world a better place to live.

Achieving Egolessness and Transcending Ego

Egolessness is a normal experience for most human beings that appear in between thoughts. But among untrained minds, this experience goes unnoticed. Lengthening the duration of that very Egolessness happens only after forcing ego to lose its hold on its basic spirit of separateness. Meditation alone is capable of breaking through outer layers of ego-defense mechanism of our projected personality and to help reach our pure inner self. Ultimately practitioner becomes capable of achieving mental stillness and calm. By the process of detoxification and reconnecting with the compassionate universal consciousness, sustained by progress in meditation, we overcome ego influence. Attempts to achieve these results without meditation are possible but run the risk of multiple psychological disorders.

Once ego is extinguished, its menaces of judgement, comparison, and criticism also disappear. This pushes out all negativity and pettiness out of our system. Side by side the continued practices of strengthened morality, sustained ethical behaviour, stronger compassion, enhanced acceptance and other general practices already mentioned, help our initiatives towards transcending ego to a level not feasible before. The boundaries of ego centric self also get loosened by practising forgiveness, honesty and gratitude as all these practices bring down our very desire for reaming in control or command. By this stage of spiritual growth, the sense of separateness starts appearing as unwanted burden. After the end of this tunnel, the practitioner also starts realising the sense of bliss in oneness of universality.

Ultimate transcendence of ego requires complete loss of subjective self-identity and a permanent loss of "attachment to a separate sense of self". Since ego is long accumulation of thoughts and emotions, de-identifying from it also takes a long route and tough navigation. One is required to go through ego death, a death which is far greater than the physical death itself. Egolessness is just a precursor to this ultimate death and makes human beings ready to accept death in all forms. Meditation plays most critical role in this entire process to unfold. That is why according to Jin Y. Park, Director of Asian Studies and Professor at Department of Philosophy and Religion at American University of Washington DC, "meditation is learning how to die by learning to "forget" the sense of self."

24

Challenging Frustrations/Obstacles for Advance Meditators

Obstructions thrown by real life keep providing rude awakening to practitioners at all stages and at all times. Powerful forces like desires, restlessness, doubts, enmity, hatred, lust, jealousy, and fears keep raising their heads. The churning arising from bringing back of buried baggage for contemplation is often scary and proves too much to be handled by poor mind. Experience suggests that practitioner at this stage has to be at his strongest to broom out this rubbish trash out of the system. Some of that debris are actually psychic in nature and pose obstructions of gigantic proportions. During this long and arduous process, the mind is bound to retaliate and doubts/frustrations are naturally expected to hover around. Maharishi Patanjali warned every practitioner against the inescapable reality of these obstacles. There will be occasions when you lower your guard and become careless or negligent or too overconfident. Resisting temptations of the real world at all times also become a losing battle.

Unfortunately, many practitioners lose steam at this stage, and it is not difficult to understand why. Self reflection process brings out one's own harsh realities in open in seven dimensions. For many people, such stark realities prove too much to take. Disturbingly unpleasant yet genuine realities of self are seen standing diametrically opposite to the perceptions carried all this while. Understanding them, accepting them and later initiating changes to correct them becomes a long drawn process and takes tumultuous journey involving arduous trails. One invariably has to deal with lot of shame and anger. This whole process ignites tons of frightful worries forcing one to feel scared and tired at the same time. The only consolation is that it is normal to expect such feelings on way to your meditation growth.

Actually, on the contrary, it is affirmation of your positive results out of your contemplative efforts.

Continuing meditation for years and years requires great measures of willpower, discipline, dedication and determination which are no mean feat. The aspirant has to erect walls to protect against such forces and must remain vigilant against them. It is here that full understanding in advance and preparation for overcoming all such obstacles become absolutely indispensable. Interestingly, these obstacles are not blatantly obvious but very subtle and discernible rather than obvious, physical, easily identifiable or simple to fight against. However, being internal in nature, fighting against these obstacles is entirely within our own control. So the practitioner can tackle them with increased chances of success through his own efforts and struggles.

These obstacles are, however, not a modern day development. Obstacles are very natural tendencies and have been posing threats since very beginning. Just imagine that thousands of years ago, in the era when wisdom was condensed in most possible brevity, where saving a single syllable was a matter of pride for the author, Maharshi Patanjali, devoted one full sutra, Yoga Sutra 1.30, explaining following nine impediments to Samadhi, the ultimate destination of meditation practice. A closer look at the list clearly suggests that their relevance in modern times remains completely unchanged.

> "1.30 *vyadhi styana samshaya pramada alasya avirati bhranti-darshana alabdha-bhumikatva anavasthitatva chitta vikshepa te antarayah.*"

This can be loosely translated as nine kinds of distractions in the process of seeking Samadhi to be naturally encountered on the way. These are physical illness, tendency of the mind to not work efficiently, doubt or indecision, lack of attention to pursuing the goal, laziness in mind and body, failure to regulate the desire for worldly objects, incorrect assumptions or thinking, failing to attain stages of the practice, and instability in maintaining a level of practice once attained.

Let us briefly look at each of these strong distractions together with practical actions suggested to guard against their impacts.

1. Vyadhi—simply means disease and include all types of physical pains, grief, infections, trauma and mental diseases. Being a wider term, it covers everything resulting in a dysfunctional relationship between the mind and body. A state of being in unhealthy condition, the body and mind prevent the aspirant from working and focusing on the practice of meditation. A healthy body and mind alone enables the consciousness to become free from irrational attachment to the objects of the senses. The remedy for overcoming this obstacle is to take required medical intervention in time and bring back the body to its optimum state. Special focus is required to maintain a healthy life style, right eating, right exercising and avoiding all types of excesses.

2. *Styana*—refers to mental state of not being able to work efficiently, mental inaction, mental dullness, or inability to put one's thoughts into action. Mind is said to be the root of all mental health issues of modern age, the age of psychological disorders. To overcome this obstacle, one has to go for a holistic psychotherapy to bring back mind to work at its full potential. Another simpler approach is to set realistic expectations and make progress and see results in baby steps. Seeing positive results, even if these are small in nature, is a sure way to remove mental dullness.

3. *Sanshaya*—means skepticism; the mindless tendency to grasp two extreme ends and failure to appreciate what lies in between. It also covers confusions and bewilderment. Skepticism is based on assumptions formed due to incomplete knowledge, stored impressions and divisions within a single individual. With reference to meditation, lack of knowledge about the concepts involved and less developed belief in basic philosophies at work are known source of allowing doubts to arise in the first place. It is here that theoretical understanding and mastering all difficult sounding concepts and techniques come very handy.

Thorough and integrated comprehension of concepts helps you refine faith and beliefs by purifying them with personal experiences. Doubt disappear when one approaches a problem with an open mind, unbiased view, and enquiring approach. With proper knowledge and practice behind you, and with determination and confidence continuing, you shall get past your all your doubts one by one.

4. *Pramada*—carelessness; negligence; loss of motivation; lacking interest in attending the object of concentration. We know that carelessness in any behaviour can result in unintentional consequences. People suffering from sharp mental reactions are generally driven by deep passions and desires. Lack of proper guidance also allows aspirants to become careless where they

start making mistakes that contribute to weakening of the practice. Indulging in too much verbal communication, indiscriminate mixing with people, engaging in gossips, reading unwholesome literature, and watching material igniting carnal desires are all common examples of activities responsible for kindling Pramada in meditation practice. One has to erect strong defenses against such activities at all times. Desire to make fast progress in meditation also leads to similar results.

Generally carelessness is identified only with young adults but this is a disorder called Attention Deficit Hyperactivity Disorder (ADHD) which impacts even grown up adults in the form of lapses in judgement and mind slips. Meditation involves bringing mind under willful surrender to direct its focus inward. So, it is natural to expect the mind to try all dirty tricks at its disposal to deny inward focus. The cure lies in training the mind, sharpening of concentration as already explained.

5. *Alaysa (Laziness).* Lack of sleep or incorrect sleep patterns are obvious major cause of laziness during meditation. Sleep deficit kills your ability to concentrate. You have to track your energy cycles and undertake meditation only when you are least on fatigue, else your session will convert to relaxation cycles.

Decreased mental energy leads to dullness followed by drowsiness and finally to sleep and we are well aware of this cycle. But the impact of dullness sets in ever so slowly that keeping track of exact point of trigger becomes tricky. Initially subtle dullness is quite likeable state where the focus gets diffused a little bit. That leads to obscure perception of sensations. Soon it turns in as strong dullness invoking drowsiness. Turning the mind inward for contemplation gives rise to dullness due to reduced flow of thoughts and sensations. Quality meditation results in overall drop of activity of mind. With falling stimulations, poor mind prefers to wind down towards relaxation followed by sleep.

The sensation dullness is very feeble and demands highly sensitive sensors in action. Every meditation practitioner has to develop ability to spot the onslaught of dullness and take corrective steps before it gathers strength. Being attentive towards distractions and maintaining strong intention to avoid subtle dullness helps avoiding it from gaining strength. Taking few deeper breaths, forced exhaling through mouth, clinching muscles while maintaining posture, and repeating these routines as many times as required, need to be mastered to fight against laziness. Awareness to spot out the dullness has to be refined and fine tuned by practice to sharpen introspective attention.

6. *Avirati*—Inability to maintain freedom from sense cravings. Unfortunately, getting flooded with lustful images from many directions and multiple sources is possible even at this stage of practice. At times, these desires can be quite overpowering and persistent. In ancient times also, a male was advised not to sleep or even sit on the bed with his female relatives. Manu Smriti finds attractions of senses being so strong that it forewarns against its danger because even knowledgeable and learned people run the risk of losing control against these cravings.

For a normal person getting rid of lustful feelings indeed continues to be a challenge. But there are also brave hearts that are able to come out of the prison of lust by practising chastity with willing freedom and without suppression. It is wrong to believe that sexual urges cannot be controlled. Nor should you feel powerless against carnal desires. Uncontrolled indulgence in these desires is sign of animalistic behaviour and is unbecoming of human beings.

Physical intimacy is designed by nature only for procreation and not for pleasure seeking. Merging of hopes, lives, love, respect, family, future, social interaction etc. are so many other things that husband and wife can do together. Chastity is the most potent weapon for dealing with lust, anger and greed. For ultimate success in long run, the practitioner has no choice but to practice chastity.

Purified intellect alone leads to awakening of right prudence and discrimination between right and wrong. This discrimination helps us abstain from entertaining all lustful thoughts.

7. *Bhrantidarsana (False views or perceptions).* These may not appear that big distractions at the first but they play a crucial role in faulting progress in advance level of meditation. There is an undeniable sequence that operates with all of us. Perceptions lead to formation of premises which leads to formation of assumptions which, in turn, leads to hasty conclusions. Ultimately, conclusions get converted to actions which define successes or failures. Thus, accurate perceptions of reality become the foundation of all actions. False perceptions, which may also be called fantasy or day dreams, are ultimately destined to failures and setbacks. On the other hand, accurate perceptions may not guarantee success but they always lead in right directions.

At times a youngish practitioner runs the risk of assuming good meditation for exceptional visions or state of dramatically altered consciousness. All such assumptions are far from truth. Even if it actually happens, best is to ignore such experiences. Such incidences can never be objective for meditation practice. Neither there is any correlation of such phenomena with any milestone on the way. Significance of such events was restricted to Tantric Traditions which have very few takers in present day.

Wrongly perceived fantasies invariably involve elements of magic, mythology or such other supernatural powers providing psychological kicks. Perceptions about such distorted events generally happen due to lack of discrimination or inability to get rid of attachments from results. For example, a practitioner may come across false lights or sounds and may assume these as great progress in his practice. Identification of fantasy may also be a difficult practice as it involves a complex associative activity in which events from the past are integrated into image of present.

These visual images are generally inner events in which sequence of behaviour is formulated on mental screen. Such false perceptions or fantasy may work wonders for poets, playwrights, painters or other artists but not for a meditation practitioner. Please stand firm against such experiences and be alive to the reality that meditation has nothing to do with spurious psychic experiences.

8. *Alabdhabhumikatva*—The essential technique of Yoga establish the mind firmly in the stages of Dharana, Dhyana and Samadhi in a step by step manner. Later alone, well after Samadhi is attained, the practitioner is to go in deeper levels of consciousness. Persistent efforts and strong will alone lead progress from one state to another. Sometimes this passage is induced with reasonable amount of effort but at other times a practitioner is unable to make any progress and a dead end starts appearing. This failure to progress into next stage can cause distraction and may disturb equanimity of the mind. Patience alone is the key to exit out of such situations. This obstacle is the strongest roadblock for advanced practitioner. Since the stages currently in vogue are different from the steps suggested by Maharishi Patanjali, this particular obstacle may impact modern day practitioners in its different manifestations.

7. *Anavasthitatva*—Inability of the mind to retain steadiness. The quality of exclusive focus on objects of choice depends on steadiness

of the mind. So long as mind is unable to achieve steadiness, the focus will keep breaking and will spontaneously keep shifting to other thoughts. Hence, steadiness is a precondition to completely ignore all things but chosen object of meditation. Steadiness alone leads to drastic decrease in the number of mental objects projected into consciousness. Some people get satisfied with series of moments where attention remains focused on breadth or other objects of choice and gets shifted to other emerging objects. No, that is not a worthwhile state to be satisfied with.

This obstacle, especially applicable for advanced levels, refers to a situation where practitioner is able to find a foothold in the next stage of progress but is unable to hold his attention for longer periods and continues to slide back to previous stage of progress. This is said to be an indication of lack of firmness to maintain inner stability. Practice, some more practice followed by some more right practice alone is the recommended way out. The entire chapter named "Regulating/ Training the Mind" contained in Fourth Stage is intended to deal with this very obstacle in greater details. At this stage, it is sufficient to get sensitised about loss of mental steadiness as a powerful obstacle that every serious meditation practitioner has to deal with.

Centuries later, Gaudapadacharya, the early medieval Hindu philosopher and scholar who inspired the likes of Adi Shankara (it is reported that Govind Bhagwatpada, the teacher of Adi Shankara is presumed to be a direct disciple of Gaudpada), compiled Manduka Karika where he elaborates four categories of obstacles faced on way to spiritual development. The first is called laya or state of mental dullness due to improper diet, sleep, activity. Second is called vikshepa or restlessness of mind due to overindulgence in worldliness, desires, activities, passions, subconscious urges and anxieties caused by plans for the future. The third obstacle is identified as kashaya or strong tendencies and impressions connected to intense attachments and aversions that bring about the ups and downs and disruptions in practice. Fourth and final obstacle explained by Mandukya Karika is rasaswada, the bliss of spiritual experiences that can cause attachment with the aspirant trying to get such blissful experience again through the contemplative practice. These four put together also represent another scholarly compilation of possible obstacles to be guarded against.

Five Obstacles as per the Bhagwad Gita

The Bhagwad Gita is the ultimate scripture aimed at seeking self-knowledge as the ultimate goal of all spiritual practice. Interestingly, Gita also has its own unique take about obstacles and their antidotes. The self-knowledge concept of the Gita is indeed similar to ultimate destination of a meditation practitioner. The Gita regards a person able to see oneself, in oneself, through oneself as a complete being. The quest for this self-knowledge is not to be searched elsewhere as all-pervading Atma is said to live within one's own gross body. Every seeker has to discover the Atma by connecting with inner consciousness using intellect. The Bhagwad Gita also prescribes a well laid out process and sequence required to be followed to achieve this goal. The Gita beautifully lays down five-fold stages for completion self-knowledge journey. Each stage allows the seeker to get rid of one obstacle for self-knowledge.

The first stage involves removing mental impurities like *Raaga, dvesha, kaama, krodha, lobha, moha, madha using the Karma yoga,* the selfless service of mankind. Second stage is called Bhakti, devotion, which is nothing but meditation for a particular manifestation of Isvara, the God with attributes. This stage is prescribed to be effective in removing the obstacle of *Vikshepa*, the restlessness of the mind. Bhakti turns focus from external objects to introverted vision. This brings desired integration of the mind. Consistent study of scriptures under the guidance of a competent teacher is the next stage intended for elimination of self-ignorance.

Svadhyaya, self contemplation, is the next stage which helps in cementing the conviction that the teachings from teacher and the scriptures are true and complete by satisfying intellectual faculties. Contemplation takes care of prevailing doubts and reservations with firm conviction allowing the mind to get energetic and alert. A doubtful knowledge is considered worse than ignorance. The very last stage deals with overcoming habitual reactions. Reactions are regular unhealthy responses, *Vasanas,* which get converted as habits, developed over time, and require long time to go away. Every disturbing reaction like anxiety, frustration, self-pity, sense of insecurity, fear, attachment are all undesirable and are bigger obstacle on achieving ultimate goal of meditation practice. Interestingly every person has to necessarily follow the sequence of removing these five stages obstacles. None of these are optional stages. They are compulsory for all.

25

Raising Self-consciousness to Cosmic Consciousness

Let us, however, first look at Self-conscious and understand it as an unknown entity. Self here is a phenomena without identity, a concept that may be comparatively familiar to people exposed to Vedantic systems where Self is called as Jeevatma, a part of Brahman, the Supreme. This Self being is not subtle essence existing within clustered space of mind because that will make it subservient to mind. On the other hand, Self also does not reside outside mind. Actually, it enjoys very special relationship with the mind where, once it is properly realised it influences entire thought process. An empowered and realised Self is capable of regulating thoughts in mind but Self itself cannot be thought through by the mind. It is different matter that among normal people with undeveloped Self, the same mind continues to have capability of reducing the powers of Self to self, the ego principle. As we may already realise, this tectonic shift appears small but involves so many transformations that only few cover this distance in their lifetime.

Consciousness is explained as one's individual awareness of perceptions, thoughts, feelings, sensations, and environments. Essentially, it is awareness of self and the world around. Comprehending Consciousness always necessitated onerous concepts where deeper interpretations are essentially fully realised for better clarity. But many philosophers have argued about consciousness being a unitary concept which is understood only intuitively; it is something to be realised and not defined in words. The term is actually definable only in very obscure terms. Disagreement about the meaning of the word indicates multiplicity attached with its meaning. In reality, it is more like an umbrella entity encompassing a variety of distinct but dissimilar meanings. However, considering its importance in spiritual advancement, we must be ready to look at its real meaning from various angles.

One way to look at Consciousness is the very sense that correlates the sensory feedback of all the organs into experiencing and recognising our emotional interface. This very interface shapes our reactions or interactions with our own internal process, with other individuals or with the world at large. It is another matter that many people fail to recognise their own conscious awareness and, ignorantly enough, keep taking actions mechanically influenced by emotions or instincts in a very un-thoughtful manner. Editors Max Velmans and Susan Schneider, in their book titled as "The Blackwell Companion to Consciousness" which happens to be a collection of 55 peer reviewed chapters written by leading authors in the field, making this book as most extensive survey of the study of consciousness available today, explain consciousness as:

> "Anything that we are aware of at a given moment forms part of our consciousness, making conscious experience at once the most familiar and most mysterious aspect of our lives."

Being much more than being awake or alert, Consciousness is also not comparable with conscience also as conscience is limited to sense of morality or sense of right versus wrong. Much wider than this, consciousness is the entire sense of being alive, which enables to feel things around with sensations, analyse everything using intellect and enables application of discretion. Consciousness is the very source of each and every mental activity including thoughts. The level of positivity, negativity or neutrality undertaken to do anything is actually linked to the level of evolution of consciousness. Happiness or satisfaction is just a small expression of the states impacted by conscious awareness.

Consciousness is also explained as an information exchange process taking place at the highest level in the mind systems and sub-systems. Authors of "The Mind Illuminated", a complete meditation guide integrating ancient Buddhist wisdom and latest brain science, define it as:

> "Consciousness is simply the inevitable result of interconnectedness of different parts of the brain, and of the shared receptivity that results in information exchange between them."

In their view, the shared receptivity of this interconnectedness takes place in the form of many different kinds of social units, from couples and families to nations and humankind as a whole and later getting extended to multiple species and ecosystems, finally reaching to entire universe as a whole.

For a long time in history, Consciousness has been studied only by philosophers or biologists. But in last 150 years or so, it has also captured interest of psychologists all over the world. But for our specific purpose in hand, it is better to rely on explanations by philosophers in general for whom consciousness suggests the relationship between the mind and the world. Also that people from spiritual or religious background look at it as a relationship between the mind and God, or the relationship between the mind and deeper truths that are thought to be more fundamental than the physical world.

In terms of understanding Consciousness by dissecting it into different categories, the classification put forward by Richard Maurice Bucke, famous Canadian Psychiatrist of late 19th century, is considered most acceptable. In his book titled "Cosmic Consciousness: A Study in the Evolution of Human Mind" Bucke provided three distinct forms or degrees of Consciousness as under:

- Simple consciousness, possessed by both animals and mankind
- Self-consciousness, possessed by mankind, encompassing thought, reason, and imagination
- Cosmic consciousness, which is "a higher form of consciousness than that possessed by the ordinary man".

Simple consciousness, as the name suggests, is easy to comprehend as it occupies bulk of normal person's life and keep him going with mundane life mostly through sub-conscious systems. Each seeker in his earlier avatar must have lived life with simple conscious before getting motivated to pursue spiritual journey. This consciousness is simply instinctive and reactive. It is similar to consciousness being enjoyed by all animals that keep them physically going, surviving against dangers and all such other normal activities including procreation and raising the family. Interestingly, consciousness is the real energy that keeps living beings moving and enabling to perform smallest possible activity including thinking. We often come across two individuals having similar level of physical and mental powers approaching a given problem in entirely non-similar manner. This is to be taken as a clear indication that degree of even this simple consciousness differs from person to person.

The second stage or form, called Self-consciousness is about refinement of simple consciousness itself. We can actually look at it as a heightened sense of self-awareness; a preoccupation with oneself. Its degree also differs from person to person where some are habitually more self-conscious than others. It is also further broken down as private self-consciousness versus public. The private branch refers to tendency of introspection of one's inner self and feelings while public self-consciousness referring to awareness of the self as it is viewed by others.

All important last degree called Cosmic Consciousness is the subject matter of our interest at this stage of spiritual evolution using meditation practice. This stage may also be known by other names like collective consciousness, Christ consciousness, Buddha consciousness, Super consciousness or God-consciousness. Those names basically project images of divinity or exceptionally high states of spiritual development. As you raise your consciousness, you get awaken to the eternal, unlimited nature of your being. Higher consciousness is spiritual or energetic awareness that transcends the mind's normal preoccupation with the past and the future. Higher consciousness is ever-increasing awareness of the meaning of existence, your spiritual essence, and of the spiritual or energetic nature in all things.

Cosmic Consciousness provides us with capability to introspect and analyse issues with the active use of intellect and discretion and enables looking at self as a distinct entity different from physical self. In this state we behave like we believe and we become what we would have liked to become. In this state a person is said to enjoy unity and equilibrium. This very perfection in unity of consciousness enabled Arjuna to correctly aim the eye of the fish mounted on a fast rotating wheel and that too by seeing only its image in the liquid placed below.

Cosmic Consciousness is an ultra high state of illumination of the human mind that is beyond self-awareness or ego-awareness. Such a mind rests in pure knowledge rather than beliefs. This mind finds solitude in multitude and silence in noise. The intensity of normal sense organs also gets heightened in proportion to growth of cosmic consciousness. Main characteristic of cosmic consciousness is continuous flowing joyfulness by reaching true meaning, purpose and unity with the entire Universe. Sense of mortality, under this state, replaces fear of death. The conflicts of right/wrong or good/ bad, all disappear. Being a state of mind, a person evolved to this state can still live a completely normal and ordinary human life having interactions with other normal people without having to live a life of monk in seclusion somewhere in remote hilltops or mountain caves.

> "Realisation is nothing new to be acquired. It is already there, but obstructed by a screen of thoughts. All our attempts are directed to lifting this screen and then realisation is revealed" — *Ramana Maharshi*

Heightened awareness under this state goes to make this very world a real, beautiful and fascinating place. It allows the person to sense the sacred aliveness of the world, its radiance, its harmony, pervading every object and living things alike. Grounded in newness of present, the awareness of surroundings, intentions, perceptions, senses, all become powerful stabilising total attention and thereby rendering the notions about past or future as completely irrelevant. Scintillating particles of cosmic energy become visible to such a person losing limitations of space and infinity. In this state a person perceives by the power of inner perceptions, with intuition heightened, without withdrawing attention to the depth of oneself through meditation.

It is said that our intensity or potency of higher consciousness is responded by the collective universal consciousness in similar proportions. If we have positive and intense consciousness, lesser are the chances that we end up getting negative occurrences within our surroundings. Exactly similar reaction is expected with negative or weak potency of consciousness shaping responses. The popular doctrine of Karma, in a way, is logical extension of this very approach. True, evolution of consciousness as a process goes beyond one life cycle but knowledge of self, questioning, reasoning and experiencing of all dimensions are the only key elements to improve the purity of our Karma. Good Karma of today may either get consumed in wiping out accumulated bad Karmas of the past or add to our kitty of good Karma life after life.

In other words, higher consciousness is the state or quality of any and every thing including an external object, individual or something well within. Yes, it is very familiar but also mysterious aspect of human life. Its presence is indication of life within a body and its absence is a clear indication of death of a person or the state of being in coma. Higher Consciousness also awakens human mind to larger and better possibilities through aroused imaginations. Improved higher consciousness strengthens the unique quality of intuition which in turn helps in seamlessly connecting with the entire external world. Similarly, enhanced inspiration goes in awakening the positive attributes that converts, for example, high net worth individuals into philanthropist, political leaders into social reformers, business leaders turning to become affordable solution providers or accomplished sport stars to open academies to nurture future champions.

People blessed with raised cosmic consciousness get bestowed with greater sense of appreciation and gratitude for the smallest of things. They start seeing God in everything. They become aware of divinity of the entire universe and become part of the same divinity. All spiritually advance personalities in history like Jesus, Buddha, Krishna, Socrates, Mohammad, or people in recent past like Vivekananda, Maharishi Ramana, Vinoba Bhave and Martin Luther King (just to name few) have all lived this very concept. The mantra here is that creation creates each one of us to create something more and, ultimately, power to create rests with God, so each one of us become part of that very God; a God which is within and also without.

Meditation and Cosmic Consciousness

By this stage the issues relating to unity in entire mind systems are well settled resulting in cohesive and harmonious functioning of thoughts and actions. Quality of meditation has also been improving progressively with mastering of all subjects explained in different stages of the journey. By this time, most of the contents accumulated in the sub-conscious should have been purified through contemplation during meditation sessions. This is the stage where practitioner is expected to develop profound insight and heightened awareness. As a result earlier divisions and fragmentations are a matter of past. The consensus in subparts of the mind and its processes ensures substantial reduction the number of competing sensations passing through the consciousness resulting in easy concentration and focused attention.

Improved integration processes and subparts improve quality of contemplation facilitating quicker unlearning and right learning of all subjects of contemplation. Practitioners regularly gain quicker access to intuitive view of reality providing powerful insights and helping transformations on all counts. As the mind gets more and more purified, the place for conflicts and contradictions keep shrinking. At some stage of this progress, the difference between meditation 'on the mat' and 'off the mat' slowly disappears completely.

With the assimilation of meditation, higher state of consciousness starts illuminating the internal contents of the practitioner making him gradually realising being a part of universe. Perceiving Self as a part of the universe allows free flow of love between the world and person. This very loving connectivity empowers him to overcome the adversarial powers, negative energy and other disturbances in normal life. Anger and disappointments may still arrive from time to time as a transient emotion that occurs momentarily before vanishing again. Once the practitioner pasts the tipping point of gaining Super Consciousness state, he is no longer susceptible of getting thrown off-balance by situations and disturbances of normal life. Gaining Super Consciousness unifies and elevates all aspects of physical, mental and spiritual existence allowing living a truly worth human life.

This very consciousness, the permanent aspect of every person, is called the Self. Scientific studies already suggest that at quantum level the whole universe is just a play of energy in some or the other form. The same energy at the helm of entire visible world is spiritually called supreme consciousness where everything moving and dead is taken as manifestation of the same consciousness and that is how the whole world is shown connected to each other in an integrated manner.

> "Real Meditation is nothing but the art of realising this very energy, this very Self."

Bibliography

Ajahn, Brahm, *Mindfulness, Bliss and Beyond: A Meditator's Handbook*, Wisdom Publications, Boston, 2005.

Badrinath, Chaturvedi, *Swami Vivekananda, The Living Vedanta*, Penguin Books, 2006.

Bucke, Richard Maurice, M.D., *Cosmic Consciousness: A Study in the Evolution of the Human Mind*, First Published in 1901.

Chinmayananda, Swami, *A Manual of Self Unfoldment*, Central Chinmaya Mission Trust, 1975.

Cooper, David A., *A Heart of Stillness—A Complete Guide to Learning the Art of Meditation*, Bell Tower, an imprint of Harmony Books, a Div. of Random House, Inc, 1999.

Cooper, David A., *Silence Simplicity and Solitude – A complete Guide to Spiritual Retreat*, Bell Tower, an imprint of Harmony Books, a Div. of Random House, Inc, 1999.

Culadasa (Johm Yates, Ph.D) and Matthew Immergut, *The Mind Illuminated, A Complete Meditation Guide Integrating Buddhist Wisdom and Brain Science for Greater Mindfulness*, Touchstone, 2015.

Dalai Lama, His Holiness and Howard C. Cutler, *The Art of Happiness; A Handbook for Living*, Hodder and Stoughton Ltd. London, 2009.

Dalai Lama, His Holiness The, *The Path To Freedom*, Abacus London, 2002.

Doniger, Wendy *The Hindus: An Alternate History*, The Penguin Press, New York, 2009.

Eknath, Easwaran, *Passage Meditation—Bringing the Deep Wisdom of the Heart Into Daily Life*, NILGIRI Press, 3rd edition 2010 by Publishing division of Blue Mountain Center for Meditation.

Gautier, Namrata and Francois Gautier, *The Art of Healing Pranayama: The Breath of Life*, HarperCollins, 2010.

Giri, Swami Satchidananda, *My Struggle for Self-Realization, An Autobiography*, Shipra Publications, 2015.

Goleman, Daniel, *Emotional Intelligence; Why it can matter more than IQ*, Bantam Books, NY, 1996.

Goleman, Daniel, *Social Intelligence: The New Science of Human Relationships*, Bantam Books, NY, 2006.

Hanh, Thich Nhat, *The Art of Mindful Living* (Audio Edition), Sounds True, 1999.

Hart, William, *Vipassana Meditation—The Art of Living as Taught by S.N. Goenka*, Vipassana Research Institute, Dhamma Giri, Igatpuri, Apollo Printing Press, Nashik, 2017.

Holiday, Ryan and Stephen Hanselman, *The Daily Stoic-366 Meditations on Wisdom, Perseverance, and the Art of Living*, Profile Books, 2016.

Jonathan, Haidt, *The Happiness Hypothesis—Finding Modern Truth in Ancient Wisdom*, Basic Books, A Member of the Perseus Books Group, 2006.

Kapleau, Philip, *The Three Pillars of ZE–Teaching, Practice and Enlightenment*, Anchor Books, New York, 2000.

Karen, Armstrong, *The Great Transformation, The Beginning of Our Religious Traditions*, Anchor Books, A Division of Random House INC, New York, 2006.

Kempton, Sally, *Meditation for the Love of It; Enjoying Your Own Deepest Experience*, Sounds True, Colorado, 2011.

Krishnamurti, J., *Inward Revolution*, Shabhala Boston and London, 2006.

Lawrence, Richard, *The Meditation Plan; 21 Keys to your inner potential*, Judy Piatkus, London, 1999.

Newbigging, Sandy C., *Mind Calm–The Modern Day Meditation Technique that gives you 'Peace with Mind'*, Hay House ISBN 978-1-78180-262-5

Radhakrishnan, S., *The Hindu View of Life*, HarperCollins, 2009.

Roberts, Bernadette, *What is Self?: A study of the Spiritual Journey in Terms of Consciousness*, Sentient Publications, 2005.

Schneider, Susan and Max Velmans, *The Blackwell Companion to Consciousness*, 2nd Edition, John Wiley and Sons UK, 2017.

Siegel, Daniel J., MD, *Aware—The Science and Practice of Presence, The Ground Breaking Meditation Practice*, A TarcherPerigee Book, New York, 2018.

Sivananda, Swami, *Concentration and Meditation,* The Divine Life Society, Shivanandanagar, 2014.

Smith, Tony, *Mindfulness for Beginners: How to Reduce Stress and Improve your Life!*, CreateSpace Independent Publishing Platforms, 2018.

Tejomayananda, Swami, *Living Vedanta* (Vedanta Cintnam), Chinmaya Prakashan, Mumbai, 2014.

The Shivananda Yoga Vedantic Centre, *The Sivananda Book of Meditation*, Gaia Books ISBN 1-85675-124-4.

Tyagi, Ashok, *All About Hinduism–From Vedas to Devas and Past to Present*, Shipra Publications, Delhi, 2015.

Tyagi, Ashok, *All About Spirituality–Practical Way for Self Realization*, Shipra Publications, 2017.

Waitley, Denis, *Empires of the Mind—Lessons to Lead and Succeed in a Knowledge Based World*, Nicholas Brealey Publishing, London, 2004.

Yogananda, Paramhansa, *Autobiography of a Yogi*, Yogoda Satsanga Society of India, 2010.

Articles, Lectures, Essays and Blogs and Various Websites

Introductions about Vipassana at www.dhamma.org/en/about/vipassana

Peter Russell, Effortless Meditation at www.Stillnessspeaks.com/meditation-efforts-russell

Meditation Benefits and Latest Scientific Research at www.tmhome.com/transcedental-meditation-benefits-research-efforts

Online Free Guided Meditation of Isha Kriya at www.ishafoundation.org/ishakriya

Various online meditation practice courses hosted at www.wisdomexperience.org

Bhante Gunaratana about structuring your meditation at www.vipassana.com/meditation/mindfulness

Workshops and events about 21 stages of meditation hosted by www.yogawest.ca/21-stages-of-meditation

Seven Pranayama; Breathing exercised by Swami Ramdev hosted at www.atmabodh.net/2015/06/pranayama

True Meditation Evolution's Tools for Ego Transcendence by Brad Reynolds at www.integralworld.net/reynolds

Articles about Sadhana under Kundalini Yoga at www.3ho.org/kundalini-yoga/sadhana-daily-spiritual-practice

Various articles by V. Jayaram hosted at www.hinduwebsite.com

Lessons I Learned from 10 days of Silence and Meditation by Tomas Laurinavicius hosted at www.tomaslau.com/silenec-meditation

Complete Guide to Ten Stages of Meditation for mastering the art of Meditation by Culadasa (John Yates Ph.D) hosted on www.consciouslifestylemag.com/ten-stages-of-meditation-complete-guide

An overview of 23 different meditational techniques explained by Giovanni at www.liveanddare.com/types-of-meditation

Listing of obstacles to be expected during meditation practice and ways to overcome them explained by Abbot George Burke (Swami Nirmalananda Giri) at www.ocoy.org/obstacles-in-meditation-and-how-to-overcome-them/

Listing of seventy six different benefits of meditation and Mindfulness by Giovanni hosted by www.liveanddare.com/benefits-of-meditation

Index